The Reader's Digest
Children's Atlas
of the Universe

$\mathcal{T}$HE READER'S DIGEST
Children's Atlas of the Universe

A Reader's Digest® Children's Book,
published 2000 by Reader's Digest Children's Publishing Ltd,
King's Court, Parsonage Lane, Bath BA1 1ER,
a subsidiary of The Reader's Digest Association, Inc.

Conceived and produced by Weldon Owen Pty Limited
59 Victoria Street, McMahons Point, NSW, 2060, Australia
A member of the Weldon Owen Group of Companies
Sydney • San Francisco

Copyright © 2000 Weldon Owen Pty Limited

READER'S DIGEST CHILDREN'S BOOKS
President: Vivian Antonangeli
Group Publisher: Rosanna Hansen
Managing Editor: Cathy Jones
Editor: Sarah Williams
Assistant Editor: Deri Robins

WELDON OWEN PUBLISHING
CEO: John Owen
President: Terry Newell
Publisher: Sheena Coupe
Creative Director: Sue Burk
Production Managers: Helen Creeke, Caroline Webber
Production Assistant: Kylie Lawson
Vice President International Sales: Stuart Laurence

Managing Editor: Jenni Bruce
Editorial Assistant: Tracey Jackson
Design Concept: John Bull
Art Director: Clare Forte
Jacket Design: John Bull
Picture Research: Jenny Mills

Illustrators: Wildlife Art Ltd:
David A. Hardy
Tom Connell
Luigi Gallant
Lee Gibbons
Sandra Pond
Star Charts: Wil Tirion

British Library Cataloguing in Publication Data.
A catalogue record for this book is available
from the British Library.

Colour Reproduction by Colourscan Co Pte Ltd
Printed by Toppan Printing Co, (H.K.) Ltd
Printed in China

A WELDON OWEN PRODUCTION

THE READER'S DIGEST
Children's Atlas of the Universe

by Robert Burnham

A Reader's Digest Children's Book

CONTENTS

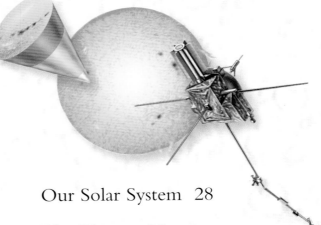

OUR SOLAR SYSTEM

DEEP SPACE

STARGAZING

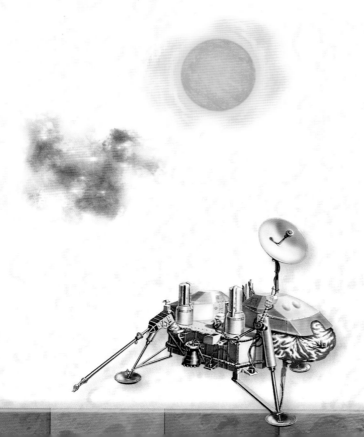

How to Use This Atlas

THE READER'S DIGEST CHILDREN'S ATLAS OF THE UNIVERSE takes you on an exhilarating journey through space. You can prepare yourself for the tour by reading the introductory section (pages 8 to 27). This section begins by explaining how Earth fits into the universe and how the universe fits together. It then guides you through the history of astronomy, from pre-historic times to the present day, with all the latest information on satellite telescopes and space probes.

Visit Earth's neighbours in the Solar System section (pages 28 to 63). Featuring detailed maps and spectacular photographs, these pages describe the Sun and all the objects that orbit it – the nine planets, 68 moons and countless asteroids and comets.

The Deep Space section (pages 64 to 87) takes you beyond the Solar System to the realm of stars and galaxies. Here you will learn about dazzling star clusters, exploding supernovas, amazing black holes and the mind-boggling birth of the universe.

Now it's time to explore space for yourself. The Stargazing section (pages 88 to 109) shows you how. It has 16 star maps to help you find the most rewarding sights in the night sky, whether you are using the naked eye, binoculars or a telescope.

At the back of the atlas, the Universe Fact File (pages 110 to 121) includes an astronomy timeline and lists a wealth of data about planets, moons, asteroids, comets, meteors, eclipses, stars and galaxies. Finally, the Glossary (pages 122 to 125) explains all the main terms used in this book, and the Index (pages 126 to 128) helps you to find any topics that especially interest you.

Our Solar System Pages (28–63)

Section Symbol
This tells you which section of the book you are in.

Photographs
The pages feature the latest photographs from space probes.

Key Facts List This provides the main facts about the object, such as its size, its distance from the Sun and its length of day.

Project By trying out these activities and experiments, you can learn more about the topic.

Stargazing Pages (88–109)

Seasonal Maps
The heading tells you what time of year and what part of the world the star maps are for.

Amazing Fact This illustrated box contains a fascinating fact about an aspect of the topic.

Star Maps Each map shows half of the sky you will see, depending on whether you are looking north or south.

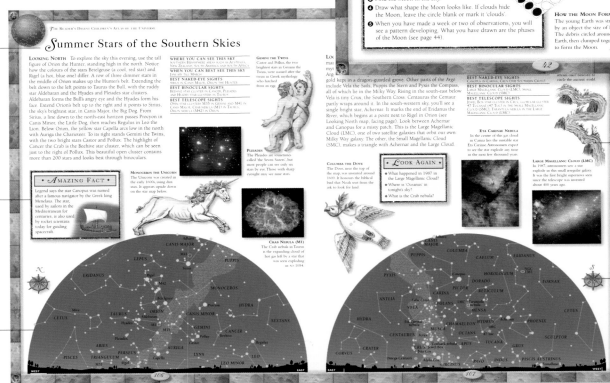

DEEP SPACE PAGES (64–87)

Main Image A powerful main image brings the topic alive. On the Star Clusters pages, the main image details the stars in a beautiful open cluster.

Cross-section A cross-section cone reveals the interior of the object.

Space Probe A space probe that has visited the object is featured in the top right-hand corner.

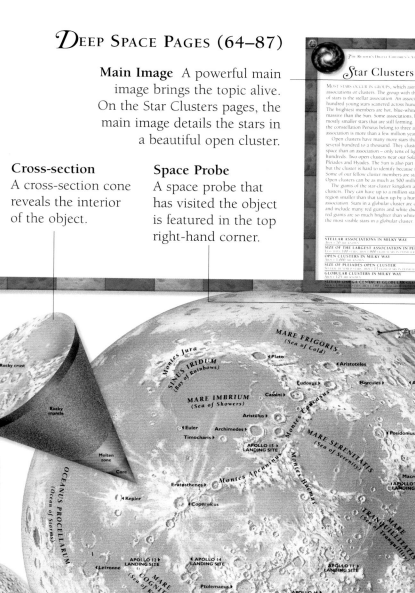

Diagrams Clear, colourful diagrams help you to understand complex ideas about objects in deep space.

Look Again To answer these questions, you need to take a close look at the information on the pages.

Map The surface features of the object are shown and labelled on the map.

UNIVERSE FACT FILE AND GLOSSARY (110–125)

Locator The object is coloured to show its position in the Solar System.

Constellation Figures These show you how to see mythological figures in the stars of the major constellations.

Additional Illustrations These give you more information about the featured object.

Coloured Border Each section of the atlas has a different coloured border.

KEY TO SECTION SYMBOLS

Compass The compass indicates whether you use this map looking north or south.

Introduction

Our Solar System

Deep Space

Stargazing

Fact File and Glossary

Our Planetary Neighbourhood

FOR MOST PEOPLE, Earth seems enormous, and life centres on nearby family and friends. Many live and work in an area only twenty or so kilometres across. So it has been for thousands of years. The study of the stars and planets – astronomy – looks far beyond this familiar world and gives a very different view. Astronomy seeks to know where our Earth fits into the universe.

Like sentries standing on a high hill to survey the country ahead, astronomers have turned their telescopes on other worlds beyond Earth and have begun to study them. They have learnt that the Sun is a star roughly 330,000 times larger than Earth. They have concluded that Earth and other planets travel in orbits around the Sun, making part of a family called the Solar System. Most of the planets have 'families' of their own. Earth has one moon that travels around it. Mars has two moons and Saturn has eighteen together with spectacular rings. Smaller bodies, including asteroids and comets, also travel in the Solar System. Asteroids are rocky or metallic mini-planets, some more than 500 kilometres (300 mi) across. Comets, made of ice and dust, may be only a few kilometres in diameter, but they can have spectacular tails that stretch for millions of kilometres.

Until the mid-1900s, astronomers used physics and telescope observations to estimate the size of the Sun and the planets and their distance from each other. They learnt, for example, that Earth is about 150 million kilometres (93 million mi) from the Sun. They called that distance the astronomical unit (or AU) and used it to describe other Solar System distances. Today, radar and spacecraft visits provide much more precise figures. But all the figures show that the Solar System is vast.

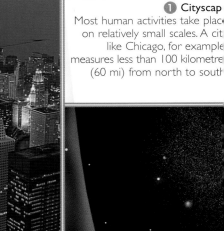

FROM CITIES TO THE SOLAR SYSTEM
A city can seem like a big place when you're walking along its streets, but it is tiny compared to the distances in the Solar System. Driving at 100 kilometres (60 mi) per hour, it would take you half an hour or so to drive across London, about 5½ months to drive to the Moon and about 175 years to drive all the way to the Sun.

GAZING INTO SPACE
Invented 400 years ago, the telescope magnifies our view of Earth's neighbours. Even with a small telescope, you can see the Moon's craters or Saturn's rings.

BRIGHT VISITORS
Comets spend most of their time in the outer parts of the Solar System, but they sometimes pass close to Earth and display spectacular tails. Comet Hyakutake was a beautiful sight in 1996.

◆ AMAZING FACT ◆

Earth travels around the Sun once every 365¼ days, covering a distance of about 940 million kilometres (584 million mi) per year. This means that at this very moment Earth is speeding through space at more than 107,000 kilometres (66,000 mi) per hour.

OUR CRATERED NEIGHBOUR
The Moon is the only one of Earth's neighbours that humans have visited in person. People had studied its surface with telescopes, but many questions about the Moon could be answered only when astronauts brought back lunar rock samples.

LANDING ON MARS

No astronaut has yet walked on Mars, but spacecraft have told us what it looks and feels like. The Viking 2 lander visited Mars in 1976, revealing a red desert strewn with rocks and boulders.

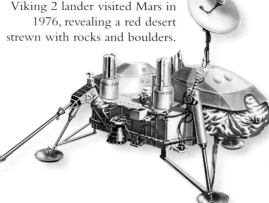

A CLEARER VIEW OF SATURN

Saturn is lovely to see in any telescope, but the visits by the Voyager spacecraft in 1980 and 1981 provided stunning images and a wealth of data.

❸ Solar System

Earth is the third of nine planets that orbit the Sun. It travels at an average distance of 150 million kilometres (93 million mi), or 1 AU. Mercury orbits at 0.4 AU, Mars at 1.5 AU, Jupiter at 5.2 AU and Neptune at 30.1 AU.

❷ Earth and Moon

The Moon is Earth's nearest celestial neighbour, but it is still far away by human standards. It orbits Earth at an average distance of 30 Earth diameters, or 384,401 kilometres (238,856 mi).

The Home Galaxy

THE SUN IS ONE of 200,000 million stars in the galaxy we call the Milky Way, and the whole Solar System is a tiny dot in the galaxy. Beyond the Solar System, astronomers measure distances in light-years – the distance light can travel in a year. At a rate of 300,000 kilometres (186,000 mi) per second, light travels about 10 billion kilometres (6 billion mi) in a year. The main part of the Milky Way is a disk-shaped spiral of stars that orbits its centre. The disk is about 100,000 light-years across and about 1,000 light-years thick.

Just as Earth is not in the centre of the Solar System, the Sun is not at the centre of the galaxy. It orbits about 33,000 light-years from the centre, roughly two-thirds of the way to the Milky Way's edge. One trip of the Sun around the centre takes about 226 million years.

Because light takes time to travel, when we see faraway things, we are looking back in time. For things close to us, our 'now' is the same as the object's. But the further away we look, the greater the difference between our present time and the time when the light left a distant body. The Moon is 1.3 light-seconds away, so we see it as it was 1.3 seconds ago. The nearest star system, Alpha Centauri, is 4.3 light-years away. We see this star system as it was 4.3 years ago. When we look at the far edge of the galaxy, we see it as it was about 80,000 years ago. An observer looking back at Earth would see our planet as it was 80,000 years ago, too!

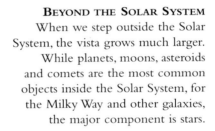

❶ Solar System
The Sun and its family of planets and moons seem vast to us, but the Solar System is a tiny speck in the millions of stars in the galaxy.

BEYOND THE SOLAR SYSTEM
When we step outside the Solar System, the vista grows much larger. While planets, moons, asteroids and comets are the most common objects inside the Solar System, for the Milky Way and other galaxies, the major component is stars.

MEASURING DISTANCES
Astronomers can work out how far away a star is by measuring its parallax – the slight shift in the star's apparent position when it is viewed from opposite sides of Earth's orbit. The greater the shift, the closer the star is to Earth.

Star's apparent position October

Star's apparent position April

Star's actual position

Earth's position April

Sun

Earth's position October

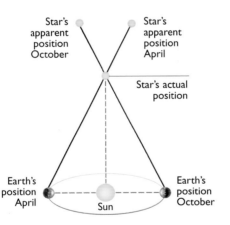

◆ PROJECT: *Parallax* ◆

❶ Hold up a pencil at arm's length in front of a bookcase or window. Close your left eye (or cover it with your free hand) and note where the pencil stands in front of the background.

❷ Without moving the pencil or your head, close (or cover) your right eye and open your left. The pencil's apparent change in position is its parallax.

Astronomers determine the distance to nearby stars by measuring their parallax six months apart, when Earth has moved from one side of the Sun to the other (see diagram, above).

STAR BIRTH AND DEATH
The Milky Way galaxy contains many clouds of gas, which are known as nebulas. In some of these, such as the Rosette nebula (above), stars are being born. Other nebulas, such as NGC 6543 (right), formed when a star shed its outer layers at the end of its life.

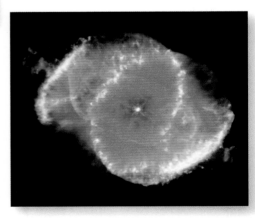

STAR CLUSTER

The star cluster known as M22 is one of more than 100 globular star clusters that orbit the Milky Way like moons. Each cluster contains 100,000 to a million stars.

INTO THE HEART

The Very Large Array in New Mexico is a collection of 27 radio telescopes. It uses radio waves to peer through the Milky Way's dust and gas into its heart.

❸ Milky Way

The Milky Way's nearest neighbours are two small galaxies called the Large and Small Magellanic Clouds. The Large Cloud (upper right) lies about 179,000 light-years away, while the Small Cloud (lower right) is 210,000 light-years away. Astronomers believe that some day these galaxies will merge with the Milky Way.

❷ Spiral Arm of Milky Way

Radio telescopes have mapped the gas and dust in the Milky Way. These maps told astronomers that the Milky Way is a spiral galaxy and that the Sun lies near the edge of one of its spiral arms.

The Cosmos

IF THE SOLAR SYSTEM IS JUST a tiny dot in the crowded Milky Way, the galaxy itself is a mere speck drifting through the universe. Surrounding the Milky Way galaxy is the Local Group of about 35 galaxies, most of them small. The Local Group has a diameter of roughly 8 million light-years, but big as it is, this cluster of galaxies is not the whole universe. It is merely one group among many.

The word *cosmos* is Greek and means 'the organization of everything'. Astronomers who study the structure of the universe are called cosmologists. They use the largest and most sensitive telescopes because only these can detect the faint light coming from the furthest galaxies. Cosmologists have found that galaxies are the basic building blocks of the universe. Galaxies tend to form in groups, such as the Local Group. And these cluster into groups of groups. (For instance, the Local Group belongs to the Local Supercluster of galaxies.) And these superclusters in turn gather into groups of groups of groups.

Where does it end? No one knows for certain. Using a special space telescope, astronomers have detected the fading echo of the Big Bang, the event in which the universe began. This echo shows that in the very early days of the universe, there were no galaxies, no stars, no structures of any kind. Somehow the cosmos changed from this smooth state into one where groups of galaxies fill the universe. Exactly how that happened is still a mystery. Astronomers estimate that the Big Bang occurred about 12,000 to 15,000 million years ago, which would make the edge of the universe 12,000 to 15,000 million light-years away.

❶ Milky Way
Galaxies are the building blocks of the cosmos. The Milky Way is a spiral galaxy. Other galaxy types are ellipticals and irregulars.

BEYOND THE MILKY WAY
Despite its size, the Milky Way galaxy is tiny compared with the rest of the universe. The distances are so vast that even the speed of light is a very small measuring stick. For example, light from the Andromeda galaxy (M31), a close neighbour, takes more than 2 million light-years to reach us.

◆ PROJECT: *Life in the Cosmos* ◆

Elsewhere in the Milky Way or even in other galaxies, there may be other planets that support life. No one knows for sure whether life exists on other worlds, but the chemistry that governs life appears to be the same all over the universe. Try inventing some alien life forms that could live on the planets listed below. Think about how big they would be, how they would breathe, how they would move around and what they would eat and drink.

❶ A planet with very weak gravity.

❷ A planet with very strong gravity.

❸ A cold planet much further from its star than Earth is from the Sun.

❹ A hot planet much closer to its star than Earth is to the Sun.

❺ A gaseous planet with no solid surface.

GALAXIES AND BLACK HOLES
The giant elliptical galaxy M87 sends out powerful radio signals. At its centre, there is probably a black hole – an extremely dense object that cannot be seen but is sucking in gas from the galaxy.

INTERACTING GALAXIES
The galaxies in a cluster of galaxies occasionally pass near one another or even collide. When this happens, few stars hit one another but both galaxies are pulled out of shape.

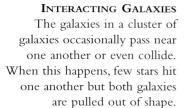

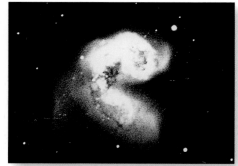

EDGE-ON GALAXY

The Sombrero galaxy belongs to the Virgo cluster of galaxies. We see the Sombrero almost sideways-on. It has a large core and a line of dust running through the middle of its disc.

SATELLITE OBSERVATORY

Astronomers used the Infrared Space Observatory to investigate water clouds in distant galaxies and dust in the Coma cluster of galaxies.

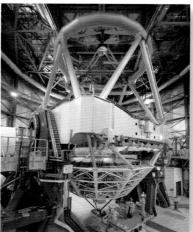

BIG TELESCOPE

The bigger the telescope, the more light it collects. Giant instruments such as the Very Large Telescope in Chile help astronomers study distant, faint galaxies.

3 Cosmic Structure
Galaxies seem to appear in groups, and groups gather in larger clusters. Cosmologists are studying how such structures form and evolve.

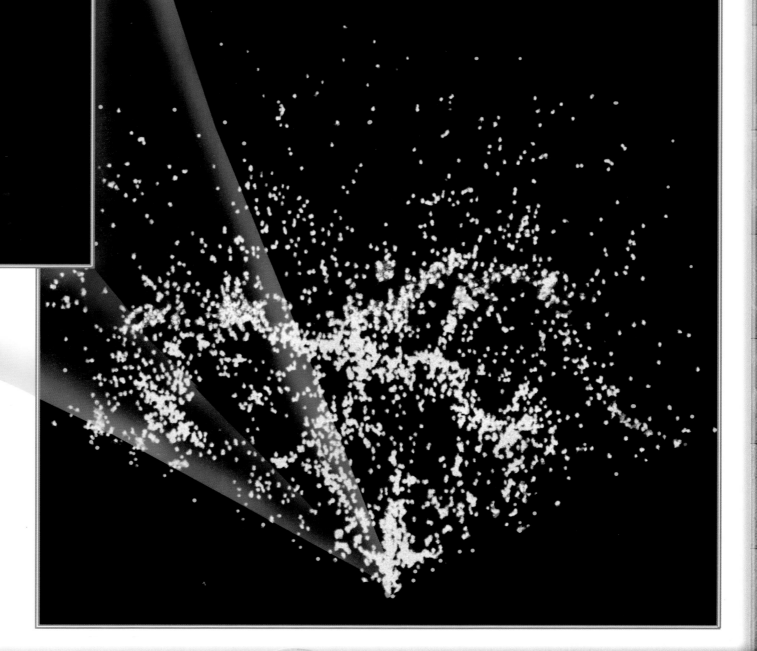

2 Local Group
With about 35 member galaxies, the Local Group is dominated by the Milky Way and two other large spiral galaxies – the Andromeda galaxy (M31), shown upper left and the Pinwheel galaxy (M33), shown right. The rest are small galaxies, some of them resembling the Magellanic Clouds.

The First Observers

SKYWATCHING IS AS OLD AS HUMANITY itself. Pre-historic people used the heavens as both a clock and a calendar. Sunrise and sunset marked day and night, while the Moon's phases indicated a lunar month. The Sun rose in a slightly different place on the horizon each day, following a cycle that marked a year. People created stories to explain how the heavens controlled events on Earth, and saw the outlines of gods and monsters in the arrangement of the stars. They named constellations, the major star formations that appear at different times of year. We use many of these formations today. Some constellations are more than 5,000 years old.

Early astronomers worked without telescopes, relying on their eyes and a few simple instruments. In ancient Sumeria, Babylonia and Egypt, astronomers recorded when stars rose and set and compiled lists of special events such as lunar and solar eclipses. They developed calendars so they would know when to plant their crops. These keen observers saw that every year the Sun appeared to travel through 12 constellations, which are now known as the zodiac. They also noticed that some stars within the zodiac moved, and they struggled to understand what they were seeing. Today we know that these moving stars are actually planets. The name comes from the Greek word meaning 'wanderer'.

Ancient Chinese astronomers figured out that the year was 365¼ days long. They also observed comets, eclipses and exploding stars called supernovas. In the New World, the Maya of southern Mexico built temples that they used for astronomy. They developed a complex calendar based on the movements of the planet Venus.

PLANET GODS
The ancient Greeks linked planets with the gods. The Romans adopted this system and gave the planets the Latin names we use today. Because Mercury was the swiftest planet, it was named after the gods' messenger.

BABYLONIAN ASTRONOMY
Astronomers in ancient Babylonia (present-day Iraq) recorded the movements of stars and planets on clay tablets more than 2,500 years ago.

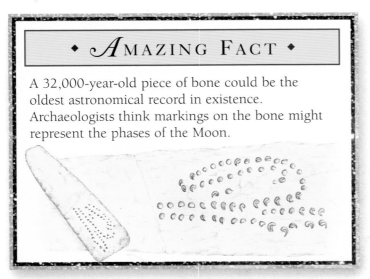

◆ AMAZING FACT ◆

A 32,000-year-old piece of bone could be the oldest astronomical record in existence. Archaeologists think markings on the bone might represent the phases of the Moon.

EARTH AT THE CENTRE
In early models of the universe such as this, the Sun, Moon and planets all revolved around Earth. Even today, we say the Sun 'rises' and 'sets', when in fact it is Earth that is moving. The animals and figures shown here mark the zodiac, the 12 constellations that lie close to the yearly path of the Sun in the sky.

EGYPTIAN CONSTELLATIONS

Constellation figures decorate the tomb of an Egyptian pharaoh. Egyptian astronomers tracked the rising and setting of bright stars like Sirius. They also divided the day and night into 12 periods each.

SUN GOD

This is a Native American Sun god mask. The Sun's importance to life led many early cultures to make it their main god. A Moon goddess usually ruled the night.

STONEHENGE

Begun more than 4,000 years ago, England's Stonehenge helped astronomers observe the Sun and Moon. At the start of summer, they could see the Sun rise between its standing stones.

• PROJECT: *Sun Movements* •

For this project, you need a place where you can watch the Sun rising or setting on the horizon.

1. Find a point facing east or west where a tree or pole lines up with a distant landmark such as a church steeple.

2. Each clear morning or evening, at dawn or dusk, note where the Sun appears or disappears on the horizon. *Warning: The Sun can permanently damage your eyes, so only ever give the Sun a quick glance at sunrise or sunset and never look at the Sun if it is higher in the sky.*

3. In about a week you will see changes. The Sun moves in one direction from late June to late December, then moves back again in the following six months.

Early people built monuments to follow the Sun's movements through the year.

(Zodiac wheel labels: TAURUS, ARIES, PISCES, AQUARIUS, CAPRICORNUS, SAGITTARIUS, JUNE, MAY, APRIL, MARCH, FEBRUARY, JANUARY, SUN, MERCURY, MOON, JUPITER, THE STARS)

Models of the Universe

THE ANCIENT GREEKS STRUGGLED to understand the universe. By the 300s BC, they had established that Earth itself is round. Most Greek astronomers believed that all the heavenly bodies revolved around Earth, but at least one, Aristarchus, thought that Earth revolved around the Sun. In the 100s BC, Hipparchus compiled a star catalogue, invented magnitudes to compare star brightness and calculated the Moon's distance from Earth. The most influential astronomer, Claudius Ptolemy, came along 300 years later. Ptolemy's model built on the work of Hipparchus and explained that all the heavenly bodies moved around Earth. It was accepted for more than a thousand years.

Nicolaus Copernicus (1473–1543) was the first modern astronomer to assert that Earth travels around the Sun. In the next hundred years, other astronomers gathered observations that supported the theory. Tycho Brahe (1546–1601) tried to combine Copernicus' ideas with Ptolemy's. Johannes Kepler (1571–1630), who worked with Tycho, formed the first accurate theory of how the planets move. Then Galileo Galilei (1564–1642) built the first astronomical telescope. He was the first human to see mountains on the Moon, and he discovered the phases of Venus and the four large moons of Jupiter.

Finally, Isaac Newton (1642–1727) proposed a theory that explained the mechanics of both the Solar System and the everyday world. Planets, including Earth, are held in their orbits by the gravity of the Sun. In the same way, the Moon is held by Earth's gravity. Using Newton's theory, astronomers could calculate the size and scale of the Solar System and accurately predict the movements of planets, moons and comets.

NICOLAUS COPERNICUS
Aware that his ideas would anger the Catholic Church, Copernicus published his Sun-centred model of the universe only when he was on his deathbed.

CLAUDIUS PTOLEMY
The Earth-centred universe developed by Ptolemy lasted more than a thousand years. It was replaced by the Sun-centred model of Copernicus.

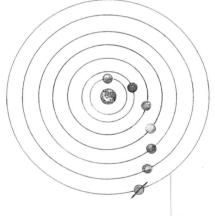

Ptolemy's model

◆ AMAZING FACT ◆

The great scientist Isaac Newton once saw an apple fall from a tree. This gave him the idea that the gravity that brought the apple to the ground might reach all the way to the Moon and keep it in orbit around Earth.

SUN AT THE CENTRE
In the Copernican model, the Sun lies at the centre of the Solar System and all the planets, including Earth, orbit it. When Copernicus published this model, no observations could prove it was right. Astronomical proof that Copernicus was correct didn't come until long after his death.

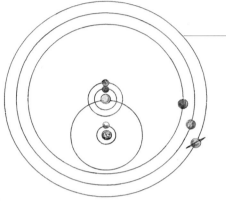

TYCHO BRAHE

Tycho Brahe wore a silver nose because his real one was cut off in a duel. This sharp-eyed astronomer made thousands of observations of the heavens. In his model, the other planets orbited the Sun, but the Sun orbited Earth.

Tycho's model

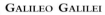

GALILEO'S TELESCOPE

Galileo used telescopes that magnified only 20 to 30 times, but they showed him celestial sights that no one had ever seen before.

GALILEO GALILEI

Galileo argued constantly and skillfully with the Church for Copernican views. He was accused of heresy and ended his life under house-arrest as a prisoner of the Inquisition.

ISAAC NEWTON

As a boy, Newton tinkered with waterwheels and windmills. When he grew up, his mathematical theories saw the universe as a giant clockwork whose movements were always predictable.

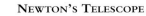

NEWTON'S TELESCOPE

Newton designed a new type of telescope using mirrors instead of lenses. Known as a reflector, it gave a clearer view. Many of today's telescopes are reflectors.

𝒢reat Leaps Forward

SINCE THE 1700S, NEW THEORIES and new technology have led to great leaps in our understanding of the universe. With Newton's mathematical tools, astronomers could calculate the orbits of planets, moons and comets. Edmond Halley (1656–1742) confirmed Newton's 'clockworks' by predicting that a particular comet would pass by Earth again. When it did return after Halley's death, it was named after him.

More powerful telescopes led to further discoveries. William Herschel (1738–1822) was a musician and amateur astronomer when he discovered the planet Uranus in 1781. He then became a full-time astronomer, building big telescopes that showed him many faint star clusters and nebulas. His goal was to understand the Milky Way galaxy and discover where the Sun lay within it.

In the 1850s, Robert Kirchoff (1824–87) and Robert Bunsen (1811–99) invented the spectroscope. In the decades that followed, this device showed that stars were balls of hot gases, while planets simply reflected sunlight. Some nebulas were found to be sheets of thin gas. Others were masses of stars. By 1900, the spectroscope had turned astronomers, who mainly studied stars' positions, into astrophysicists, who study what the universe is made of.

The 20th century has seen huge advances. Albert Einstein (1879–1955) became world famous after his theory of relativity was tested at a solar eclipse in 1919. His theories suggested the universe was expanding, a fact that astronomers such as Edwin Hubble (1889–1953) were discovering at about the same time. More recently, spacecraft have revealed details of the planets, while high-tech telescopes have provided clearer views of distant objects and shown us the universe in wavelengths invisible to the eye.

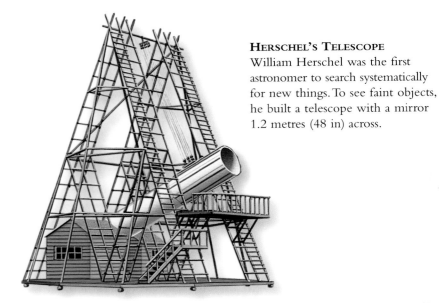

HERSCHEL'S TELESCOPE
William Herschel was the first astronomer to search systematically for new things. To see faint objects, he built a telescope with a mirror 1.2 metres (48 in) across.

ALBERT EINSTEIN
As they investigate the universe, astronomers now use Einstein's work daily. Computers calculate model stars and galaxies based on his theories. The models are then checked against telescope observations.

◆ 𝒜MAZING FACT ◆

The idea of black holes – objects whose gravity is so strong that light rays can't escape – was first proposed in the 1700s. But the idea was ignored until the 20th century because no astronomer could imagine how such a strange object could ever exist.

Slit helps the spectrograph to produce a clean spectrum

Lens makes the light entering the prism parallel

Light from star

Telescope

SPECTROSCOPE
A spectroscope can break light into the colours it is made up of. The result is called a spectrum. A spectrograph is a device that records this spectrum. Astronomers study a star's spectrum to learn about the chemical elements that make it shine. A spectrum can also show how fast a star, nebula or galaxy is moving towards us or away from us.

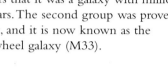

SPIRAL GALAXY
In the early 1900s, astronomers argued about spiral-shaped objects like this. Some said it was a young solar system, others that it was a galaxy with millions of stars. The second group was proved right, and it is now known as the Pinwheel galaxy (M33).

EDWIN HUBBLE
Hubble's discoveries revealed that spiral galaxies were immense collections of individual stars. He also showed that the universe was expanding and calculated its rate of expansion.

◆ PROJECT: *Splitting Light* ◆

For this project, you need a piece of cardboard, a straight glass filled with water and a sheet of paper.

❶ Make a long, narrow slit in the piece of cardboard.

❷ Put the glass of water on the sheet of paper near a sunny window, with the piece of cardboard between the Sun and the glass.

As the Sun shines through the slit into the water, you can see sunlight break into the colours of its spectrum – just as a spectroscope splits the light from stars and planets into its spectral colours.

Prism splits light into its component colours

Photographic plate records spectrum of star

❶ No shift = galaxy at rest

❷ Shift to the red = galaxy moving away from Earth

❸ Shift to the blue = galaxy approaching Earth

DOPPLER SHIFT
If a light source stays at about the same distance from Earth, its spectrum has characteristic lines (1). If the source is moving away from Earth, the light waves are longer and the spectrum lines shift towards the red (2). If the object is moving towards Earth, the waves are shorter and the lines shift towards the blue (3). This effect is named after its discoverer, Christian Doppler.

Astronomy from the Ground

MOST OBJECTS IN THE NIGHT SKY are faint and give off only dim beams of light. To make more discoveries, astronomers always need to collect more light. The answer lies in building ever-bigger telescopes. The first telescopes were refractors, but astronomers soon learnt how to make much bigger telescopes using mirrors. In the 1700s, William Herschel built one with a mirror 1.2 metres (48 in) across (see page 18). It was a giant for its day and impressive even now. Larger and larger telescopes followed. Completed in 1948, the 5 metre (200 in) Hale Telescope on Palomar Mountain in California was used to discover distant objects known as quasars. For a long time, this was the world's largest telescope, but today more than a dozen bigger telescopes exist.

It is hard for a telescope to get a clear view of the night sky. City lights wash out the stars, and Earth's atmosphere distorts the starlight passing through it, creating an effect like the shifting bright and dark bands on the bottom of a swimming pool. Most big telescopes are on remote mountain tops, far from cities and above the most distorting part of Earth's atmosphere.

Traditional telescopes are optical, which means they collect the kind of light that our eyes can see. Stars, planets and galaxies also send out invisible radiation (see page 22). This includes radio waves, which are less affected by Earth's atmosphere and so can be studied from the ground. Radio waves are much longer than visible light waves, so radio telescopes must be much larger than optical telescopes. The antenna of the largest single radio telescope, the Arecibo in Puerto Rico, measures 305 metres (1,000 ft) across. Astronomers can connect several radio telescopes together and make them work as a single instrument. This technique is called interferometry. It lets radio telescopes capture details more sharply than optical telescopes can.

MOUNTAIN TOP VIEWS
An international array of telescopes, including the two Keck telescopes, covers the top of Hawaii's Mauna Kea mountain. With an altitude of 4,200 metres (13,800 ft), it is the world's best astronomy site.

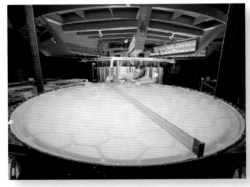

GIANT MIRRORS
Big telescope mirrors tend to sag under their own weight, so they need special designs. The mirror of the Vatican Telescope (shown here) has a very thin surface supported by a honeycomb of glass.

Keck II dome

Each Keck Telescope stands eight storeys high and weighs 270 tonnes (300 tons).

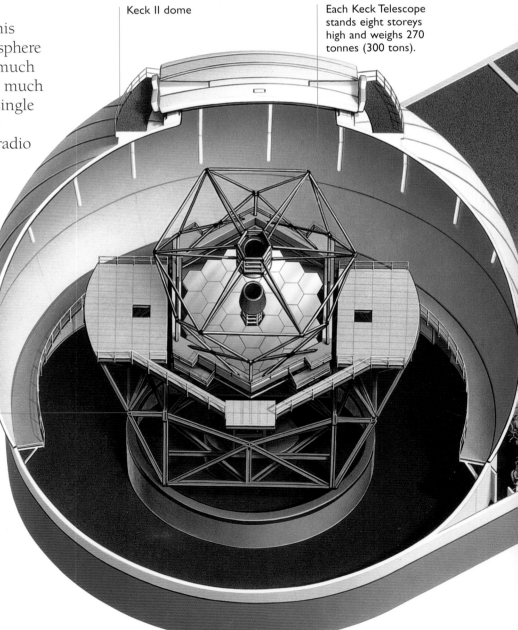

KECK TELESCOPES
The two Keck Telescopes on Mauna Kea are among the world's largest. Each dome contains a reflector telescope with a mirror nearly 10 metres (400 in) across. These two giant eyes can work independently or they can work together to provide a sharper view than either telescope could achieve alone.

As Earth turns, stars and galaxies rotate across the sky. The telescope is mounted on a moveable base so it can track their movement.

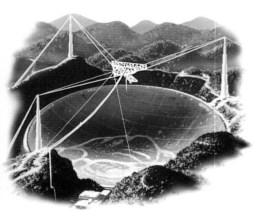

ARECIBO TELESCOPE
The enormous Arecibo Radio Telescope is set in a natural hollow on the island of Puerto Rico. It studies planets and stars, and also listens for radio signals that might come from extraterrestrial life.

Refractor

Reflector

REFRACTORS

Refractor telescopes use lenses to collect light and form images. Lenses are expensive to make and cannot be any larger than 1 metre (40 in) in diameter.

REFLECTORS

Reflector telescopes collect light and produce images with mirrors. They can be built in giant sizes. Today, nearly all professional and most amateur telescopes are reflectors.

The giant mirror that collects the light is not a single sheet of glass. It is made up of 36 individual hexagonal segments, each almost 1.8 metres (6 ft) wide.

Keck I dome

Moveable shutter

Electronics workshop

Instrument assembly

Moveable shutter

In the control room, operators use computers to move and point the telescope. The light collected is sent through a suite of high-tech instruments, producing images and data for astronomers to analyse.

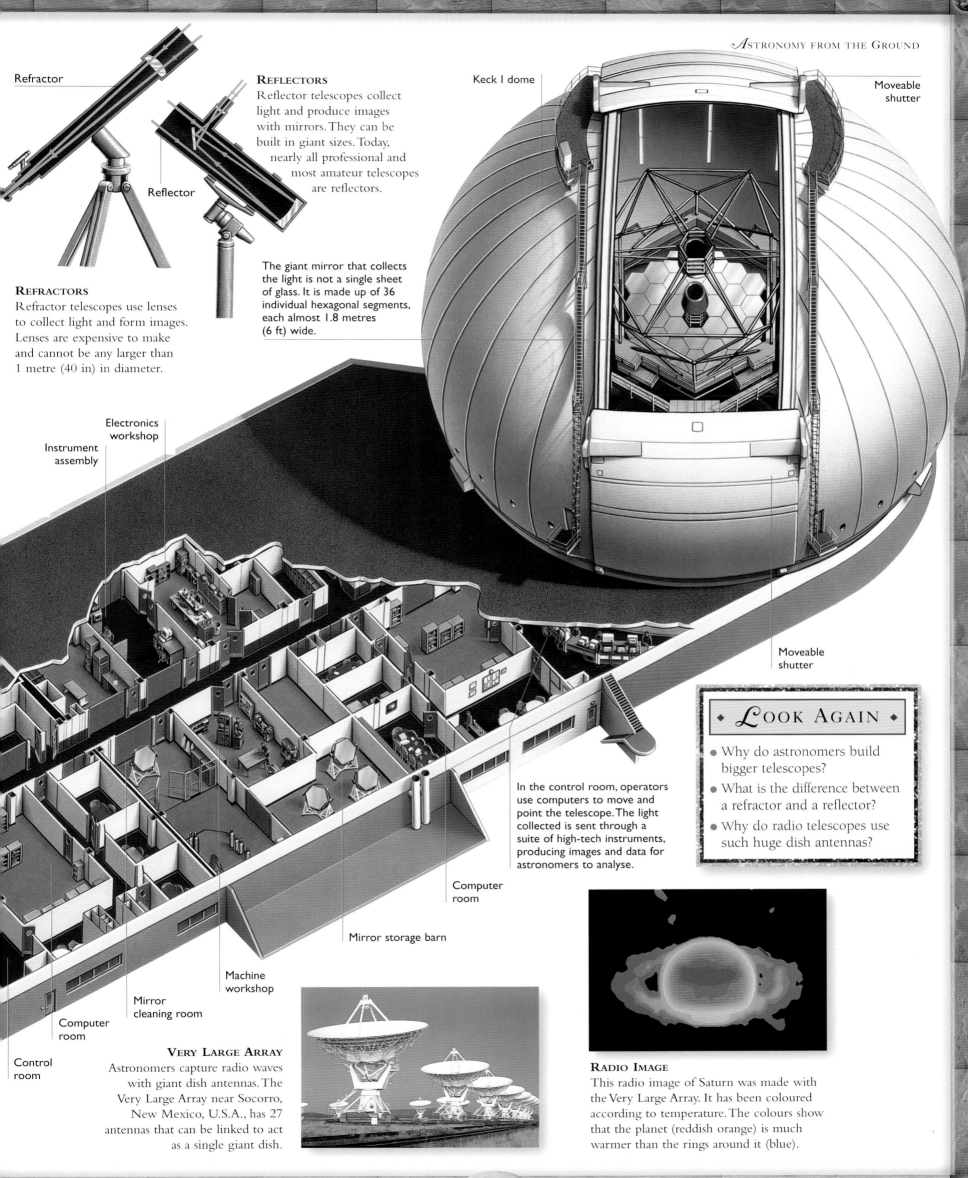

Computer room

Mirror storage barn

Machine workshop

Mirror cleaning room

Computer room

Control room

· LOOK AGAIN ·

- Why do astronomers build bigger telescopes?
- What is the difference between a refractor and a reflector?
- Why do radio telescopes use such huge dish antennas?

VERY LARGE ARRAY

Astronomers capture radio waves with giant dish antennas. The Very Large Array near Socorro, New Mexico, U.S.A., has 27 antennas that can be linked to act as a single giant dish.

RADIO IMAGE

This radio image of Saturn was made with the Very Large Array. It has been coloured according to temperature. The colours show that the planet (reddish orange) is much warmer than the rings around it (blue).

Astronomy from Orbit

EVEN BEFORE THE FIRST artificial satellites were put into orbit in 1957, astronomers were planning ways to send up space observatories. They knew that they would be able to see deeper into space without the distortion of Earth's atmosphere, and they hoped to detect new kinds of signals that don't reach Earth's surface. The Orbiting Solar Observatory, launched in 1962, was the first of many astronomical satellites that have sent new information to astronomers on Earth.

Some space telescopes capture visible light, but many explore the other kinds of radiation that planets, stars and galaxies give off. The full range of radiation is known as the electromagnetic spectrum. Radio and infrared radiation travel in longer waves than visible light, while ultraviolet, X-ray and gamma-ray radiation have shorter waves.

The best-known satellite observatory is the Hubble Space Telescope (HST). Launched in 1990, HST is the first of four Great Observatories planned by the United States' National Aeronautics and Space Administration (NASA). Each Great Observatory will explore one part of the electromagnetic spectrum. HST covers the visible part of the spectrum plus the ultraviolet and part of the infrared. On the short-wave side of visible light, the Chandra X-Ray Observatory and the Compton Gamma-Ray Observatory are designed to detect radiation from hot stars, supernova explosions and colliding black holes. On the long-wave side of visible light, the Space Infrared Telescope Facility (SIRTF, due for launch in 2001) will study clouds of gas and dust that give birth to stars and other solar systems.

CHANDRA X-RAY OBSERVATORY
The Chandra Observatory is surveying the entire sky. It is looking for X-rays from objects such as distant exploding stars and merging clusters of galaxies.

HUBBLE SPACE TELESCOPE
The Hubble Space Telescope has studied almost everything in the universe, from the most distant known galaxies to minerals found around lunar craters. Astronauts visit from time to time to upgrade instruments and fix failing parts.

X-RAY GALAXIES
ROSAT, a German-built X-ray satellite, took images showing very hot gases surrounding two galaxies in the Coma galaxy cluster.

HUBBLE HOURGLASS
The Hubble Space Telescope captured this spectacular image of the Hourglass nebula. The nebula is made up of rings of glowing gas around a fading star.

ELECTROMAGNETIC SPECTRUM
The Sun shines strongest in the visible part of the spectrum, but the universe gives off radiation with both longer and shorter waves. Because our atmosphere blocks most of these other signals, astronomers send telescopes into space to see them.

♦ AMAZING FACT ♦

A doctor's X-ray machine produces X-rays that travel through our skin and tissue but not through our bones. The X-rays that pass through can make a photographic image showing our bones. An X-ray telescope receives natural X-rays from outer space and can tell us about the objects that send out the rays. Some are gas clouds hotter than a million degrees Celsius.

RADIO WAVES

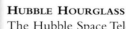

Radio telescopes

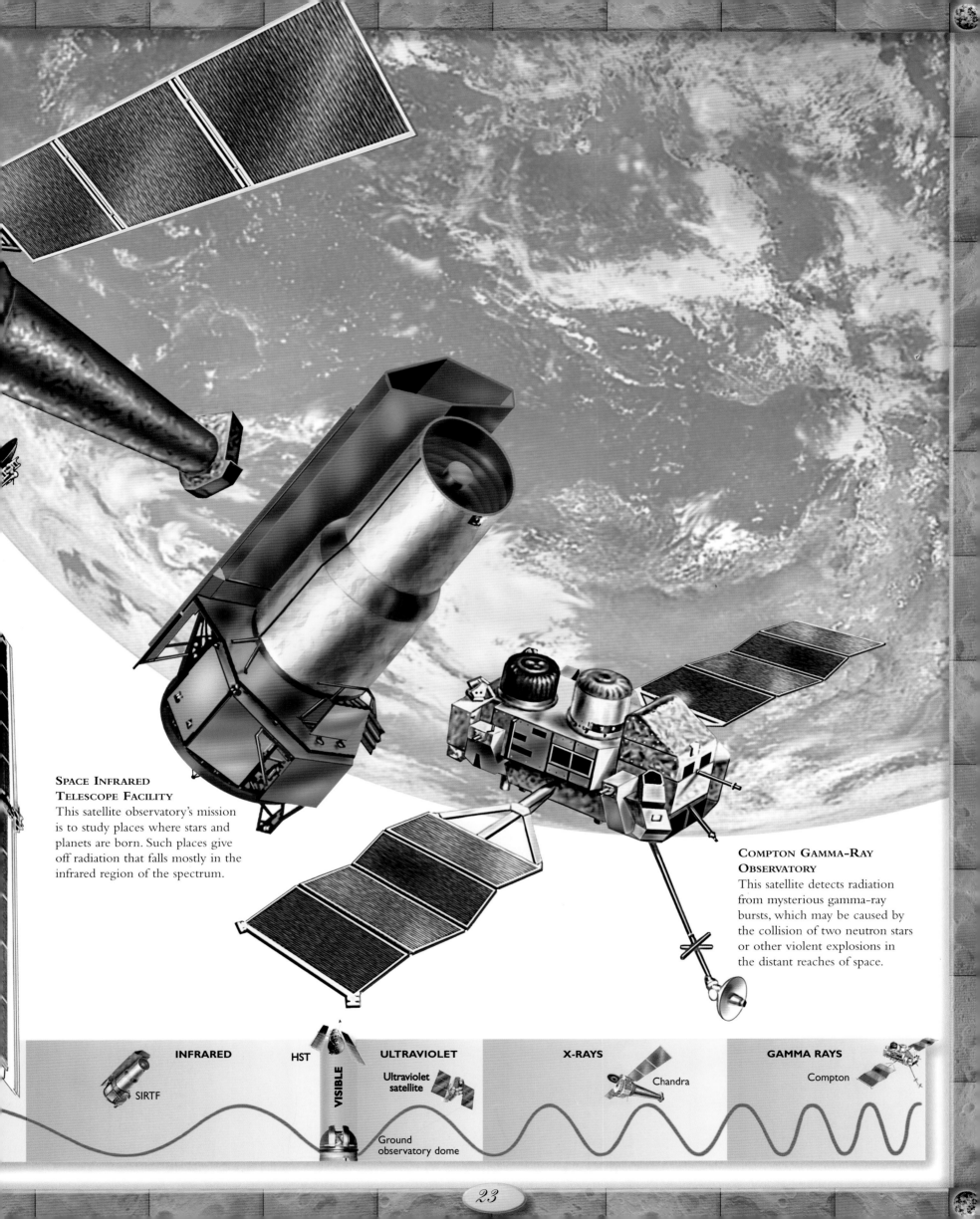

SPACE INFRARED TELESCOPE FACILITY
This satellite observatory's mission is to study places where stars and planets are born. Such places give off radiation that falls mostly in the infrared region of the spectrum.

COMPTON GAMMA-RAY OBSERVATORY
This satellite detects radiation from mysterious gamma-ray bursts, which may be caused by the collision of two neutron stars or other violent explosions in the distant reaches of space.

INFRARED   HST   **ULTRAVIOLET**   **X-RAYS**   **GAMMA RAYS**

SIRTF   VISIBLE   Ultraviolet satellite   Chandra   Compton

Ground observatory dome

Visiting Space

PEOPLE DREAMT OF FLYING INTO SPACE for centuries, but the dream only became a reality in the late 1950s. Using rockets developed from the weapons of World War II, Soviet scientists sent the first satellite into space in 1957. In 1961, Soviet Yuri Gagarin became the first human to orbit Earth. Soon afterwards, the United States announced a programme called Apollo to send people to the Moon.

A trip to the Moon required a giant booster rocket and a complex mission plan. After several Apollo test flights around Earth, Apollo 8 took three astronauts to orbit the Moon in December 1968. They didn't land because the lander craft had not yet been built. More test flights followed. Then Apollo 11's Neil Armstrong and Buzz Aldrin landed on the lunar Sea of Tranquillity on 20 July, 1969. Five more Apollo Moon landings followed, collecting hundreds of lunar rock samples.

As Apollo ended in 1972, the United States was designing a new spaceship, the space shuttle. A shuttle can hold seven astronauts and orbit Earth for two weeks or more. Shuttles have been used for launching satellites and planet probes, but their main purpose is building the International Space Station.

A space station orbits Earth and can be occupied by people for long periods of time. The first space stations were launched in the early 1970s, but the most successful was the Russian Mir station, which was almost continuously occupied from 1986 to 1999. The International Space Station will use crews from many nations. They will study how to fly to Mars. Bases on the Moon and Mars are the next steps for humanity in space.

◆ PROJECT: *Moon Base* ◆

Construct a base on the Moon. You can use cardboard, old cartons, craft sticks, soil, modelling clay, thin plastic sheets, aluminium foil, wire, paints and glue. There's no particular recipe – use your imagination. But remember that a Moon base must have these things:

1. Places for people to live, grow food, do scientific studies and repair equipment.
2. A radio antenna to communicate with Earth.
3. Vehicles to carry astronauts on exploration trips.
4. A rocket to bring astronauts back to Earth.

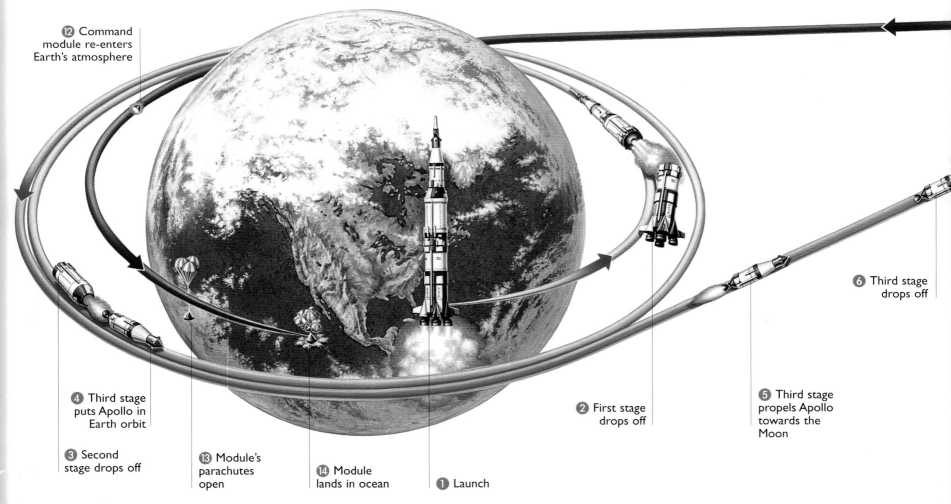

12 Command module re-enters Earth's atmosphere

4 Third stage puts Apollo in Earth orbit

3 Second stage drops off

13 Module's parachutes open

14 Module lands in ocean

1 Launch

2 First stage drops off

5 Third stage propels Apollo towards the Moon

6 Third stage drops off

ROVING THE MOON

This folding Moon buggy helped astronauts travel further and collect more rock samples. It had four-wheel drive – and four-wheel steering!

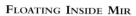

INTERNATIONAL SPACE STATION

The station will include more than 100 components from 16 countries. When finished, it will be more than 100 metres (300 ft) long and weigh more than 450 tonnes (500 tons).

FLOATING INSIDE MIR

The Russian space station Mir was cramped, but it taught crews – Russian, American and many others – how to live and work in space.

SPACEWALKING

Construction workers in space need to leave their spacecraft to move big things around. Backpacks with small thrusters can turn an astronaut into a mini-spaceship.

7 Command and service modules stay in orbit while lunar module separates

11 Service module discarded

10 Lunar module discarded

9 Lunar module meets up with command and service modules

8 Lunar module lands on Moon

JOURNEY TO THE MOON

The Apollo spacecraft was launched by a powerful rocket, the Saturn 5. The rocket had three stages that propelled the craft and then dropped off, leaving the light Apollo craft to travel into space. Once Apollo reached the Moon, two astronauts landed in the lunar module, while a third orbited in the command and service modules.

◆ AMAZING FACT ◆

It took Apollo astronauts three days to travel to the Moon (and three days to come back). But a trip to Mars would take at least six months each way – and you would have to stay on Mars for almost a year and a half, waiting for the planets to be lined up correctly for your return.

SPACE SHUTTLE LAUNCH

Designed as 'space trucks', the four space shuttles are the workhorses for assembling the International Space Station. The shuttles will need to make several dozen flights to build the station.

Probing Space

To explore beyond the Moon, scientists have relied on robot probes. These are cheaper and safer than manned spacecraft and can go places where people can't. Sending spacecraft to planets follows a time-tested pattern. Fly-by spacecraft go first – these take photographs and collect data as they travel past the planet. They are followed by orbiters, which travel around the planet like a moon. And then come the landers, spacecraft that actually touch down on the planets. Each type of mission sends back information via radio waves that tells scientists and engineers about the conditions the next probe will meet.

Several missions have been launched from space shuttles, but most probes now leave Earth on rockets because they are cheaper. Probes often loop around the Solar System, flying past a number of planets before reaching their goal. For example, the Cassini probe goes past Venus (twice), Earth and Jupiter before arriving at Saturn. The gravity of each planet speeds up the spacecraft and sends it onwards – and scientists get a free fly-by of three extra planets.

Every planet except Pluto has been visited by at least one robot probe. Uranus and Neptune have had only a single fly-by, but others have had many visits. Mars, for instance, has been visited by fly-bys, orbiters, landers and a rover. Pluto's turn is being planned. The Pluto-Kuiper Express mission would fly past Pluto and its moon Charon, then continue into the outer reaches of the Solar System to visit a comet.

Other mission plans include a close fly-by of the Sun, rock sample returns from Mars, orbiters for Mercury and Neptune, a lander for Neptune's moon Triton and an orbiter to look at Europa, a mysterious moon of Jupiter.

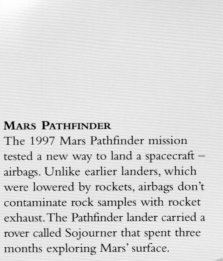

1 Pathfinder lander separates from orbiter

2 Parachute opens, slowing the lander's descent

3 Airbags around lander inflate

MARS PATHFINDER
The 1997 Mars Pathfinder mission tested a new way to land a spacecraft – airbags. Unlike earlier landers, which were lowered by rockets, airbags don't contaminate rock samples with rocket exhaust. The Pathfinder lander carried a rover called Sojourner that spent three months exploring Mars' surface.

◆ PROJECT: *Aiming a Probe* ◆

Launching a spacecraft at a distant planet is extremely difficult. Both Earth and the planet are moving. It's much more difficult than threading a needle from across the room. To get some idea of what it's like, try this project:

1 Cut a ring out of cardboard, making a 25 centimetre (10 in) hole in it.

2 Use a piece of string to hang the ring from the branch of a tree.

3 Take several steps back and try to toss balls of paper through the hole. A windy day just makes it more realistic!

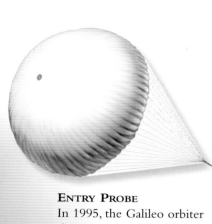

Entry Probe

In 1995, the Galileo orbiter shot an entry probe into Jupiter's dense atmosphere. The probe sampled gases as it fell, radioing data to the orbiter.

Lander

Between 1970 and 1982, ten Soviet Venera landers reached Venus' surface. The immense heat and pressure made each lander malfunction after a few minutes, but four of the landers managed to photograph their surroundings, showing gritty sand and slabs of volcanic rock.

Fly-by

Between 1979 and 1989, a fly-by probe known as Voyager 2 visited the four gas-giant planets – Jupiter, Saturn, Uranus and Neptune. As it flew past, the probe collected lots of data about each planet.

Orbiter

Arriving at Saturn in July 2004, the Cassini spacecraft will orbit the ringed planet for four years. It will also drop a lander probe on to Titan, Saturn's biggest moon.

Comet Probe

The Stardust probe will fly past comet Wild 2 and capture particles from its tail, bringing them back to Earth in 2006.

Rover

Rover craft let scientists explore beyond the reach of a lander. Here Pathfinder's Sojourner rover examines the Martian boulder Yogi, about a 1 metre (3 ft) across.

• Amazing Fact •

Voyager 1 is the most distant human-made object, at more than 11,000 million kilometres (6,900 million mi) from Earth. Launched in 1977, it visited Jupiter and Saturn in 1979–80 and is now heading towards the edge of the Solar System. Voyager 1 should keep sending back data until at least 2020.

4 Lander cocooned in airbags lands

5 Airbags deflate

6 Airbags retract and petals of lander open

7 Sojourner rover leaves lander and explores nearby

Our Solar System

AT THE CENTRE of the Solar System is the enormous Sun, which makes up 99.9 per cent of the Solar System's mass. Orbiting the Sun are the nine planets along with smaller bodies called asteroids and comets, all controlled by the Sun's powerful gravity. Just as planets orbit the Sun, most planets have at least one moon orbiting them. The four largest planets also have rings, Saturn's being the biggest and most famous.

The nine planets travel in the same direction almost on the same level, or plane. Their orbits are flattened circles called ellipses. If a planet had a perfectly circular orbit, the distance between the planet and the Sun would always be the same. In an elliptical orbit, the distance varies – Mars, for example, travels as far from the Sun as 249 million kilometres (155 million mi) and as near as 207 million kilometres (129 million mi). But planet orbits are still much more circular than the orbits of comets. Some comets have such elliptical orbits that they travel from the scorching zone around the Sun to an icy darkness half-way to the nearest stars.

Thousands of years ago, people tracked the motions of planets and comets with the unaided eye. When the telescope was invented 400 years ago, astronomers could start to study the details of the planets. Since about 1960, spacecraft have revealed many more features, including the red rocks of Mars, a giant storm on Neptune and erupting volcanoes on Jupiter's moon, Io. We used to think that ours was the only solar system, but scientists have recently found planets circling distant Sun-like stars. There may even be other planets like Earth.

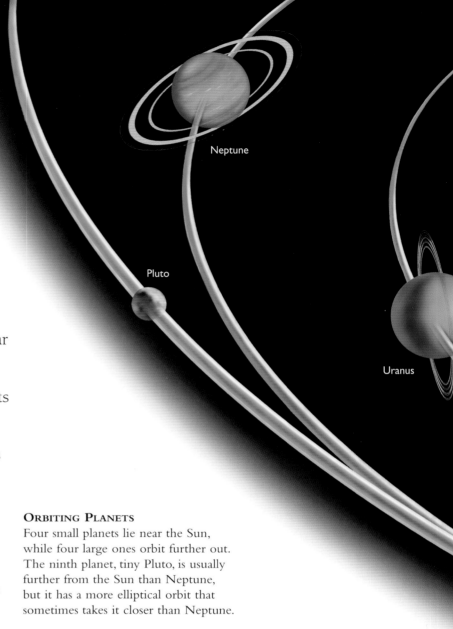

Neptune

Pluto

Uranus

ORBITING PLANETS
Four small planets lie near the Sun, while four large ones orbit further out. The ninth planet, tiny Pluto, is usually further from the Sun than Neptune, but it has a more elliptical orbit that sometimes takes it closer than Neptune.

SOLAR SYSTEM STARS
JUST 1, WHICH WE CALL THE SUN

SOLAR SYSTEM PLANETS
9: MERCURY, VENUS, EARTH, MARS, JUPITER, SATURN, URANUS, NEPTUNE, PLUTO

SOLAR SYSTEM MOONS
68 MOONS FOUND SO FAR (2 ORBITING ASTEROIDS)

SOLAR SYSTEM ASTEROIDS
MILLIONS, BUT ONLY ABOUT 10,000 HAVE WELL-MAPPED ORBITS

SOLAR SYSTEM COMETS
ASTRONOMERS GUESS BILLIONS

DISTANCE FROM THE SUN
The diagram shows each planet, its average distance from the Sun, and part of the Sun itself, all to scale. Light from the Sun can reach us in only eight minutes, but takes four hours to travel out to Neptune.

◆ PROJECT: *Draw an Orbit* ◆

For this project, you need two drawing pins, a pencil, letter-size (A4) paper, cardboard as big as the paper and a length of light string or strong thread about a 30 centimetres (1 ft) long.

❶ Tape the paper to the cardboard, then push the two pins into the middle of the paper about 12 centimetres (5 in) apart.

❷ Tie the string ends to make a loop and place it over the two pins.

❸ With the pencil holding the loop taut as shown, trace an oval.

❹ Change the spacing of the pins to vary the shape of the oval.

The oval curve is called an ellipse, the path that planets and comets follow. The closer together the two pins are, the more the ellipse will look like a planet's orbit. When you put the pins further apart, the ellipse becomes more elongated and comet-like.

Mercury: 58 million km (36 million mi)
Venus: 108 million km (67 million mi)
Earth: 150 million km (93 million mi)
Mars: 228 million km (142 million mi)

Asteroid belt

Jupiter: 778 million km (483 million mi)

Saturn: 1,432 million km (890 million mi)

Uranus: 2,871 million km (1,784 million mi)

Trojan asteroids

Mars

Venus

Mercury

Earth

Jupiter

Asteroid belt

Saturn

Comet

DAY AND YEAR

The time a planet takes to make one trip around the Sun is called its year. A planet also rotates on its axis – an imaginary line through its centre. One full rotation is the planet's time of rotation, or sidereal day. Earth's time of rotation is 23 hours and 56 minutes; its solar day – the time from noon one day to noon the next – is 24 hours.

I revolution around
Sun = I year

I rotation on
axis =
I sidereal day

✦ AMAZING FACT ✦

Distances in the Solar System mean long journeys for space probes. It took the Lunar Prospector more than four days to reach the Moon. The Mars Pathfinder (shown right) took seven months to get to Mars. And Voyager 2 travelled two years on its way to Jupiter, then another ten years to reach Neptune.

Neptune: 4,498 million km
(2,795 million mi)

Pluto: 5,914 million km
(3,675 million mi)

The Planets

THE PLANETS FALL INTO TWO MAIN GROUPS — small rocky worlds and large gas-rich ones. They are like this because of how they formed. About 5,000 million years ago, the Sun and planets were born from a cloud of dust and gas. The thickest part of the cloud became the core and grew even thicker as it sucked in matter. This core, called the proto-Sun, grew hotter as it collapsed. Eventually nuclear reactions began inside it and it started to shine as a star — our Sun.

Meanwhile, the rest of the cloud settled into a disc called the solar nebula, which was slowly turning. The nebula was hot where it lay near the proto-Sun and icy cold at its edges. Particles in the nebula collided and stuck together, forming small bodies, which attracted more particles and grew larger. The bodies closest to the proto-Sun were too hot to hold much water or ice. They evolved into small, rocky planets — Mercury, Venus, Earth and Mars. Further from the Sun's heat, Jupiter, Saturn, Uranus and Neptune formed. They are called gas giants because of their great size and because they are rich in hydrogen, helium and other gases.

Between Mars and Jupiter is a band of asteroids — rocky or metallic fragments that never formed a planet. Finally, out where the Sun's heat barely reached, icy bodies took shape. These were small, very cold and loaded with frozen water and some rocky elements. A few collided to form objects such as Pluto. Others became comets.

PLANETS KNOWN SINCE PRE-HISTORY
MERCURY, VENUS, MARS, JUPITER, SATURN

PLANETS RECENTLY DISCOVERED
URANUS   1781 BY WILLIAM HERSCHEL
NEPTUNE   1846 BY URBAIN LEVERRIER AND J.C. ADAMS
PLUTO   1930 BY CLYDE TOMBAUGH

PLANETS VISITED BY PROBES
ALL PLANETS EXCEPT PLUTO HAVE BEEN VISITED BY AT LEAST ONE SPACE PROBE.

PLANETS WITH MOONS
7 PLANETS ARE ORBITED BY MOONS: EARTH, MARS, JUPITER, SATURN, URANUS, NEPTUNE, PLUTO

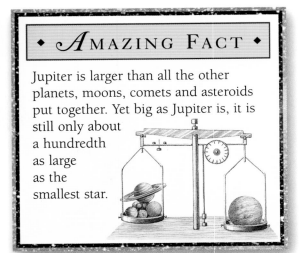

◆ *A*MAZING FACT ◆

Jupiter is larger than all the other planets, moons, comets and asteroids put together. Yet big as Jupiter is, it is still only about a hundredth as large as the smallest star.

ROCKS AND GAS

Shown here to scale are all of the Sun's planets. They divide naturally into two main types — small rocky planets like Earth and big gas-giant planets like Jupiter. (Tiny Pluto is something of a special case all by itself.) Each planet rotates at a particular angle around its axis (an imaginary line through the planet's centre, indicated here by the small grey markers).

Mercury

Venus

Earth

Mars

Jupiter

THE ROCKY PLANETS

The four inner planets are made mostly of rock and are small compared with the gas-giant planets. Mercury is airless, but Venus, Earth and Mars have relatively thin atmospheres that were mostly erupted from volcanoes.

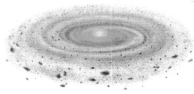

❶ SOLAR SYSTEM BIRTH
The Solar System begins when a cloud of dust and gas collapses to form a dense core surrounded by a broad disc called the solar nebula.

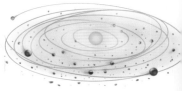

❷ PROTO-SUN FORMS
The nebula's densest part quickly attracts dust and gas. It grows larger and hotter and becomes the proto-Sun.

THE GAS GIANTS

The four gas-giant planets formed from icy and gaseous materials, the same sorts of materials that made up the Sun. These planets all have thick, deep atmospheres of hydrogen and helium.

Saturn

PLUTO

The little world of Pluto is unlike either the rocky planets or the gas giants. It probably formed from icy materials beyond Neptune's orbit. The gravity of the gas-giant planets then moved Pluto to its present orbit.

Pluto

Uranus

◆ LOOK AGAIN ◆

● What are the two main kinds of planet?

● How many planets have been discovered in recent times?

● Which is the smallest planet? Which is the largest?

Neptune

❸ SMALL BODIES FORM
Particles stick together into fragments of rock and ice called planetesimals – the building blocks of planets.

❹ PROTO-PLANETS FORM
The planetesimals clump together, often in violent collisions, to form larger bodies called proto-planets.

❺ NINE PLANETS EMERGE
The Sun becomes a star, and its radiation blows away any left-over dusty gas, leaving behind nine planets.

The Sun

To us, the most important object in our sky is the Sun. Its energy powers Earth's climate and supports life. Yet the Sun is an ordinary star like a million others in the Milky Way galaxy.

Like other stars, the Sun is a huge ball of hot gas, mostly hydrogen (92.1 per cent) and helium (7.8 per cent). In its core, extremely high temperatures and pressures fuse hydrogen into helium. This nuclear fusion releases energy that slowly travels to the surface and makes the Sun shine.

The Sun's heat and light make it dangerous to look at, so astronomers use telescopes fitted with special filters to study its surface, which is known as the photosphere. They can see that the photosphere is split into granules, cells formed by currents of gas rising from inside the Sun. Small dark regions known as sunspots come and go, and giant loops of gas called prominences leap from the surface. Occasionally, part of the photosphere erupts in a solar flare, one of nature's most powerful explosions.

The Sun's life is not quite half over, with about 7,000 million years to go. Eventually, our star will run out of hydrogen to turn into helium. It will first swell to become a red giant star and then shed its outer layers, leaving behind a tiny hot star called a white dwarf (see page 68).

ORIGIN OF NAME
Sunne, the Anglo-Saxon word for 'Sun'
DIAMETER
1,392,000 km (865,000 mi)
MASS
332,946 x Earth's mass
SURFACE TEMPERATURE
5,500°C (9,900°F)
CORE TEMPERATURE
15,500,000°C (27,900,000°F)
TIME OF ROTATION
25 Earth days at equator, 34 Earth days near poles

◆ LOOK AGAIN ◆
- How much longer does the Sun have to live?
- How long does it take energy from the Sun's core to reach the surface?
- Why are sunspots dark?

MAP OF THE SUN
The photosphere's sunspots and prominences appear and vanish over time. Beneath the photosphere, energy from the core trickles out through the radiative zone, then moves in currents through the convective zone, like water boiling in a pot. The energy takes 200,000 years to travel from core to surface.

CORONA
The Sun's corona is a dim halo of super-hot gas. Because it is faint compared with the rest of the Sun, it can be seen clearly only when the Sun is completely hidden by the Moon during a total solar eclipse.

◆ AMAZING FACT ◆
The Sun rings like a bell! Sound waves bounce around inside the Sun every several minutes. These waves are too low frequency for humans to hear, but astronomers use special devices to analyze them. This 'ringing' helps astronomers study the Sun's structure.

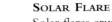

LOOPS OF GAS
The Sun's powerful magnetic fields bend and twist gas near the surface into loops. If the magnetic lines break, gas sprays out into space.

SOLAR FLARE
Solar flares erupt mainly when there are many sunspots on the Sun. The enormous energy a flare releases can disrupt communications and cause electrical power blackouts on Earth.

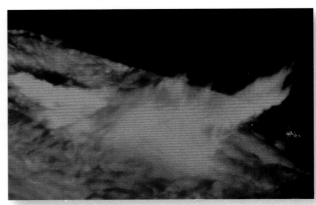

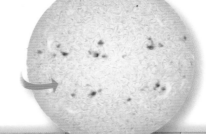

Year 1 Sunspot minimum — Year 5 Sunspot maximum — Year 9 Approaching minimum

SUNSPOT CYCLE
The number of sunspots waxes and wanes every 11 years. As the spots increase, they occur closer to the solar equator. As the last spots of one cycle fade, the first of a new cycle appear.

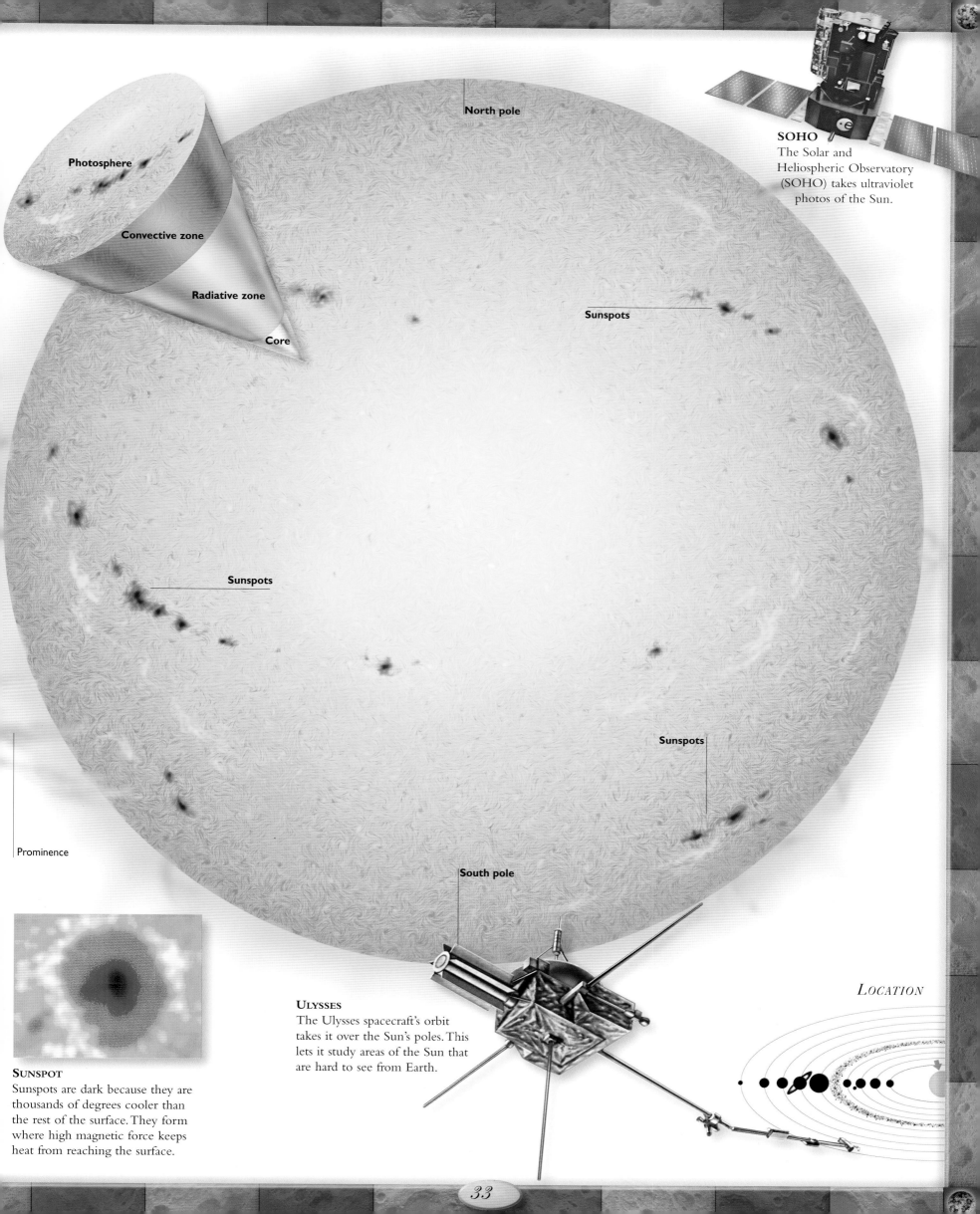

North pole

Photosphere

Convective zone

Radiative zone

Core

Sunspots

Sunspots

Sunspots

Prominence

South pole

SOHO
The Solar and Heliospheric Observatory (SOHO) takes ultraviolet photos of the Sun.

ULYSSES
The Ulysses spacecraft's orbit takes it over the Sun's poles. This lets it study areas of the Sun that are hard to see from Earth.

SUNSPOT
Sunspots are dark because they are thousands of degrees cooler than the rest of the surface. They form where high magnetic force keeps heat from reaching the surface.

LOCATION

Mercury

MERCURY IS THE CLOSEST planet to the Sun. This makes it hard to see from Earth because it always lies near the Sun's glare. It also makes Mercury's sunny side very hot – temperatures can reach 427°C (800°F), but since there is little atmosphere to trap the Sun's energy, they plunge to –173°C (–280°F) on its night side. At the planet's north and south poles, some craters are always in shadow and may contain patches of underground ice. If so, the water probably came from collisions with icy comets.

In 1974–75, photos from the Mariner 10 spacecraft showed that Mercury's surface looks like the Moon (see page 43). It is covered with craters and basins – the scars of impacts. The biggest basin, Caloris, is 1,300 kilometres (800 mi) across. But Mercury is not just a bigger version of the Moon. It has a huge iron core, which is probably the source of Mercury's magnetic field. Mysteriously, this field is only a hundredth as strong as Earth's.

Mercury's year – one orbit of the Sun – is only 88 Earth days long, but its day – one rotation on its axis – lasts 59 Earth days. This means that an astronaut on the planet's surface would see sunrise occur once every 176 Earth days.

ORIGIN OF NAME
MERCURIUS, THE ROMAN MESSENGER OF THE GODS

DISTANCE FROM THE SUN
58 MILLION KM (36 MILLION MI)

DIAMETER
4,875 KM (3,029 MI)

MASS
55% X EARTH'S MASS

ATMOSPHERE
NONE

MOONS
NONE

LENGTH OF DAY (in Earth days)
ROTATION TIME: 59 / SOLAR DAY: 176

LENGTH OF YEAR
88 EARTH DAYS

MAP OF MERCURY

Mercury's cratered surface was mapped by the Mariner 10 spacecraft. Because of its flight path, Mariner mapped only half the planet. We won't know what's on the other side until another probe visits. Many of Mercury's features are named after musicians, artists and writers.

CRATERS AND LAVA FLOWS

Thousands and thousands of impact craters cover Mercury, but between the craters lies a surface built by flows of lava (molten rock). In this photo, you can see fractures in the surface.

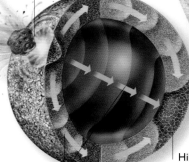

Rocky crust

Rocky mantle

CALORIS BASIN
(behind cross-section cone)

TIR PLANITIA

◄ Fet

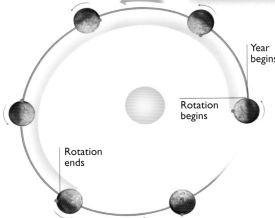

Year begins

Rotation begins

Rotation ends

LONG DAY, SHORT YEAR

During its year of 88 Earth days, Mercury turns on its axis one and a half times. The marker on its surface shows that it completes only half of a solar day in this time. A full solar day from noon to noon lasts 176 Earth days.

Caloris Basin impact

A GIANT IMPACT

The Caloris Basin formed when a huge object crashed into Mercury. The impact sent such powerful shock waves through the iron core that it created hills almost 5,000 kilometres (3,000 mi) away on the other side of the planet.

Hills

Shock waves

◆ PROJECT: *Making Craters* ◆

For this project, you need a baking tin, flour and water, and a few round objects of different sizes such as a ball bearing, a marble and a golf ball. Do this project outdoors – it can get a bit messy.

1. Mix the flour with water until it is soft, but not runny.
2. Fill a baking tin nearly to the top with the flour mixture.
3. Put the tin on the ground.
4. Stand over the tin and drop objects into the mixture from various heights. Remove them carefully after each impact, leaving the crater.
5. Try dropping a larger object from a low height, then throwing a smaller one from the same height at higher speed. Which makes a bigger crater?

◆ AMAZING FACT ◆

Mercury has wrinkles! After the planet formed and cooled, its core shrank. The crust buckled, pushing up giant wrinkles of rock called scarps.

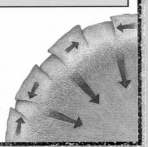

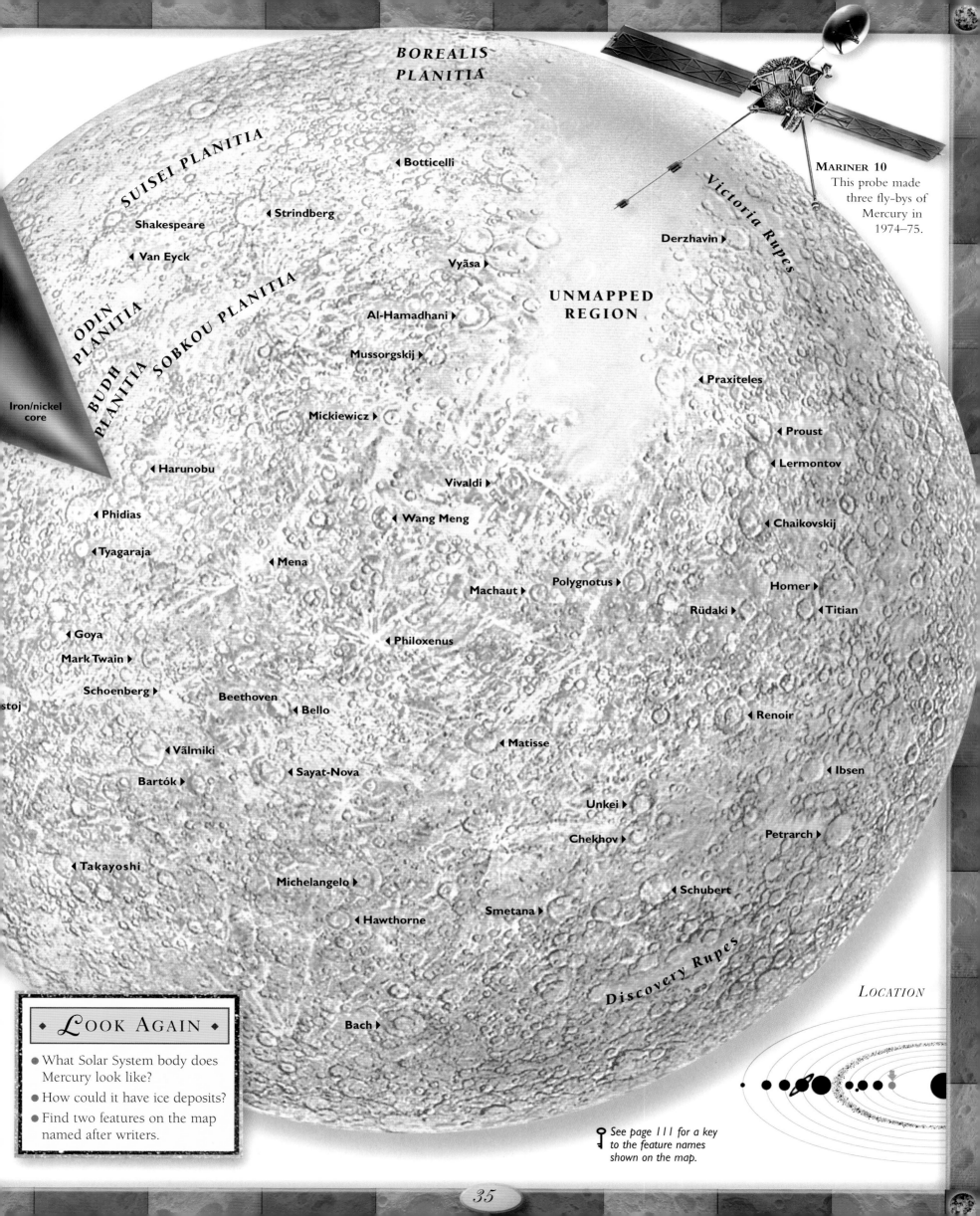

BOREALIS
PLANITIA

SUISEI PLANITIA

◄ Botticelli

Shakespeare

◄ Strindberg

◄ Van Eyck

Vyăsa ▶

ODIN
PLANITIA

SOBKOU PLANITIA

BUDH
PLANITIA

Al-Hamadhani ▶

UNMAPPED
REGION

Derzhavin ▶

Victoria Rupes

MARINER 10
This probe made
three fly-bys of
Mercury in
1974–75.

Mussorgskij ▶

◄ Praxiteles

Iron/nickel
core

Mickiewicz ▶

◄ Harunobu

Vivaldi ▶

◄ Proust

◄ Lermontov

◄ Phidias

◄ Wang Meng

◄ Chaikovskij

◄ Tyagaraja

◄ Mena

Polygnotus ▶

Homer ▶

Machaut ▶

Rüdaki ▶

◄ Titian

◄ Goya

◄ Philoxenus

Mark Twain ▶

Schoenberg ▶

Beethoven

◄ Renoir

stoj

◄ Bello

◄ Matisse

◄ Vălmiki

◄ Ibsen

Bartók ▶

◄ Sayat-Nova

Unkei ▶

Chekhov ▶

Petrarch ▶

◄ Takayoshi

◄ Schubert

Michelangelo ▶

Smetana ▶

◄ Hawthorne

Discovery Rupes

Bach ▶

See page 111 for a key
to the feature names
shown on the map.

LOCATION

◆ LOOK AGAIN ◆

- What Solar System body does
  Mercury look like?
- How could it have ice deposits?
- Find two features on the map
  named after writers.

Venus

VENUS IS THE SECOND PLANET from the Sun, and the one most like Earth in size. We often see Venus shining like a bright star in the morning or evening sky. The brightness comes from sunlight reflected off a layer of white sulphuric acid clouds about 50 to 70 kilometres (30 to 40 mi) above the planet's surface. Venus has a dense atmosphere – it is mostly carbon dioxide and presses down nearly 100 times more heavily than Earth's. The thick gases let sunlight through, but block outgoing heat. This greenhouse effect has given Venus the Solar System's hottest surface, with a temperature of 470°C (880°F).

Between 1978 and 1994, the Pioneer, Venera and Magellan spacecraft used radar to map Venus' surface. Volcanoes and lava flows dominate the landscape, but there are only about a thousand impact craters, far fewer than on Mercury. Lava flows from volcanoes and cracks in the surface have repaved the planet, covering up early craters. Some scientists think Venus may even have volcanoes that still erupt.

Two unexplained oddities are that Venus takes longer to rotate once on its axis than it does to travel once around the Sun, and that it rotates backwards compared with Earth.

ORIGIN OF NAME
VENUS, THE ROMAN GODDESS OF BEAUTY

DISTANCE FROM THE SUN
108 MILLION KM (67 MILLION MI)

DIAMETER
12,104 KM (7,521 MI)

MASS
82% X EARTH'S MASS

ATMOSPHERE
CARBON DIOXIDE, 96 TIMES DENSER THAN EARTH'S AIR

MOONS
NONE

LENGTH OF DAY (in Earth days)
ROTATION TIME: 243 / SOLAR DAY: 117

LENGTH OF YEAR
225 EARTH DAYS

BRIGHT CLOUDS
Sulphuric acid clouds show up as swirls in this ultraviolet photo. The clouds race around the planet every four days.

♦ PROJECT: *Jam-Jar Greenhouse* ♦

For this project, you need an outdoor thermometer, a glass jar with a lid and a sunny day.

❶ Place the jar outside in the sunshine with its mouth up and the lid off. Put the thermometer inside with the bulb pointing down.

❷ Wait a few minutes for the temperature to stop rising, then make a note of the temperature.

❸ Now put the thermometer inside the jar with the bulb pointing up. Screw on the lid, and place the jar on its lid back in the sunshine.

❹ Again, wait for the temperature to stabilize. Has the temperature changed?

What you have done is to create a mini-greenhouse effect. By sealing the top of the jar, sun-warmed air cannot escape and it grows hotter.

MAP OF VENUS
Spacecraft have mapped all of Venus' surface, revealing mountain ranges, volcanoes and lava flows. Most of these features have been named after women. Venus lacks the moving crustal plates that join and divide Earth's land masses.

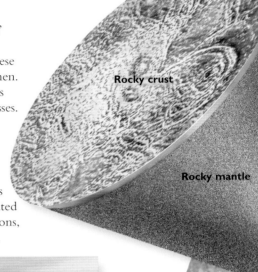

Rocky crust

Rocky mantle

VENUSIAN VOLCANOES
Volcanoes are common on Venus and many impact craters show signs of flooding by lava. This image created from Magellan data shows Maat Mons, a volcano 8 kilometres (5 mi) high.

Ovda Regio

ISHTAR TERRA
AUDRA PLANITIA
APHRODIT

Lakshmi Planum
Cleopatra
Tellus Tessera

Beta Regio
GUINEVERE PLANITIA
Maxwell Montes

Devana Chasma

Sappho Patera
Pavlova Corona

Eistla Regio

NAVKA PLANITIA
Heng-o Corona
TINATIN PLANITIA
APHRODITE TERRA

Phoebe Regio

AINO PLANITIA

Dione Regio
Alpha Regio

Hathor Mons
Innini Mons
Eve Corona

Alpha Regio hemisphere

Clouds reflect much of Sun's energy

Some solar energy passes through clouds and heats surface

GREENHOUSE EFFECT
Venus suffers from a runaway greenhouse effect. Strong sunlight filters through the clouds and heats the surface, but the clouds and carbon dioxide in the atmosphere keep the heat from escaping back into space. Venus just cannot cool down.

Carbon dioxide keeps heat from escaping into space

VELLAMO
PLANITIA

◄ Cauteovan
Corona

◄ Maria Celeste

Greenaway

NIOBE
PLANITIA

*Nokomis
Montes*

Atla Ganis Chasma *Regio*

◄ Sapas Mons

◄ Ozza Mons

RUSALKA PLANITIA

◄ Maat Mons

◄ Maram Corona

Iron/nickel
core

*Thetis
Regio*

APHRODITE TERRA

Diana Chasma *Dali Chasma*

◄ Stanton

◄ Isabella

*Phoebe
Regio*

TERRA

*Artemis
Corona*

AINO

Juno Chasma

Bonnevie

Artemis Chasma

PLANITIA

LADA TERRA

HELEN
PLANITIA

NSOMEKA PLANITIA

KAWELU PLANITIA

MAGELLAN
From 1990 to 1994,
NASA's Magellan
probe used radar
to map Venus.

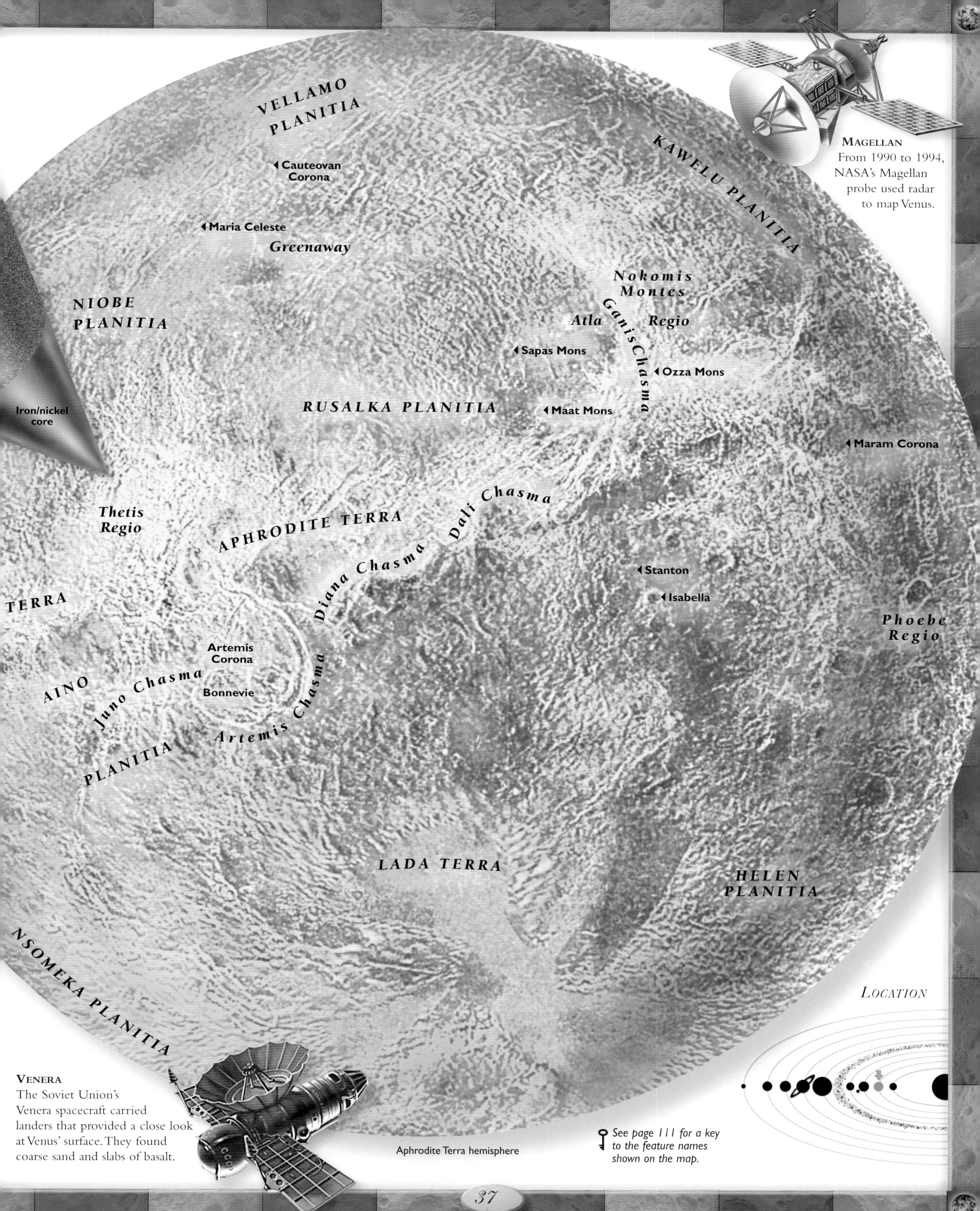

LOCATION

VENERA
The Soviet Union's
Venera spacecraft carried
landers that provided a close look
at Venus' surface. They found
coarse sand and slabs of basalt.

Aphrodite Terra hemisphere

See page 111 for a key
to the feature names
shown on the map.

Earth

THE THIRD PLANET FROM THE SUN, Earth is the largest of the small rocky planets. Seen from space, it is the Blue Planet, due to the soft blue haze of its atmosphere and the deep blue of the oceans that cover 71 per cent of it. Earth is the only planet whose surface has water in all three of its forms – solid, vapour and liquid – and appears to be the only planet with life. The oceans help reduce the extremes of hot and cold by absorbing solar energy at hot regions around the Equator and moving it to cooler regions towards the poles. These differences in heat and cold drive our weather and climate.

When Earth formed, it was hot enough for its rocks to melt. Iron and nickel sank to form a core, while lighter materials separated into a middle layer – the mantle – and an upper layer – the crust. The outer core remains molten, but the crust cooled and became hard. It broke into pieces called plates, which fit together like the pieces of a jigsaw puzzle. Thin plates lie under the oceans, and thick plates carry continents. Heat from the core drives mantle rocks in slow convection currents that push the plates together and pull them apart. Called plate tectonics, this process has moved continents all over the globe.

ORIGIN OF NAME
EORTHE, THE ANGLO-SAXON WORD FOR 'GROUND'

DISTANCE FROM THE SUN
150 MILLION KM (93 MILLION MI)

DIAMETER
12,756 KM (7,926 MI)

MASS
1.0 EARTH MASS = 5.5 x 10^{24} TONNES (6 x 10^{24} TONS)

ATMOSPHERE
NITROGEN 78%, OXYGEN 21%

MOONS
1: THE MOON

LENGTH OF DAY (in hours/minutes)
ROTATION TIME: 23 H 56 M / SOLAR DAY: 24 H

LENGTH OF YEAR
365.25 DAYS

VOLCANIC ACTIVITY

Molten rock, or magma, rises from Earth's mantle and erupts at weak parts of the crust, building volcanoes in repeated eruptions. This is how the Hawaiian Islands formed – volcanoes are still erupting there.

SHAPING THE LANDSCAPE

Erosion by waves, wind and rain shape the landscape. These cliffs, for example, will be slowly pushed back as waves batter them down. Erosion has erased many ancient features and made Earth's surface among the youngest in the Solar System.

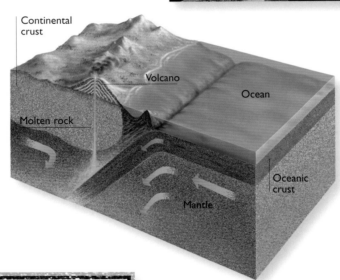

Continental crust

Volcano

Ocean

Molten rock

Oceanic crust

Mantle

COLLIDING PLATES

When a thin plate of oceanic crust and a thick continental plate collide, the oceanic plate dives beneath the continent and melts. Molten rock from deep within Earth rises to create volcanoes. These collisions happen about as fast as a fingernail grows.

EUROPE

Caspian Sea

Hindu Kush

Sahara Desert

Arabian Peninsula

Arabian Sea

AFRICA

Great Rift Valley

Lake Victoria

Madagascar

◆ PROJECT: *Erosion in a Tray* ◆

Do this project out of doors. You need a large shallow tray, enough sand to almost fill the tray and a hose and a supply of water.

❶ Fill the tray with sand and soak it thoroughly with water.

❷ Hold up one end of the tray about 2 or 3 centimetres (1 in).

❸ Hold the hose over the edge of the tray's high end and trickle a thin stream of water into the tray.

❹ Let the water run steadily and observe how it erodes channels in the sand.

❺ To experiment, increase the tray's elevation or the flow of water. Place small rocks in the stream's path and see how it flows around them. Smooth the sand and scratch a straight groove – how long does the stream flow within it?

LIFE ON EARTH

Life flourishes everywhere on Earth and takes almost endless forms. Because of its distance from the Sun, Earth is neither too hot nor too cold and there is plenty of liquid water. Scientists don't know where life came from, but liquid water appears crucial to life.

Plants

Birds

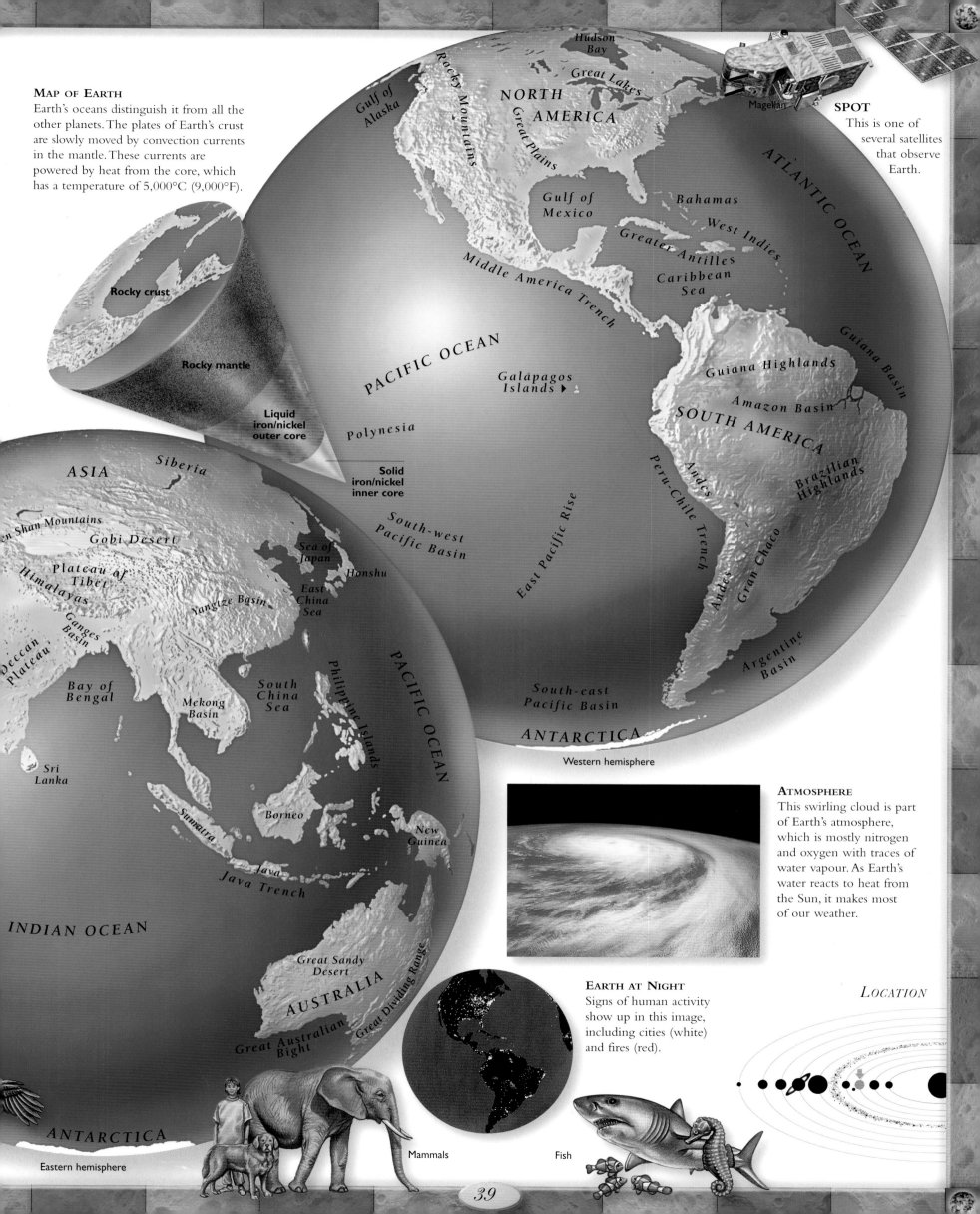

MAP OF EARTH

Earth's oceans distinguish it from all the other planets. The plates of Earth's crust are slowly moved by convection currents in the mantle. These currents are powered by heat from the core, which has a temperature of 5,000°C (9,000°F).

Rocky crust

Rocky mantle

Liquid iron/nickel outer core

Solid iron/nickel inner core

SPOT
This is one of several satellites that observe Earth.

Magellan

Western hemisphere

ATLANTIC OCEAN

NORTH AMERICA

Hudson Bay

Great Lakes

Gulf of Alaska

Rocky Mountains

Great Plains

Gulf of Mexico

Bahamas

West Indies

Greater Antilles

Caribbean Sea

Middle America Trench

PACIFIC OCEAN

Galápagos Islands ▸

Polynesia

South-west Pacific Basin

East Pacific Rise

Guiana Highlands

Guiana Basin

Amazon Basin

SOUTH AMERICA

Peru-Chile Trench

Andes

Brazilian Highlands

Gran Chaco

Andes

Argentine Basin

South-east Pacific Basin

ANTARCTICA

ATMOSPHERE
This swirling cloud is part of Earth's atmosphere, which is mostly nitrogen and oxygen with traces of water vapour. As Earth's water reacts to heat from the Sun, it makes most of our weather.

ASIA

Siberia

n Shan Mountains

Gobi Desert

Plateau of Tibet

Himalayas

Deccan Plateau

Ganges Basin

Yangtze Basin

Sea of Japan

East China Sea

Honshu

Bay of Bengal

Mekong Basin

South China Sea

Philippine Islands

PACIFIC OCEAN

Sri Lanka

Sumatra

Borneo

New Guinea

Java

Java Trench

INDIAN OCEAN

Great Sandy Desert

AUSTRALIA

Great Dividing Range

Great Australian Bight

ANTARCTICA

Eastern hemisphere

EARTH AT NIGHT
Signs of human activity show up in this image, including cities (white) and fires (red).

LOCATION

Mammals

Fish

Earth and the Sun

As EARTH SPINS ON ITS AXIS, we have day and night, and as it moves around the Sun, we have changing seasons. The seasons happen because Earth is tilted – its rotation axis tips 23.5 degrees to its orbit. This means that the amount of sunlight and solar energy falling on most parts of Earth varies during the year.

Around 21 June each year, the North Pole is tilted most directly towards the Sun. This day is called the solstice. In the Northern Hemisphere, it marks the Sun's highest path across the sky and the start of summer (winter in the Southern Hemisphere). Around 21 December, another solstice occurs when the North Pole is tilted most directly away from the Sun. This marks the Sun's lowest path across the sky and the start of winter in the Northern Hemisphere (summer in the Southern Hemisphere). In March and September, the Sun is directly over the Equator, and day and night are equally long everywhere on Earth. This is the equinox and the start of spring or autumn in much of the world.

Some parts of the globe do not experience four seasons. The regions around the Equator receive the most direct sunlight and stay warm all year round. The polar regions receive the least sunlight – in winter there is no sunlight for several months.

The Sun influences Earth in other ways, too. The solar wind, a flow of charged particles from the Sun, is always flowing past Earth. Earth's magnetic field deflects most of the particles, but some get through. They strike the upper atmosphere near the north and south magnetic poles, making the air glow. From the ground, we see rippling curtains of light called auroras.

EARTH CLOSEST TO THE SUN
EARLY JANUARY – 147 MILLION KM (91.5 MILLION MI)

EARTH FURTHEST FROM THE SUN
EARLY JULY – 152 MILLION KM (94.5 MILLION MI)

DISTANCE EARTH TRAVELS PER YEAR
940 MILLION KM (584 MILLION MI)

AVERAGE SPEED OF EARTH
107,000 KM (66,000 MI) PER HOUR

HOTTEST TEMPERATURE
HOTTEST TEMPERATURE EVER RECORDED ON EARTH – 58°C (136°F) AT AZIZIA, LIBYA, 13 SEPTEMBER, 1922

COLDEST TEMPERATURE
COLDEST TEMPERATURE EVER RECORDED ON EARTH – –89°C (–129°F) AT VOSTOK STATION, ANTARCTICA, 21 JULY, 1983

· AMAZING FACT ·

The sunlight warming your face right now left the Sun's surface just over 8 minutes ago. (And moonlight is sunlight that bounced off the Moon only 1.3 seconds ago.)

SEASONS
The seasons change as the amount of sunlight falling on your part of Earth changes. Around 21 June, the North Pole tilts most directly towards the Sun, making summer in the Northern Hemisphere and winter in the Southern Hemisphere. Six months later, the situation is reversed.

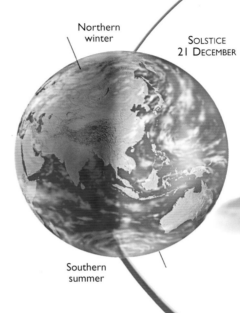

Northern winter

SOLSTICE
21 DECEMBER

Winter scene in the Northern Hemisphere

Southern summer

AURORA
Also known as the Northern or Southern Lights, auroras are stronger and more frequent when the Sun is very active and displays many sunspots.

Solar wind | Aurora | Magnetic field

Earth

Aurora

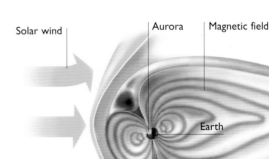

MAGNETIC FIELD
Generated by the iron in Earth's core, a magnetic field surrounds our planet like a web. It helps to protect Earth from the charged particles of the solar wind. When particles do get through to our atmosphere, they cause auroras.

AURORA FROM SPACE
Astronauts on the space shuttle Discovery photographed this Southern Hemisphere aurora from above.

Northern
autumn

EQUINOX
21 SEPTEMBER

Southern
spring

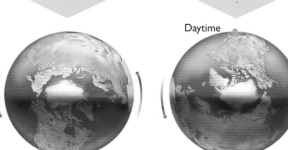

Autumn scene in the
Northern Hemisphere

Northern
summer

SOLSTICE
21 JUNE

Southern
winter

Summer scene in the
Northern Hemisphere

Earth's rotation axis
tilts 23.5°

Northern
spring

EQUINOX
21 MARCH

Spring scene in the
Northern Hemisphere

Southern
autumn

THE SUN AND CLIMATE

At the Equator, the Sun's rays hit Earth almost directly all year long. This is the hottest zone on Earth. As you move further away from the Equator, the rays hit at more of an angle and the climate is cooler.

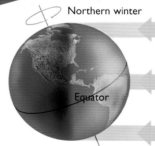

Northern winter   Northern summer

Sunlight

Equator

Equator

Equator

Southern summer   Southern winter

Sunlight

Sunlight

Daytime

DAY AND NIGHT

Day begins when your part of the world turns to face the Sun, and night falls when it turns away. At any moment, parts of the world are experiencing sunrise and sunset, noon and midnight.

Night-time

The Moon

THE MOON IS EARTH'S ONLY natural satellite. It formed soon after Earth did, from the debris that flew out when another body crashed into Earth. As the Moon formed, it was constantly bombarded by meteorites. These punched countless craters into its surface, and big impacts dug broad basins. The scars can still be seen today. The youngest craters have rays, bright streaks of shattered rock flung across the landscape.

Dark lava (molten rock) flowed from under the surface to fill the lowlands and basins. Early astronomers thought these dark areas were the dried-up beds of oceans, so they called them maria, which means 'seas' in Latin. In 1959, an early Soviet probe photographed the unseen far side of the Moon and found that nearly all the maria lie on the side facing Earth.

The Moon's gravity is one-sixth of Earth's. This is too weak to hold on to an atmosphere, so the lunar sky always looks black, even in daytime. The lack of an atmosphere also means that the Moon's surface becomes very hot (117°C or 243°F) when it is facing the Sun, and very cold (–153°C or –243°F) when it turns away.

Recently, the Lunar Prospector spacecraft found ice at the Moon's poles. This probably came from impacts with comets, which mostly contain frozen water.

ORIGIN OF NAME
MONA, THE ANGLO-SAXON WORD FOR 'MOON'

DISTANCE FROM EARTH
384,401 KM (238,856 MI)

DIAMETER
3,476 KM (2,160 MI)

MASS
1.2% X EARTH'S MASS

ATMOSPHERE
NONE

LENGTH OF DAY (in Earth days)
ROTATION TIME AND SOLAR DAY: BOTH 29.5

MAP OF THE MOON
The near side hemisphere is the side of the Moon that always faces Earth. The far side hemisphere was revealed only when probes first visited. The Moon has a small, hot core, a thick mantle and a heavily cratered crust.

Rocky crust

Rocky mantle

ON THE SURFACE
From 1968 to 1972, six Apollo missions landed astronauts on the Moon and brought back rock samples. Here, astronaut James Irwin stands near the Apollo 15 lunar module and rover in 1971.

OCEANUS PROCELLARUM (Ocean of Storms)

LUNAR ICE
The Lunar Prospector spacecraft found ice (white) in craters at the Moon's south pole.

Birkhoff ▶
D'Alembert ▶
Landau ▶
Kovalevskaya ▶
MARE MOSCOVIENSE (Sea of Moscow)
Fitzgerald ▶ ◀ Cockcroft
◀ Mach
Mendeleev ▼ ◀ Anderson Hertzsprung ▶
◀ Schuster
Chaplygin ▶ Korolev ▶
Keeler ▶ ◀ Heaviside ◀ Galois
Tsiolkovskiy ◀ Aitken
Gagarin ▶ MARE INGENII (Sea of Cleverness) ◀ Van de Graaff
Pavlov ▶ ◀ Leeuwenhoek
Roche ▶ Leibnitz ▶ ◀ Apollo
Oppenheimer
◀ Planck
MARE ORIENTALE (Eastern Sea)

Far side hemisphere

♦ PROJECT: *Drawing Moonlight* ♦

For this project, you need a piece of paper and a pencil.

① Draw 31 circles, arranged in lines, on a piece of paper. You can make them big or small, but all 31 should fit on the paper, neatly drawn to the same size. (Try tracing around a glass or a coin.)

② Write today's date next to the first circle and continue until all 31 circles have dates.

③ Find the Moon in the sky.

④ Draw what shape the Moon looks like. If clouds hide the Moon, leave the circle blank or mark it 'clouds'.

⑤ When you have made a week or two of observations, you will see a pattern developing. What you have drawn are the phases of the Moon (see page 44).

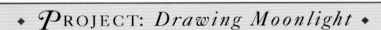

HOW THE MOON FORMED
The young Earth was struck by an object the size of Mars. The debris circled around Earth, then clumped together to form the Moon.

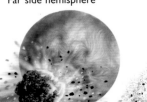

MARE FRIGORIS
(Sea of Cold)

Montes Jura

SINUS IRIDUM
(Bay of Rainbows)

◄ Plato

◄ Aristoteles

Eudoxus ▶

Hercules ▶   ◄ Atlas

Cassini ▶

MARE IMBRIUM
(Sea of Showers)

Aristillus ▶

◄ Euler   Archimedes ▶

Timocharis ▶

Montes Caucasus

MARE SERENITATIS
(Sea of Serenity)

Posidonius ▶

Cleomedes ▶

APOLLO 15 ▶
LANDING SITE

Molten
zone

Core

Eratosthenes ▶

Montes Apenninus

Montes Haemus

Macrobius ▶

APOLLO 17 ▶
LANDING SITE

MARE
CRISIUM
(Sea of
Crises)

◄ Kepler

◄ Copernicus

MARE
TRANQUILLITATIS
(Sea of Tranquillity)

APOLLO 12 ▶
LANDING SITE

◄ APOLLO 14
LANDING SITE

APOLLO 11 ▶
LANDING SITE

MARE
FECUNDITATIS
(Sea of Fertility)

◄ Letronne

MARE
COGNITUM
(Sea of Knowledge)

Ptolemaeus ▶

APOLLO 16 ▶
LANDING SITE

◄ Gassendi

Alphonsus ▶

◄ Albategnius   Theophilus ▶

MARE
HUMORUM
(Sea of Moisture)

MARE
NUBIUM
(Sea of Clouds)

Arzachel ▶

Catharina ▶

MARE
NECTARIS
(Sea of Nectar)

Pitatus ▶

◄ Purbach

Fracastorius ▶

◄ Deslandres

◄ Piccolomini

Tycho ▶

Near side hemisphere

LUNAR PROSPECTOR
Launched in 1998,
this NASA probe
has studied the
composition
of the
Moon.

LOCATION

LUNA 16
The Soviet Union's Luna 16
was the first spacecraft to collect
Moon rocks automatically.

Earth and the Moon

About once every month, the Moon orbits Earth. It always keeps the same side turned towards us, so it appears to us that the Moon does not spin on its axis. But if we watched the Moon from Mars, we would see that it turns once on its axis each month – the same time it takes to revolve once around Earth. For astronauts on the Moon, the lunar day and night last about two weeks each.

The Moon shines only because it is reflecting the light of the Sun. Throughout the month, we see different amounts of the Moon lit up, depending on where it is in its orbit. These changes are called phases. At new Moon, the Sun is shining on the far side of the Moon, so the side that faces us – the near side – is dark and we cannot see it. At full Moon, the near side is fully lit. At other phases, we see only part of the Moon's sunlit surface.

Occasionally, the Moon, Earth and Sun line up and we see eclipses. During a solar eclipse, the Moon passes directly between Earth and the Sun, and its shadow passes over part of Earth. For people in the narrow path of the shadow, the Sun is blacked out partially or totally. Solar eclipses occur because the Moon is just large enough and close enough to Earth to cover the Sun.

Lunar eclipses are much easier to see. When the Moon passes directly behind Earth, Earth blocks direct sunlight. The Moon darkens but doesn't disappear altogether – instead, it glows a deep copper-orange, coloured by sunlight that filters through Earth's atmosphere. A lunar eclipse can last more than an hour. During that time, anyone on the night-time side of Earth can see the eclipsed Moon.

DURATION OF THE MOON'S ORBIT
Seen from Earth (from one New Moon to the next) – 29.5 Earth days
Relative to the stars – 27.3 Earth days

MAXIMUM DURATION OF A TOTAL SOLAR ECLIPSE
7 minutes 40 seconds

HOW OFTEN TOTAL SOLAR ECLIPSES OCCUR
About once a year, but only along a narrow path

USUAL DURATION OF A TOTAL LUNAR ECLIPSE
About 1 hour to 1 hour 40 minutes

HOW OFTEN LUNAR ECLIPSES OCCUR
1 to 3 times a year, over a wide area

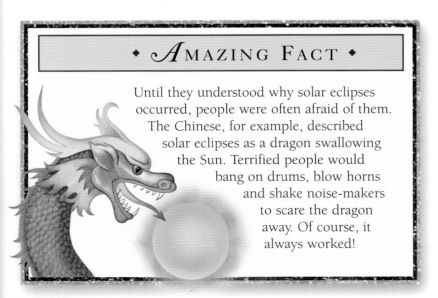

✦ Amazing Fact ✦

Until they understood why solar eclipses occurred, people were often afraid of them. The Chinese, for example, described solar eclipses as a dragon swallowing the Sun. Terrified people would bang on drums, blow horns and shake noise-makers to scare the dragon away. Of course, it always worked!

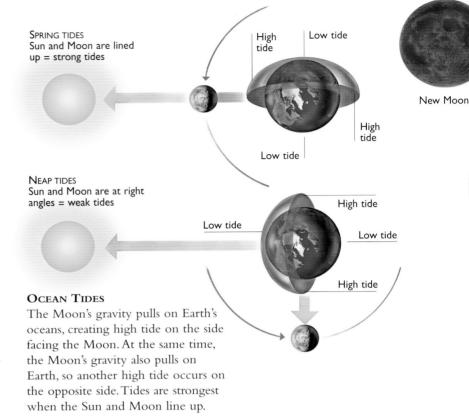

Spring Tides
Sun and Moon are lined up = strong tides

High tide
Low tide
High tide
Low tide

New Moon

Neap Tides
Sun and Moon are at right angles = weak tides

High tide
Low tide
Low tide
High tide

Ocean Tides
The Moon's gravity pulls on Earth's oceans, creating high tide on the side facing the Moon. At the same time, the Moon's gravity also pulls on Earth, so another high tide occurs on the opposite side. Tides are strongest when the Sun and Moon line up.

Earthshine
A pale, ghostly light can sometimes be seen inside the Moon's bright crescent. This is earthshine – sunlight reflecting from Earth's clouds, land and oceans.

Lunar Eclipse
When the Moon passes through Earth's shadow it causes a lunar eclipse. The Moon turns dark and often copper-orange in colour. The colour comes from sunlight filtering through Earth's atmosphere.

Sun

Solar Eclipse
Moments before the Moon completely covers the Sun in a total solar eclipse, sunlight streams through valleys on the Moon and makes a diamond-ring effect. An edge of the Sun is the diamond, and its corona – or outer atmosphere – is the ring itself.

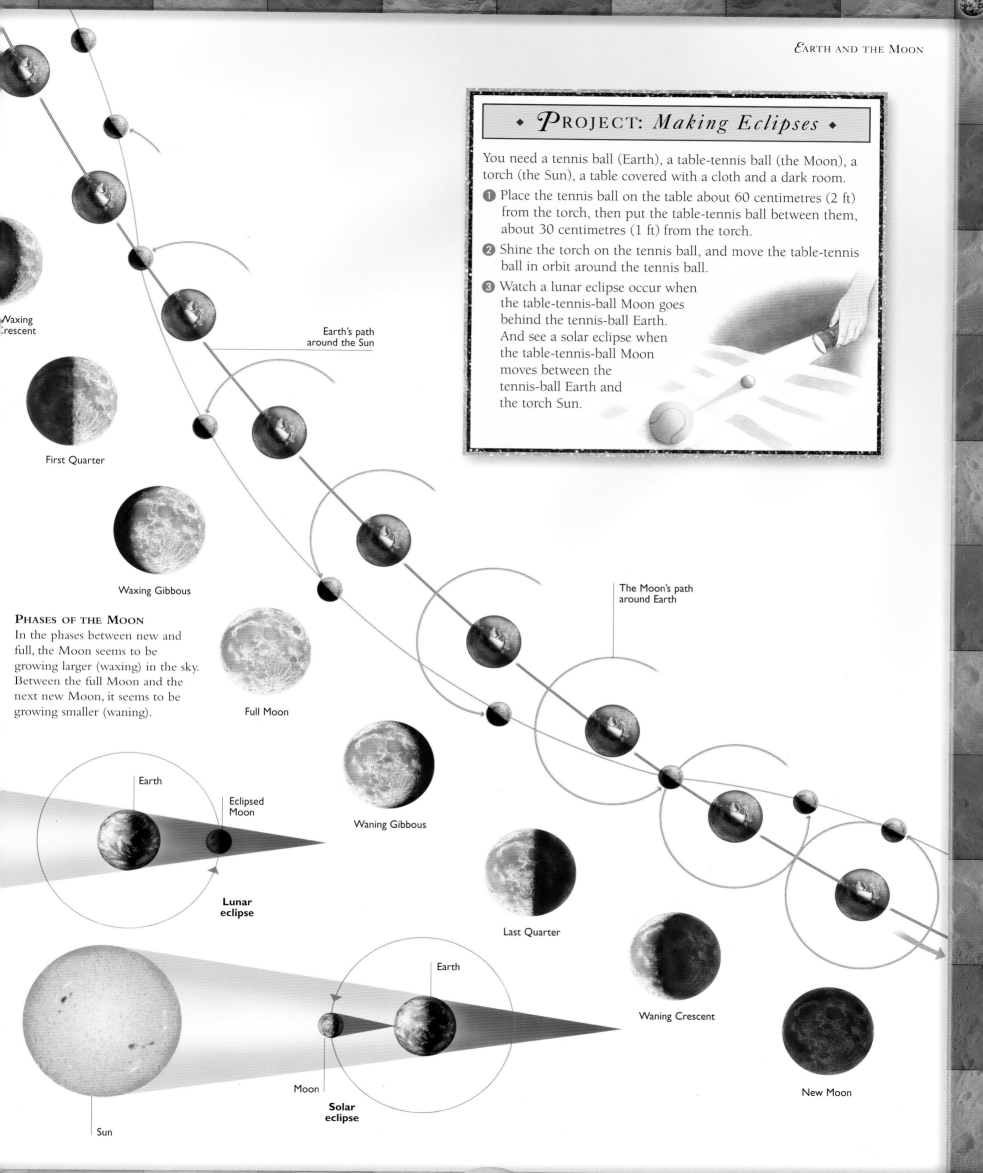

Waxing Crescent

· PROJECT: *Making Eclipses* ·

You need a tennis ball (Earth), a table-tennis ball (the Moon), a torch (the Sun), a table covered with a cloth and a dark room.

1. Place the tennis ball on the table about 60 centimetres (2 ft) from the torch, then put the table-tennis ball between them, about 30 centimetres (1 ft) from the torch.

2. Shine the torch on the tennis ball, and move the table-tennis ball in orbit around the tennis ball.

3. Watch a lunar eclipse occur when the table-tennis-ball Moon goes behind the tennis-ball Earth. And see a solar eclipse when the table-tennis-ball Moon moves between the tennis-ball Earth and the torch Sun.

Earth's path around the Sun

First Quarter

Waxing Gibbous

The Moon's path around Earth

PHASES OF THE MOON
In the phases between new and full, the Moon seems to be growing larger (waxing) in the sky. Between the full Moon and the next new Moon, it seems to be growing smaller (waning).

Full Moon

Earth

Eclipsed Moon

Lunar eclipse

Waning Gibbous

Last Quarter

Waning Crescent

New Moon

Earth

Moon

Solar eclipse

Sun

Meteors and Meteorites

MORE THAN 180 TONNES (200 tons) of space debris enter Earth's atmosphere every day. Dust grains, bits of cosmic debris the size of peas and occasional larger pieces of rock or iron continually enter Earth's atmosphere. Because these objects travel at more than 13 kilometres (8 mi) per second, friction with air molecules causes most of the material to burn up in the atmosphere. The result is a bright streak of light called a meteor, or shooting star. Before it enters the atmosphere, a piece of debris is called a meteoroid. If it survives to hit the ground, the debris is called a meteorite.

Most meteoroids come from asteroids, the bodies that orbit mainly between Mars and Jupiter, or from comets, which travel in huge elliptical orbits through the Solar System. When asteroids collide, pieces break off and become meteoroids drifting through space. Comets shed dust as their ices boil away in sunlight. This dusty debris becomes a swarm of small meteoroids that may eventually enter Earth's atmosphere. Some meteoroids were once part of the Moon or Mars. These pieces were blasted off the surface when it was hit by a large asteroid.

Meteorites are usually small enough to hold in your hand, but they can be bigger than houses. In the past, giant meteorites have created huge craters on Earth. And even small meteorites can do damage. In 1992, one destroyed a car in Peekskill, New York. Another killed a dog when it fell in Egypt in 1911.

METEORITE CRATER

When a big meteorite falls, it leaves a crater in the ground. Meteor Crater in Arizona is 1,220 metres (4,000 ft) across and 200 metres (650 ft) deep. It formed 50,000 years ago when a house-sized nickel-iron meteorite struck at 11 kilometres (7 mi) per second.

METEOR

The streak of light in this photo is a meteor. On a clear night, you might see three or four meteors an hour. Very bright meteors are known as fireballs.

ORIGIN OF NAME
METEOR COMES FROM THE GREEK WORD FOR 'THINGS IN THE ATMOSPHERE'

ALTITUDE WHERE METEORS BURN OUT
110–80 KM (70–50 MI)

SIZE OF METEOROIDS
METEOROIDS RANGE FROM TINY SPECKS TO HOUSE-SIZE.

SIZE OF METEORITES
METEORITES ARE USUALLY FIST-SIZE, BUT CAN BE HUGE. THE LARGEST ONE FOUND ON EARTH IS THE HOBA METEORITE IN NAMIBIA, WHICH WEIGHS 60 TONNES (65 TONS).

LARGEST KNOWN CRATER ON EARTH
VREDEFORT, SOUTH AFRICA: 300 KM (190 MI) ACROSS

STONY METEORITE
Stony meteorites make up 92 per cent of all meteorites. They formed early in Solar-System history and can tell scientists what the young Solar System was like.

IRON METEORITE
Iron meteorites make up only 7 per cent of all meteorites, but are the kind most commonly found because they look extraterrestrial.

◆ AMAZING FACT ◆

On 17 November, 1833, people on North America's east coast saw a spectacular meteor storm, with up to 200,000 meteors falling per hour. Thousands of meteors lit up the sky every minute.

STONY-IRON METEORITE
A minority (1 per cent) of meteorites are a mixture of stony material and iron. Scientists think they come from asteroids that have completely melted.

MARS METEORITE ALH 84001
In 1996, several NASA scientists reported finding evidence for ancient life in this meteorite from Mars called ALH 84001. Most scientists now disagree.

Meteoroids drift among the planets controlled by the gravity of the Sun and planets, and by the pressure of sunlight.

Small meteoroids usually come from comets, which leave behind a trail of dust as their ices boil away in sunlight.

SPACE DEBRIS

If you see a quick streak of light in the night sky, it is probably a meteor. The meteoroid might burn up completely or land on the ground as a meteorite.

On certain dates, many meteors appear to come from one part of the sky. These meteor showers (see page 113) occur when Earth passes through a stream of dust from a comet.

To survive passing through the atmosphere, a meteorite must be large and tough – or else very small and light, so it slows before burning up.

Although no large meteorite impact has happened in human history, scientists expect that the next big impact is just a matter of time and chance.

◆ LOOK AGAIN ◆

● What's the difference between a meteor and a meteorite?

● Where do most meteorites come from?

● What happens when a big meteorite falls?

Mars

MARS IS THE PLANET MOST like our own. It has four seasons, polar ice caps, channels carved by water and a rotation time just 41 minutes longer than Earth's. On the young Mars, conditions were probably like those on the early Earth, so life may have begun there as well. But spacecraft have found no signs of life, and scientists think Mars became too hostile for living things long ago.

Mars looks red in the sky, earning it the nickname the Red Planet. The colour comes from its rusty-orange rocks and fine red sand. It is a cold desert – the planet's atmosphere of carbon dioxide is too thin to stop heat from the Sun escaping into space. Temperatures can peak at 27°C (81°F) by day but drop to a chilly –123°C (–190°F) at night.

The southern half of the planet is heavily cratered. The northern plains are smoother and flatter, and may once have had large lakes or even an ocean. Giant extinct volcanoes include Olympus Mons, which is 24 kilometres (15 mi) high. The Valles Marineris is a canyon as long as the United States is wide.

Mars is the most studied planet, apart from Earth. More than 10 probes have visited and others are on their way. Scientists are now investigating ways to send astronauts to our red neighbour.

ORIGIN OF NAME
MARS, THE ROMAN GOD OF WAR

DISTANCE FROM THE SUN
228 MILLION KM (142 MILLION MI)

DIAMETER
6,780 KM (4,213 MI)

MASS
64% x EARTH'S MASS

ATMOSPHERE
CARBON DIOXIDE – 0.01% AS DENSE AS EARTH'S AIR

MOONS
2: PHOBOS AND DEIMOS

LENGTH OF DAY (in Earth hours/minutes)
ROTATION TIME: 24 H 37 M / SOLAR DAY: 24 H 40 M

LENGTH OF YEAR
687 EARTH DAYS

PROJECT: Making a Red Planet

For this project, you need a piece of clean steel wool, tap water, a dish or saucer and rubber gloves to protect your hands.

❶ Stretch the steel wool to loosen its weave, then put it in the dish and wet it. Leave it for several days.

❷ Pick up the steel wool with rubber gloves, and examine it closely. The rusted wool will be fragile and crumbly, leaving a reddish-orange residue.

As the iron in the steel wool mixes with water and oxygen in the air, it rusts. Many Mars rocks contain iron-bearing minerals. These minerals have slowly rusted, leaving a ruddy dust on the surface and in the atmosphere.

MAP OF MARS
Space probes have mapped the surface of Mars in detail, revealing giant volcanoes and deep canyons. Traces of magnetism suggest that the rocky mantle and crust may once have had moving plates like Earth's.

Rocky crust / Rocky mantle

ON THE SURFACE
The Pathfinder spacecraft landed where streams from the highlands once emptied onto the northern plains. It found many rock types and a landscape unchanged for more than a billion years.

THE POLES
The northern polar ice cap is frozen water, covered in winter by a layer of carbon dioxide snow mixed with dust.

THE TWO MOONS OF MARS
Phobos and Deimos, the two Martian moons, are covered in craters and a layer of dusty shattered rock. They have irregular shapes and may be asteroids captured by Mars' gravity.

Deimos

Phobos

RED ROVER
Rovers like Sojourner, carried by Mars Pathfinder (see pages 26–27), move around on a planet's surface and can explore a wider area than a fixed landing craft can.

VASTITAS BOREALIS
Lyot
Moreux UTOPIA PLANITIA
ELYSIUM PLANIT
Cassini Antoniadi
ARABIA TERRA ISIDIS PLANITIA
Schiaparelli TYRRHENA TERRA
Terra Sabaea Huygens
Herschel
HELLAS PLANITIA
PROMETHEI TERRA
PLANUM AUSTRALE
Eastern hemisphere

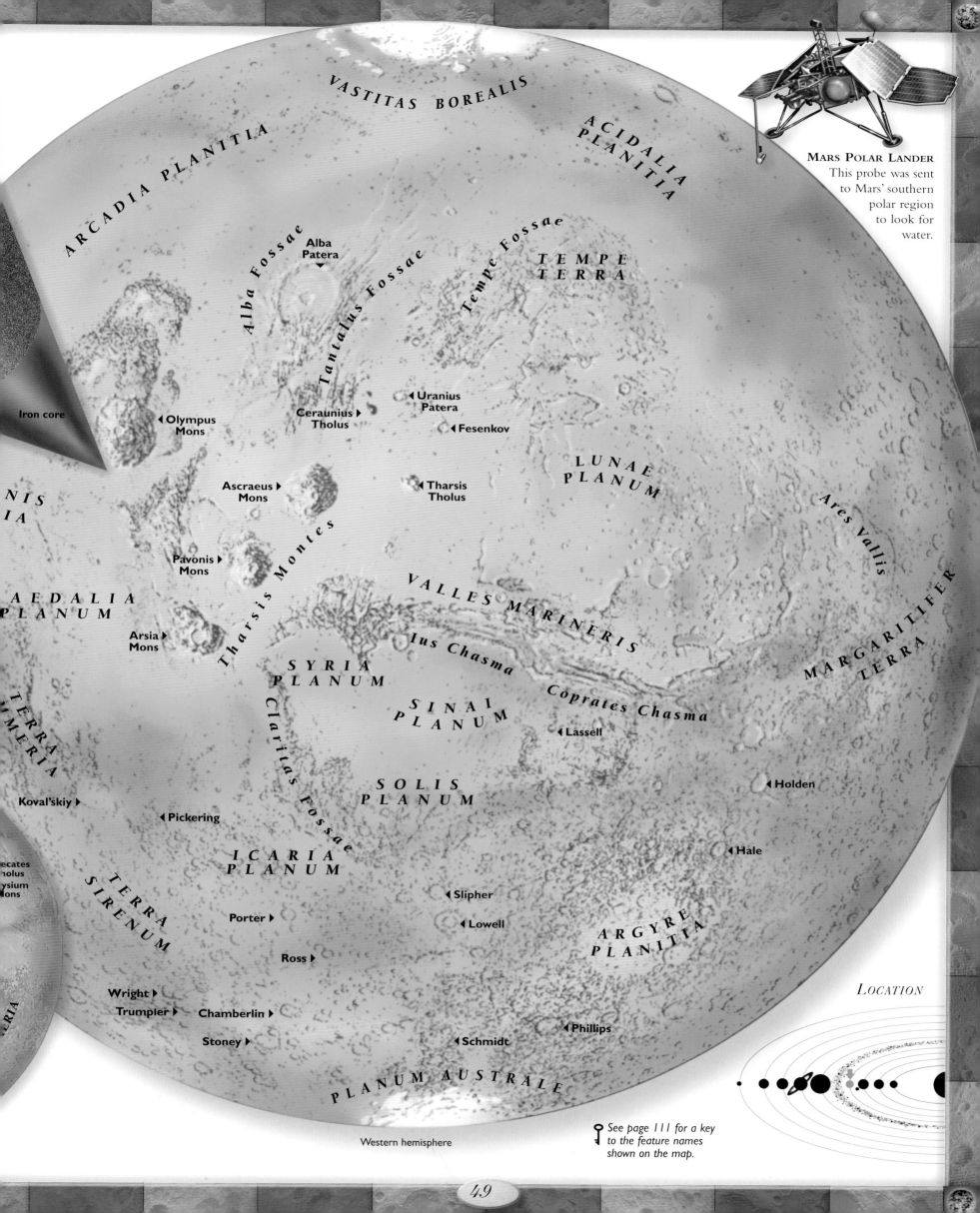

VASTITAS BOREALIS

ARCADIA PLANITIA

ACIDALIA PLANITIA

Iron core

◄ Olympus Mons

Alba Fossae

Alba Patera ▼

Tantalus Fossae

Tempe Fossae

TEMPE TERRA

Ceraunius ▶ Tholus

◄ Uranius Patera

◄ Fesenkov

◄ Tharsis Tholus

LUNAE PLANUM

Ares Vallis

Ascraeus ▶ Mons

NIS IA

Pavonis ▶ Mons

Tharsis Montes

VALLES MARINERIS

AEDALIA PLANUM

Arsia ▶ Mons

Ius Chasma

Coprates Chasma

MARGARITIFER TERRA

SYRIA PLANUM

Claritas Fossae

SINAI PLANUM

TERRA MERIA

◄ Lassell

SOLIS PLANUM

◄ Holden

Koval'skiy ▶

◄ Pickering

ICARIA PLANUM

◄ Hale

ecates holus ysium ons

TERRA SIRENUM

Porter ▶

◄ Slipher

◄ Lowell

ARGYRE PLANITIA

Ross ▶

Wright ▶

Trumpler ▶   Chamberlin ▶

Stoney ▶

◄ Schmidt

◄ Phillips

ARIA

PLANUM AUSTRALE

Western hemisphere

LOCATION

See page 111 for a key to the feature names shown on the map.

Asteroids

BETWEEN MARS AND JUPITER, there are millions of asteroids, small irregular bodies made of rock or metal left over from the Solar System's birth. The strong gravity of Jupiter keeps them from clumping together to become a planet like Earth or Mars. Asteroids are sometimes called minor planets.

The biggest, and first to be discovered, asteroid is Ceres, almost 1,000 kilometres (600 mi) across. It was first spotted in 1801. Ceres is round like the rocky planets, but smaller asteroids have odd shapes because their gravity is not strong enough to pull the asteroid material into a sphere. Spacecraft visits to asteroids such as Gaspra and Ida reveal that they have cratered surfaces covered by a dusty layer of shattered rock.

Not all asteroids orbit in the main belt. The Trojan asteroids travel in Jupiter's orbit. They don't collide with Jupiter because they are moving at the same speed as the giant planet. Other asteroids have wide elliptical orbits that cross the orbits of Earth and other large planets. Astronomers watch these near-Earth asteroids carefully. If a large one collided with Earth, the impact could create tidal waves, huge forest fires and great clouds of dust and ash that would block out sunlight for months.

Our planet was built up by countless collisions of asteroid-like materials, and scientists believe that asteroids today can tell us about the Solar System's early history. Space probes such as the Near-Earth Asteroid Rendezvous (NEAR) and MUSES-C are visiting asteroids. MUSES-C may bring back a rock sample.

ORIGIN OF NAME
ASTEROID MEANS 'STAR-LIKE', WHICH IS HOW AN ASTEROID LOOKS IN A TELESCOPE.

DISTANCE OF MAIN BELT FROM THE SUN
FROM 329 MILLION KM (204 MILLION MI) TO 539 MILLION KM (335 MILLION MI)

SIZE
ASTEROIDS RANGE FROM LESS THAN A METRE (A FEW FEET) ACROSS UP TO CERES, THE LARGEST ASTEROID AT 913 KM (567 MI) IN DIAMETER.

NUMBER OF MAIN BELT ASTEROIDS
UNKNOWN – PROBABLY HUNDREDS OF MILLIONS

NUMBER OF NEAR-EARTH ASTEROIDS
PROBABLY SEVERAL THOUSAND – ABOUT 1,000 KNOWN

IDA
Seen by the Jupiter-bound spacecraft Galileo, Ida is about 60 kilometres (37 mi) long. The speck beside Ida in this photo is its tiny moon Dactyl, which is just 1.6 kilometres (1 mi) wide.

GASPRA
Also photographed by Galileo, Gaspra is about 18 kilometres (11 mi) long. With fewer craters than Ida, Gaspra appears to have a younger surface.

EROS
The NEAR probe took this snapshot of Eros in 1998. Eros is a piece of rock about 33 kilometres (21 mi) long, irregular in shape and pocked with craters. It rotates once every 5¼ hours.

MATHILDE
Before Eros, NEAR visited Mathilde. About 66 kilometres (41 mi) across, Mathilde is as dark as coal and has large craters. Scientists think it may be like a giant pile of rubble.

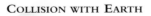

COLLISION WITH EARTH
Asteroids have struck Earth many times in the past, but the most recent big impact was 65 million years ago. This led to such a change in Earth's climate that dinosaurs became extinct.

◆ PROJECT: *Lighting Up Asteroids* ◆

For this project, you need a bright torch, a dark room and some rocks, balls and other objects. Some should be rough, others smooth. Try covering one object in silver foil.

❶ Put the objects on the table in front of you. Take a few steps back and shine the torch on them.

❷ Notice how different objects reflect different amounts of light.

❸ See how the appearance of each object changes as you shine the torch directly or from one side.

Scientists study asteroids as they rotate, showing changing textures and patterns of shadow and light.

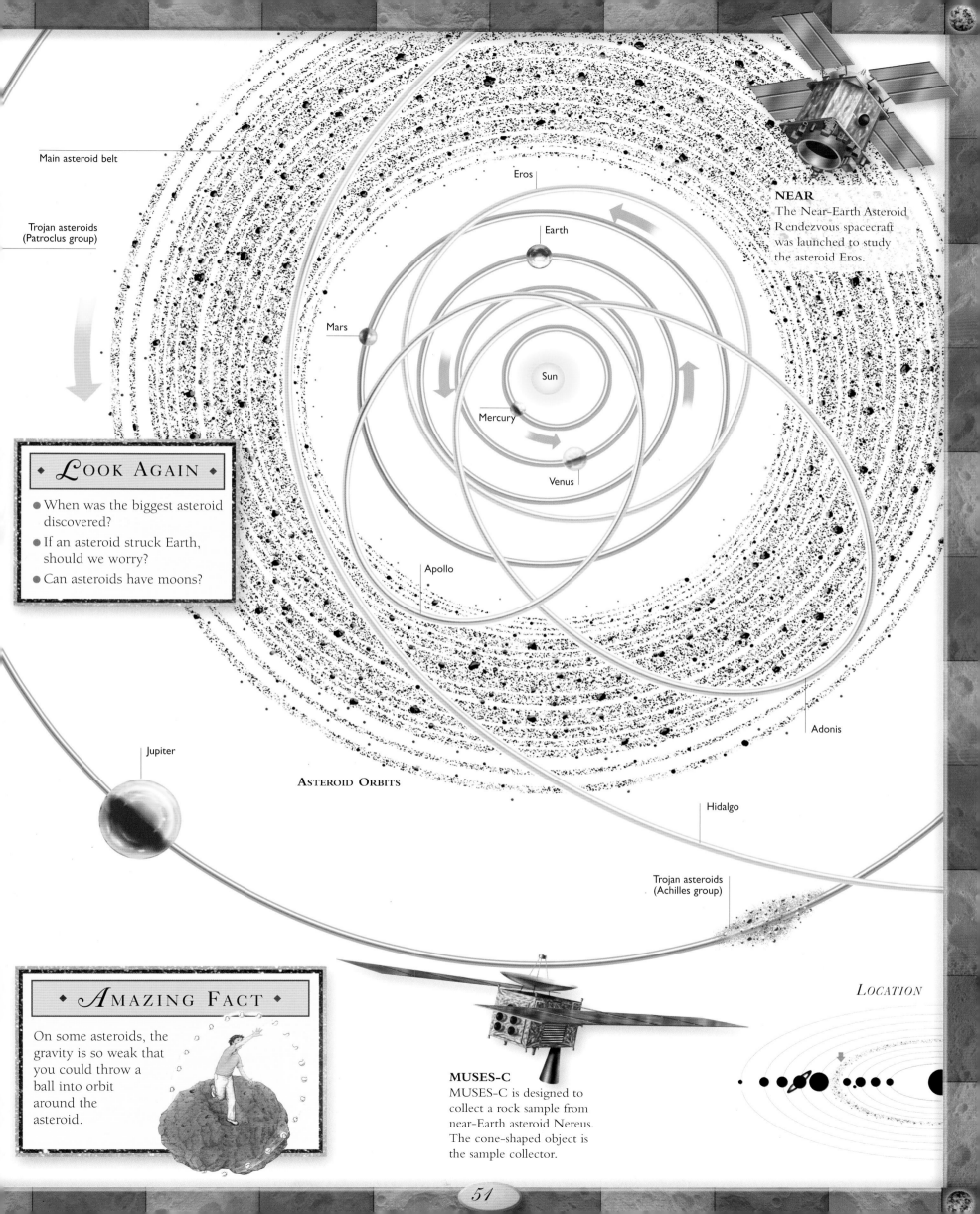

Main asteroid belt

Trojan asteroids
(Patroclus group)

Eros

Earth

Mars

Sun

Mercury

Venus

Apollo

Jupiter

ASTEROID ORBITS

Adonis

Hidalgo

Trojan asteroids
(Achilles group)

NEAR
The Near-Earth Asteroid
Rendezvous spacecraft
was launched to study
the asteroid Eros.

◆ 𝓛OOK AGAIN ◆

● When was the biggest asteroid
discovered?

● If an asteroid struck Earth,
should we worry?

● Can asteroids have moons?

◆ 𝒜MAZING FACT ◆

On some asteroids, the
gravity is so weak that
you could throw a
ball into orbit
around the
asteroid.

MUSES-C
MUSES-C is designed to
collect a rock sample from
near-Earth asteroid Nereus.
The cone-shaped object is
the sample collector.

LOCATION

Jupiter

THE LARGEST OF all the planets, Jupiter is an enormous ball of gas – mostly hydrogen and helium, like the Sun, along with small amounts of water, methane and ammonia. This planet lacks a solid surface. The upper layers are gaseous but deeper down, as pressures and temperatures increase, the hydrogen and helium become more like a liquid. Deeper still, the hydrogen behaves like a liquid metal. At the centre is a small, rocky core more than three times hotter than the surface of the Sun.

A day on Jupiter lasts less than 10 hours. This rapid spin creates winds that blow at up to 500 kilometres (300 mi) per hour and whip its colourful clouds into long bands. The light bands are called zones. The dark bands, known as belts, show deeper layers. Among the zones and belts are a number of oval spots. These are giant storms that thrive on the energy of the winds and heat from Jupiter's core. They can persist for years – the biggest storm, the Great Red Spot, has been visible for at least 300 years.

In 1610, astronomer Galileo Galilei discovered Jupiter's four largest moons – Io, Europa, Ganymede and Callisto. Today, we know of 16 moons, ranging from Ganymede, at 5,268 kilometres (3,273 mi) across, to Leda, at 16 kilometres (10 mi) across. In 1979, the Voyager 1 probe discovered that Jupiter also has a thin system of rings. These are mostly made of microscopic dust particles.

COMET IMPACTS
In July 1994, more than 20 fragments of comet Shoemaker-Levy 9 struck Jupiter. The impacts left dusty smudges that lasted months.

MAP OF JUPITER
Jupiter's top layer shows light zones and dark belts of fast-moving clouds, as well as storms such as the Great Red Spot. These icy features conceal an extremely hot interior. The giant planet is still cooling off from its formation, which occurred nearly 5,000 million years ago.

Rings

ORIGIN OF NAME
JUPITER, THE MOST POWERFUL OF THE ROMAN GODS

DISTANCE FROM THE SUN
778 MILLION KM (483 MILLION MI)

DIAMETER
142,984 KM (88,846 MI)

MASS
317.8 x EARTH'S MASS

MOONS
16 – LARGEST ARE IO, EUROPA, GANYMEDE AND CALLISTO

LENGTH OF DAY (in Earth hours and minutes)
ROTATION TIME AND SOLAR DAY: BOTH 9 H 55 M

LENGTH OF YEAR
11.9 EARTH YEARS

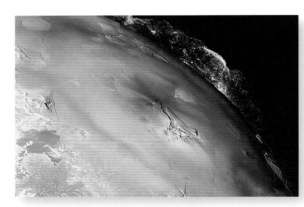

ERUPTION ON IO
In this photo of Jupiter's moon Io, a plume of sulphur shoots from one of its many volcanoes. The gravity of Jupiter and its other moons continually tugs at Io, creating internal heat that escapes through eruptions.

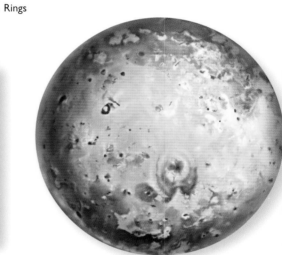

MOON: IO
The innermost Galilean moon has an iron core and a rocky mantle and crust. Unlike Jupiter's other large moons, Io has no ice or water because it formed near the planet, where temperatures were high.

◆ PROJECT: *Jupiter in a Pie-Dish* ◆

You need a glass or aluminium pie-dish, a coin, tap water and a bottle of food colouring.

1 Place the coin on a level kitchen worktop, under the centre of the pie-dish so that it turns easily.

2 Pour about 1 or 2 cm (½ in) of tap water into the dish.

3 Place a large drop of food colouring in the dish at the edge, and spin the dish slowly. See how streams of food colouring take the same shapes as Jupiter's bands of clouds.

ICE ON EUROPA
In this photo of Europa's surface, the red lines are dusty water that has leaked through cracks in the moon's bright icy shell. We do not know whether the water under the shell is still liquid or has frozen.

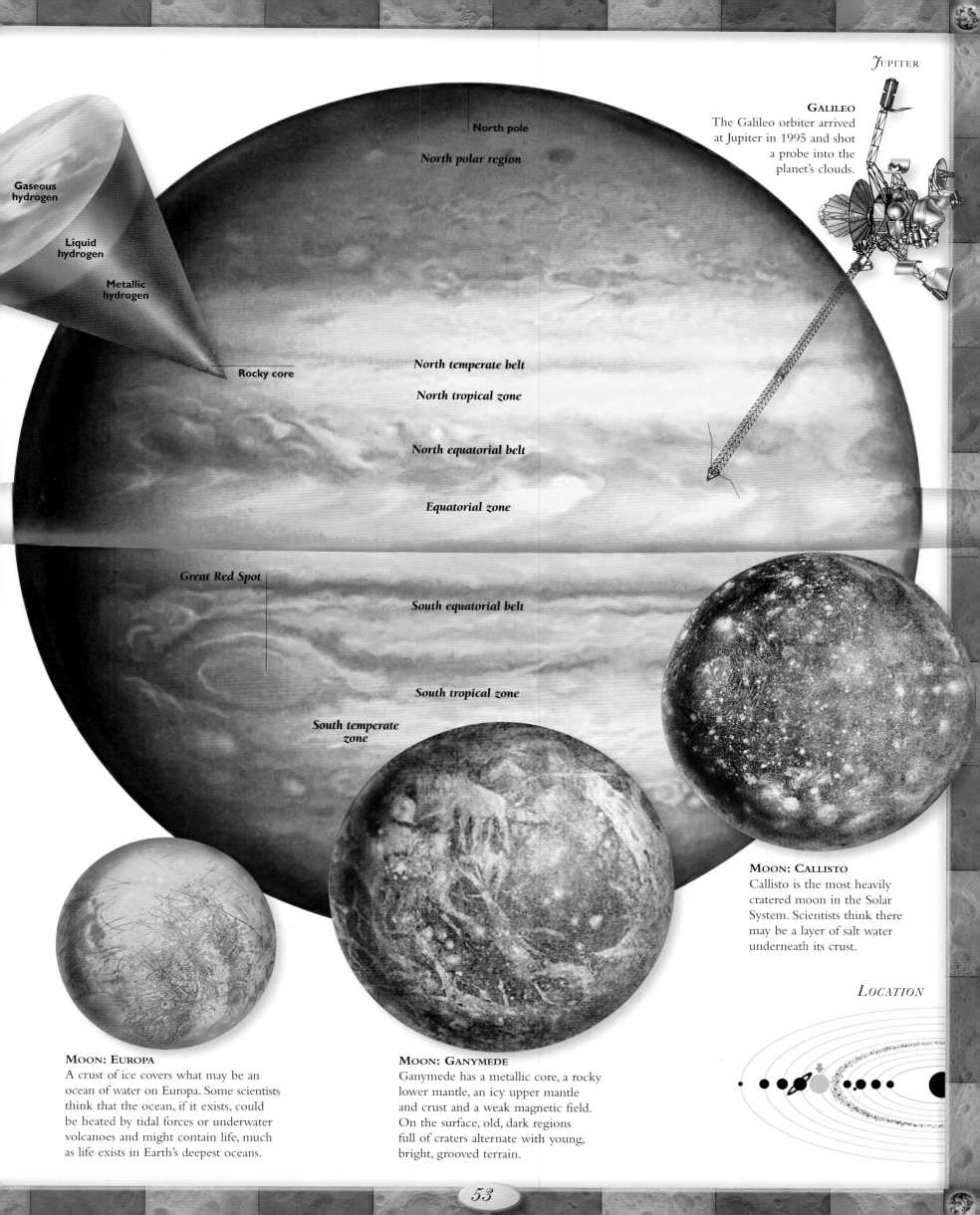

Gaseous
hydrogen

Liquid
hydrogen

Metallic
hydrogen

Rocky core

North pole

North polar region

North temperate belt

North tropical zone

North equatorial belt

Equatorial zone

Great Red Spot

South equatorial belt

South tropical zone

South temperate
zone

GALILEO
The Galileo orbiter arrived
at Jupiter in 1995 and shot
a probe into the
planet's clouds.

MOON: CALLISTO
Callisto is the most heavily
cratered moon in the Solar
System. Scientists think there
may be a layer of salt water
underneath its crust.

LOCATION

MOON: EUROPA
A crust of ice covers what may be an
ocean of water on Europa. Some scientists
think that the ocean, if it exists, could
be heated by tidal forces or underwater
volcanoes and might contain life, much
as life exists in Earth's deepest oceans.

MOON: GANYMEDE
Ganymede has a metallic core, a rocky
lower mantle, an icy upper mantle
and crust and a weak magnetic field.
On the surface, old, dark regions
full of craters alternate with young,
bright, grooved terrain.

Saturn

SATURN IS KNOWN AS the Ringed Planet. Jupiter, Uranus and Neptune also have rings, but Saturn's are the most magnificent. From Earth, we can see what look like three broad, smooth rings. The A ring is the outside one. Next comes the Cassini division, a dark gap 4,670 kilometres (2,900 mi) wide. The B ring is the widest and brightest, 25,750 kilometres (16,000 mi) across. The narrower C ring appears pale and semi-transparent.

Three spacecraft – Pioneer 11 and Voyagers 1 and 2 – have visited Saturn since 1979. They revealed that the rings are made up of thousands of ringlets, each made up of icy chunks. Even the empty-looking Cassini division contains many particles. Scientists think that the rings are the remains of several broken moons. As time passes, ring particles collide and slowly spiral into Saturn. Millions of years from now, the rings will be gone.

Saturn seems like a pale copy of Jupiter. It has no solid surface and, like Jupiter, is nearly all hydrogen and helium, with traces of other gases such as methane and ammonia. Although Saturn is nearly as big as Jupiter, it has only 30 per cent as much mass. A bit like a giant marshmallow, Saturn would float if you could find a large enough ocean.

The winds at Saturn's equator blow at more than 1,600 kilometres (1,000 mi) per hour. Saturn has fewer storms than Jupiter because it has less internal heat, but large clouds of ammonia ice crystals break out at its equator about every 30 years.

Outside the main rings orbit 18 moons, ranging from Titan, 5,150 kilometres (3,200 mi) in diameter, to Pan, just 20 kilometres (12 mi) across. Titan is the target for the Huygens probe carried by the Cassini spacecraft, due to reach Saturn in 2004.

ORIGIN OF NAME
SATURNUS, THE ROMAN GOD WHO WAS FATHER TO JUPITER

DISTANCE FROM THE SUN
1,432 MILLION KM (890 MILLION MI)

DIAMETER
120,533 KM (74,896 MI)

MASS
95.2 X EARTH'S MASS

MOONS
18 – LARGEST IS TITAN

LENGTH OF DAY (in Earth hours and minutes)
ROTATION TIME AND SOLAR DAY: BOTH 10 H 39 M

LENGTH OF YEAR
29.4 EARTH YEARS

♦ AMAZING FACT ♦

When Galileo Galilei first discovered the rings of Saturn in 1610, he didn't know what he was looking at because his telescope lens was not very sharp. He thought the planet had 'ears' or 'handles'.

MAP OF SATURN
Saturn has numerous rings, but only the A, B and C rings can be easily seen from Earth. Near the surface, Saturn's hydrogen and helium are gaseous, but they become fluid, and then metallic, deeper inside. The rocky core has about twice the Sun's surface temperature.

Gaseous hydrogen

Liquid hydroge

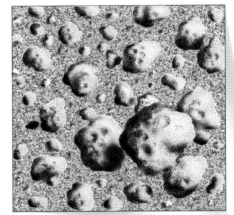

INSIDE THE RINGS
Saturn's rings are made of chunks of ice and rock. The rings are thousands of kilometres wide but only some 12 to 120 metres (40 to 400 ft) thick.

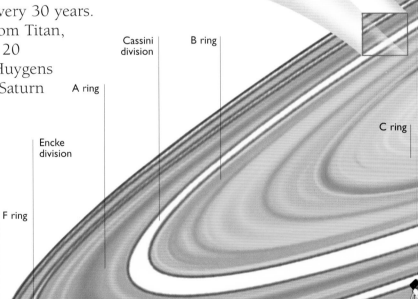

A ring

Cassini division

B ring

D ring

C ring

Encke division

F ring

HUYGENS PROBE
Huygens will parachute through Titan's atmosphere to its surface. Titan might have organic chemicals like those on the early Earth.

CASSINI
The Cassini orbiter will take more than six years to reach Saturn.

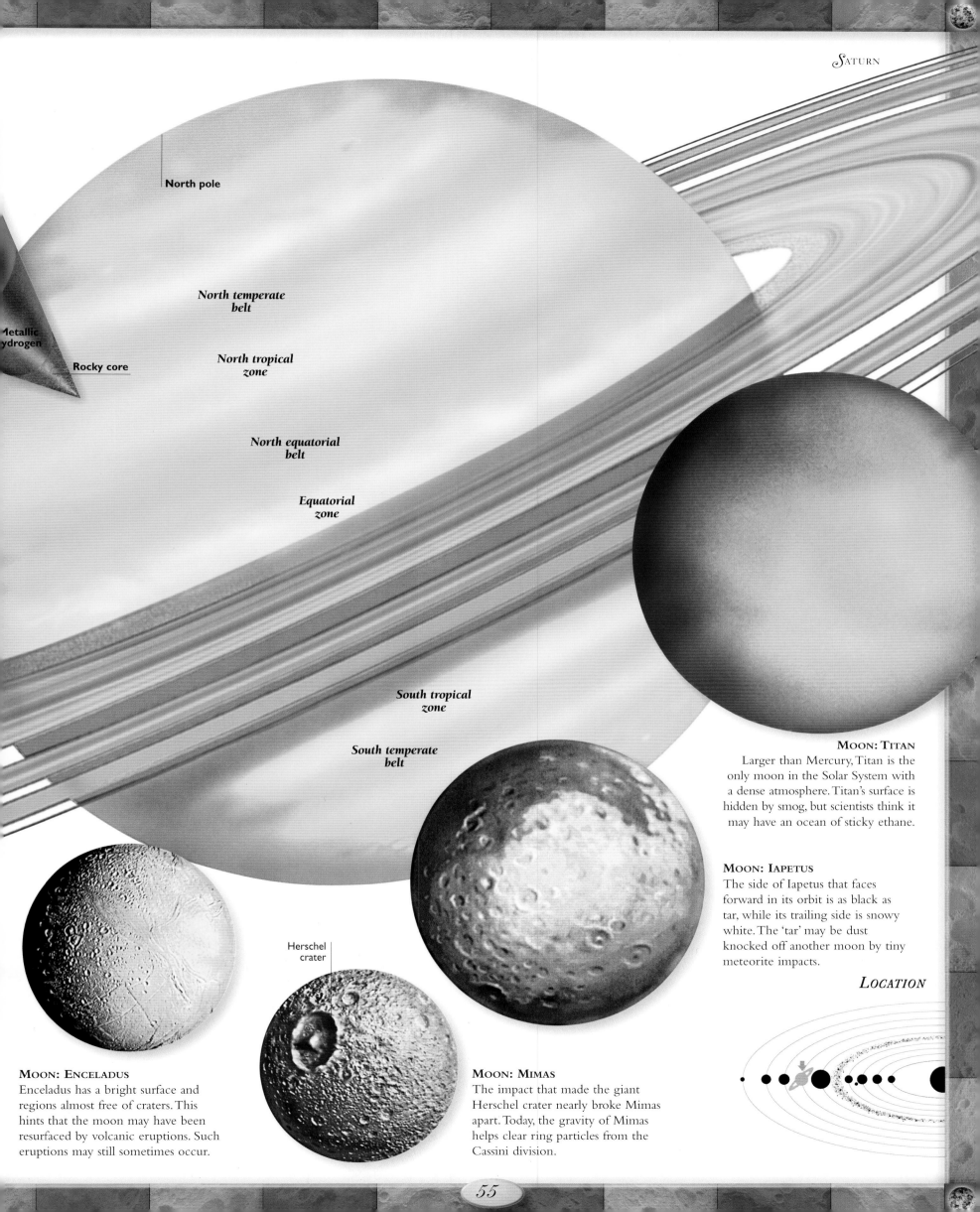

North pole

North temperate
belt

Metallic
Hydrogen

Rocky core

North tropical
zone

North equatorial
belt

Equatorial
zone

South tropical
zone

South temperate
belt

MOON: TITAN
Larger than Mercury, Titan is the
only moon in the Solar System with
a dense atmosphere. Titan's surface is
hidden by smog, but scientists think it
may have an ocean of sticky ethane.

MOON: IAPETUS
The side of Iapetus that faces
forward in its orbit is as black as
tar, while its trailing side is snowy
white. The 'tar' may be dust
knocked off another moon by tiny
meteorite impacts.

LOCATION

Herschel
crater

MOON: ENCELADUS
Enceladus has a bright surface and
regions almost free of craters. This
hints that the moon may have been
resurfaced by volcanic eruptions. Such
eruptions may still sometimes occur.

MOON: MIMAS
The impact that made the giant
Herschel crater nearly broke Mimas
apart. Today, the gravity of Mimas
helps clear ring particles from the
Cassini division.

Uranus

In 1781, William Herschel looked through his telescope and found Uranus, the first planet discovered in modern times. Uranus' diameter is about four times greater than Earth's, but it orbits so far from the Sun that Herschel and other observers could tell little about the planet. Most of what we now know about Uranus was learnt from the Voyager 2 spacecraft fly-by in 1986.

Uranus might be called the planet-on-its-side – Earth's axis tilts 23.5 degrees to its orbit, but Uranus' axis tips almost 98 degrees. When Voyager 2 flew past, Uranus' south pole was pointing almost directly at the Sun, and the northern hemisphere was in darkness. Voyager saw a featureless, blue-green Uranus. Scientists using the Hubble Space Telescope are now seeing signs of storms in Uranus' northern hemisphere as it emerges from its long, dark winter.

The blue-green colour of Uranus comes from traces of methane in its upper atmosphere. The methane reflects the blue wavelengths of sunlight and absorbs the red. Most of Uranus is hydrogen and helium, like the Sun. And like the other gas-giant planets, it has no solid surface.

In 1977, astronomers watched a star wink on and off before disappearing behind Uranus. This revealed that Uranus has a set of narrow, dark rings. Eleven rings are now known. The grey ring particles are 10 centimetres to 10 metres (4 in to 30 ft) across.

Uranus has five large moons, including Miranda, which has a surface unlike any other moon in the Solar System. In recent years, many smaller moons have been discovered. There are at least 15 of these dark asteroid-like objects.

◆ Look Again ◆

● How were Uranus' rings discovered?
● Why are storms starting to appear on Uranus?
● How did Uranus end up with a large tilt to its axis?

Map of Uranus
So far, the face of Uranus has appeared featureless, but that might change as it continues its orbit. Beneath Uranus' gaseous top layer is a dense liquid layer and a hot rocky core. The planet is circled by 11 rings.

Seasons
Uranus' orbit takes 84 Earth years, so each pole receives a long period of constant sunlight followed by a long period of darkness. The atmosphere is growing more active as Uranus approaches its equinox, when the Sun is over its equator.

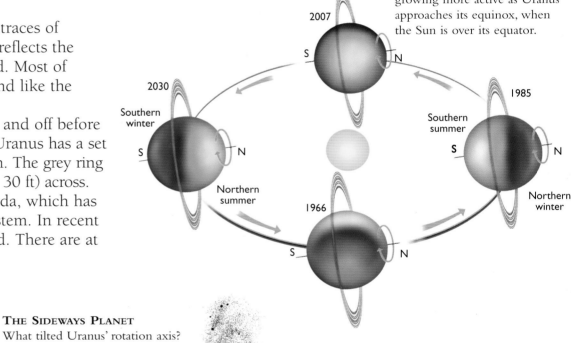

2007
S   N

2030
Southern winter
S   N

1985
Southern summer
S   N

1966
S   N

Northern summer

Northern winter

Origin of Name
Uranus, the most ancient of the Roman gods

Distance from the Sun
2,871 million km (1,784 million mi)

Diameter
51,118 km (31,763 mi)

Mass
14.5 x Earth's mass

Moons
At least 20 – largest is Titania

Length of Day (in Earth hours and minutes)
Rotation time and solar day: both 17 h 14 m

Length of Year
84.1 Earth years

The Sideways Planet
What tilted Uranus' rotation axis? Scientists speculate that as Uranus was forming, a large object struck and knocked it over on its side. The impact may also have created the moons and rings, which orbit in line with Uranus' equator.

❷ Uranus tips on its side, debris from impact circles equator to form rings

North pole

Surface of Miranda
Scientists believe Miranda's grooves (seen in the top left and bottom right of this photo) mark where eruptions were starting to resurface the moon. When Miranda's internal heat ran out, the landscape froze in place.

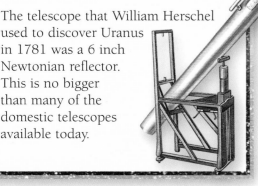

◆ Amazing Fact ◆

The telescope that William Herschel used to discover Uranus in 1781 was a 6 inch Newtonian reflector. This is no bigger than many of the domestic telescopes available today.

North pole

❶ Large object strikes Uranus

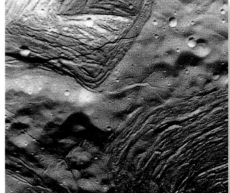

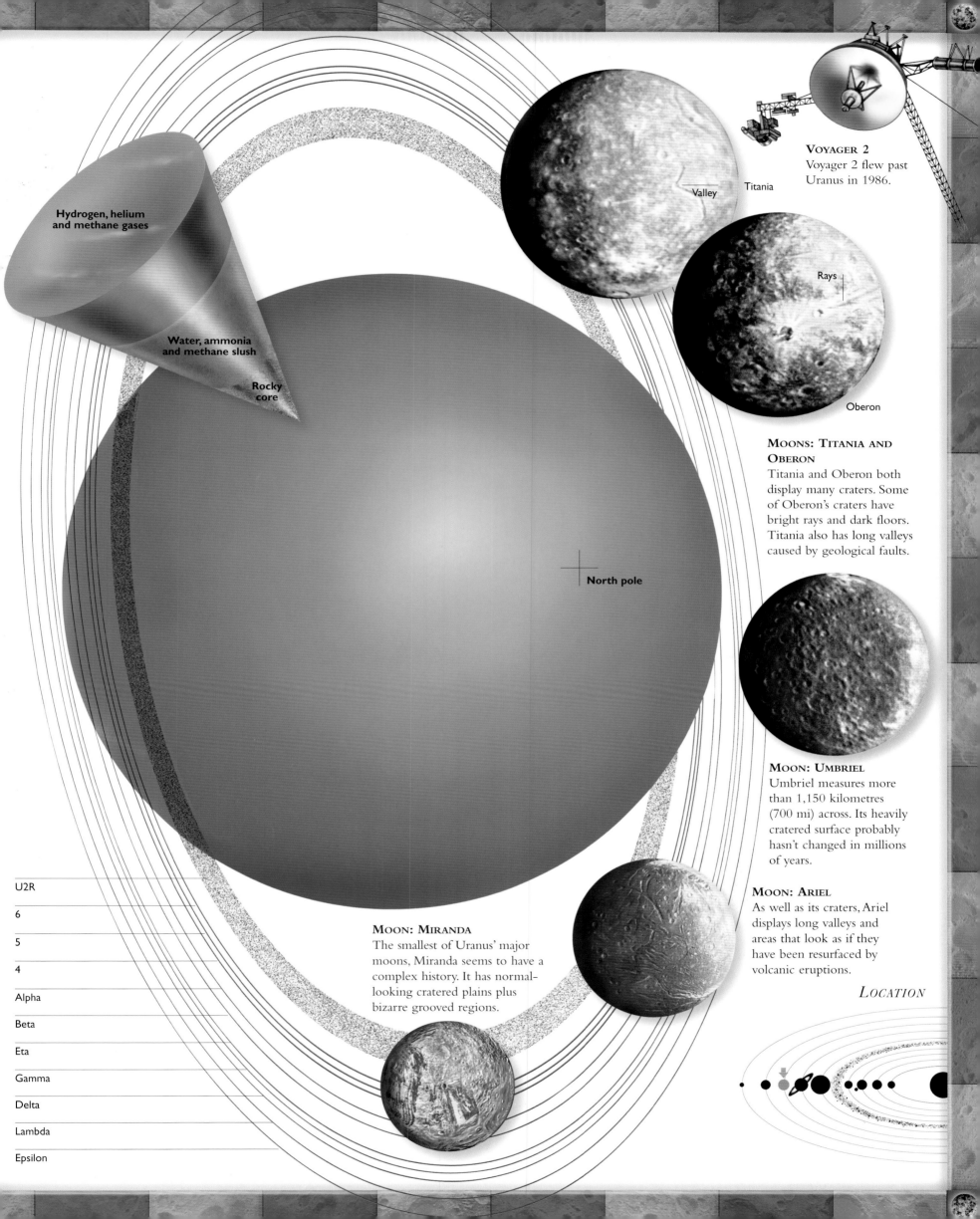

Hydrogen, helium and methane gases

Water, ammonia and methane slush

Rocky core

North pole

Valley

Titania

VOYAGER 2
Voyager 2 flew past
Uranus in 1986.

Rays

Oberon

MOONS: TITANIA AND OBERON
Titania and Oberon both display many craters. Some of Oberon's craters have bright rays and dark floors. Titania also has long valleys caused by geological faults.

MOON: UMBRIEL
Umbriel measures more than 1,150 kilometres (700 mi) across. Its heavily cratered surface probably hasn't changed in millions of years.

MOON: ARIEL
As well as its craters, Ariel displays long valleys and areas that look as if they have been resurfaced by volcanic eruptions.

LOCATION

MOON: MIRANDA
The smallest of Uranus' major moons, Miranda seems to have a complex history. It has normal-looking cratered plains plus bizarre grooved regions.

U2R

6

5

4

Alpha

Beta

Eta

Gamma

Delta

Lambda

Epsilon

Neptune

NEPTUNE IS THE SUN'S last gas-giant planet. It was first spotted in 1846 after astronomers noticed that Uranus wasn't moving along its orbit exactly as it should. Guessing that an unknown planet was orbiting further out and influencing Uranus, the astronomers John Couch Adams in England and Urbain Leverrier in France independently calculated where the new planet might be. When observers Johann Galle and Heinrich d'Arrest checked, they found the new planet right where Adams and Leverrier had predicted.

Since Neptune orbits far from Earth, little was known about it until the Voyager 2 spacecraft paid a fly-by visit in 1989. The spacecraft showed that Neptune is a cold, blue echo of Uranus, with some important differences. Like Uranus, Neptune is a ball of hydrogen, helium and methane. The tilt of Neptune's axis (29.6 degrees) is not as extreme as Uranus', so its seasonal changes are less dramatic. Neptune has raging storms. Voyager photographed a storm known as the Great Dark Spot and a fast-moving cloud of methane ice crystals called the Scooter. Observations from Earth show that storms come and go over the years, probably driven by Neptune's internal heat.

Two Neptunian moons were known before Voyager. Its fly-by added six. They range from Triton, with a diameter of 2,706 kilometres (1,681 mi), to Naiad, just 58 kilometres (36 mi) wide. Triton has erupting geysers, but the other moons are inactive worlds.

Astronomers discovered the rings of Neptune in 1984. They found that one of the six rings has clumps in it, caused perhaps by moons that are yet to be discovered.

ORIGIN OF NAME
NEPTUNUS, THE ROMAN GOD OF THE OCEAN

DISTANCE FROM THE SUN
4,498 MILLION KM (2,795 MILLION MI)

DIAMETER
49,528 KM (30,775 MI)

MASS
17.2 X EARTH'S MASS

MOONS
8 – LARGEST IS TRITON

LENGTH OF DAY (in Earth hours and minutes)
ROTATION TIME AND SOLAR DAY: BOTH 16 H 7 M

LENGTH OF YEAR
164.9 EARTH YEARS

◆ LOOK AGAIN ◆

- What led astronomers to discover Neptune?
- Is Triton volcanically active?
- Are Neptune's storms permanent?

GREAT DARK SPOT
This 1989 photo from Voyager 2 shows the Great Dark Spot (upper left), the white Scooter (centre) and the Dark Spot 2 (lower right). All the features have vanished since the photo was taken.

MAP OF NEPTUNE
Neptune is circled by six faint rings. The planet is coloured blue by traces of methane in its gaseous surface. Beneath the surface, Neptune probably has a deep 'ocean' of water, ammonia and methane and a hot rocky core.

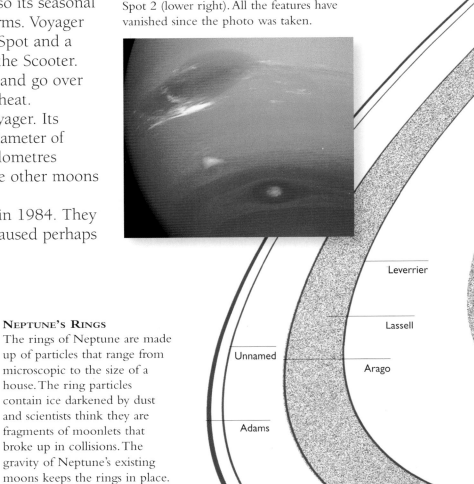

Galle

Leverrier

Lassell

Unnamed

Arago

Adams

NEPTUNE'S RINGS
The rings of Neptune are made up of particles that range from microscopic to the size of a house. The ring particles contain ice darkened by dust and scientists think they are fragments of moonlets that broke up in collisions. The gravity of Neptune's existing moons keeps the rings in place.

◆ AMAZING FACT ◆

Since Neptune was first seen from Earth in 1846, it still has not made a full orbit around the Sun. The trip takes 165 Earth years, so it completes the trip in 2011.

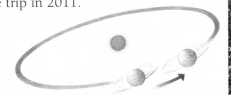

TRITON'S SURFACE
Triton is volcanically active, with geysers shooting plumes of dark material 8 kilometres (5 mi) high. With few craters, Triton's surface is covered in frosts of nitrogen, methane and other ices.

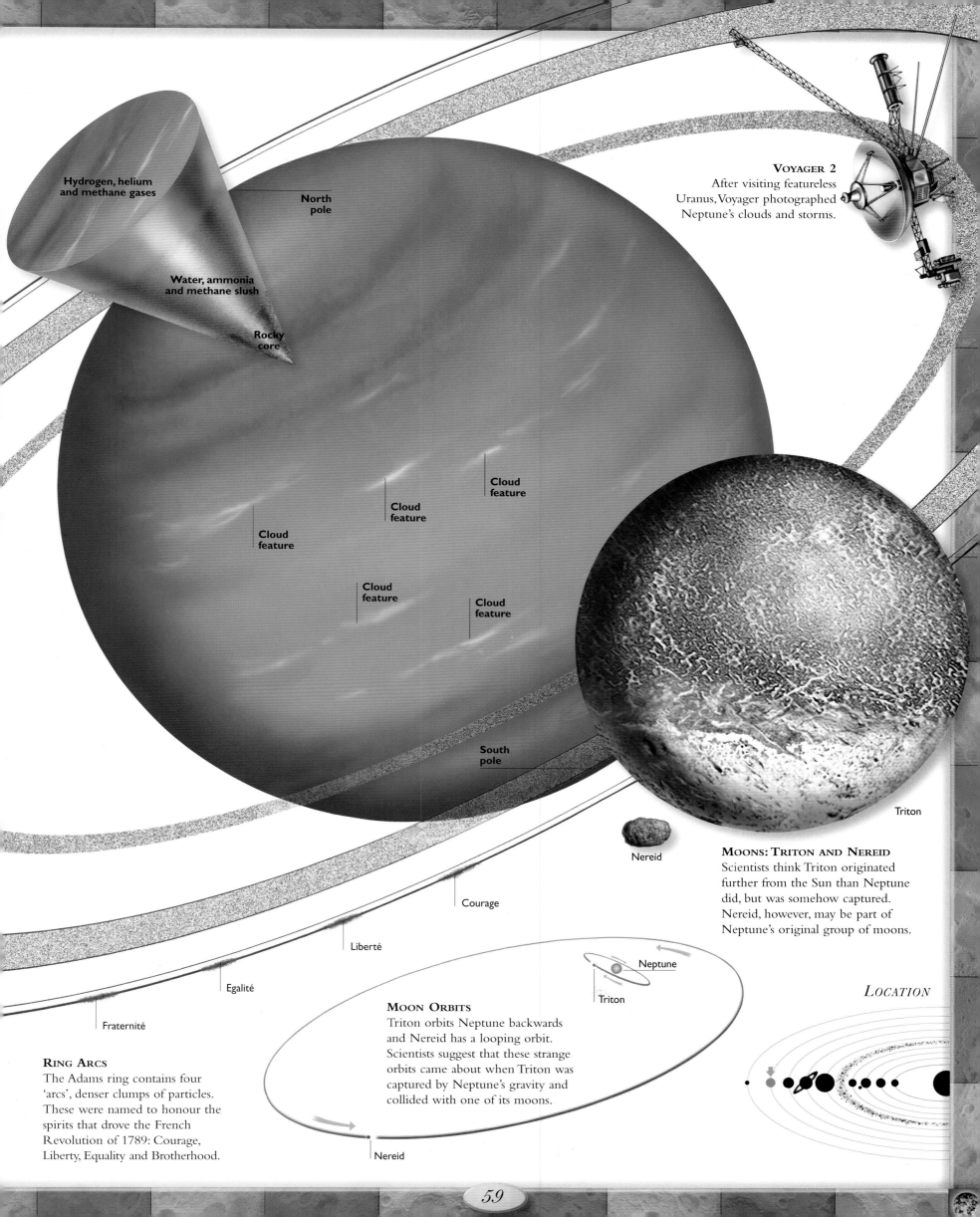

Hydrogen, helium
and methane gases

North
pole

Water, ammonia
and methane slush

Rocky
core

VOYAGER 2
After visiting featureless
Uranus, Voyager photographed
Neptune's clouds and storms.

Cloud
feature

Cloud
feature

Cloud
feature

Cloud
feature

Cloud
feature

South
pole

Triton

Nereid

MOONS: TRITON AND NEREID
Scientists think Triton originated
further from the Sun than Neptune
did, but was somehow captured.
Nereid, however, may be part of
Neptune's original group of moons.

Courage

Liberté

Egalité

Fraternité

Neptune

Triton

LOCATION

MOON ORBITS
Triton orbits Neptune backwards
and Nereid has a looping orbit.
Scientists suggest that these strange
orbits came about when Triton was
captured by Neptune's gravity and
collided with one of its moons.

Nereid

RING ARCS
The Adams ring contains four
'arcs', denser clumps of particles.
These were named to honour the
spirits that drove the French
Revolution of 1789: Courage,
Liberty, Equality and Brotherhood.

Pluto

THE NINTH AND LAST PLANET is Pluto. It was discovered in 1930 by Clyde Tombaugh, after a long search. In 1978, James Christy found that Pluto has a large moon, now called Charon. Pluto is very small and icy, unlike either the rocky planets or the gas giants. Scientists think Pluto is a different kind of Solar System object – an icy planetesimal.

Icy planetesimals probably formed in the Kuiper Belt, a region beyond the orbit of Neptune. From there, the gravity of the gas giants sent most of them careening among the planets. Some planetesimals were destroyed in collisions. Others were captured and became moons (Neptune's big moon Triton may be an icy planetesimal captured in this way). Some planetesimals were thrown out and formed the distant Oort Cloud (see page 62), and some became comets. And one, perhaps, became Pluto.

During its long year, Pluto's distance from the Sun varies from about 30 times Earth's distance from the Sun to about 50 times. As it nears the Sun and grows warmer, its atmosphere springs into existence. The rest of the time, Pluto's temperature hovers around −238°C (−396°F). This is so cold that its atmosphere stays frozen as a layer of frost and snow on the surface.

No spacecraft has yet visited Pluto, but the Pluto-Kuiper Express is planned. After passing Pluto, the spacecraft will head into the Kuiper Belt to visit at least one other icy planetesimal.

NAME
PLUTO, THE ROMAN GOD OF THE UNDERWORLD

DISTANCE FROM THE SUN
5,914 MILLION KM (3,675 MILLION MI)

DIAMETER
2,304 KM (1,432 MI)

MASS
0.2% × EARTH'S MASS

MOONS
1, CHARON

LENGTH OF DAY (in Earth days/hours/minutes)
ROTATION TIME AND SOLAR DAY: BOTH 6 D 9 H 17 M

LENGTH OF YEAR
248 EARTH YEARS

◆ AMAZING FACT ◆

The Pluto-Kuiper Express spacecraft will take eight years to reach Pluto. Once it arrives, its radio signals will take almost five hours to travel back to Earth.

PLUTO AND ITS MOON
Charon's diameter is about half Pluto's, making almost a double planet. Scientists speculate that Pluto and Charon may have formed together after a catastrophic collision.

MAP OF PLUTO
Scientists don't know what Pluto's surface features look like, but observations show that it has a thin crust of nitrogen and methane ice. What lies below the surface is also guesswork until a probe visits, but there may be a mantle of water ice and a large rocky core.

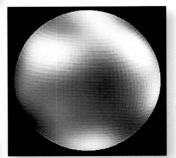

PLUTO SNAPSHOT
Images taken by the Hubble Space Telescope suggest that Pluto is much like Neptune's moon Triton. They are nearly the same size and temperature and have similar surface ices.

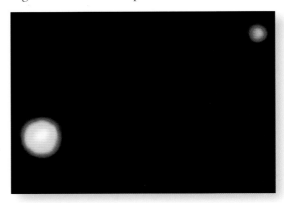

Pluto's orbit — Pluto — Kuiper Belt

THE OUTER REACHES
This cutaway view shows planet orbits and the Kuiper Belt. Pluto's eccentric orbit tilts 17 degrees to the orbits of the other planets. Scientists think Pluto came from the Kuiper Belt, a region beyond Neptune populated by small, icy bodies.

◆ PROJECT: *Weighing It Up* ◆

1 Weigh yourself on a household scale and write down your weight on Earth at the top of a piece of paper.

2 Write down the name of every planet you want to visit. (Draw its picture too if you like.)

3 Go to the Universe Fact File on pages 110–11 and find the surface gravity of each planet. Write it next to the planet's name.

4 Multiply your weight on Earth by the surface gravity for each planet. That's what you'd weigh on each body. (Of course, you wouldn't actually be able to stand on the gas-giant planets because their surfaces aren't solid!)

Pluto — Moon — Ganymede

SIZE COMPARISON
Not only is Pluto smaller than all the other planets, it is even smaller than some of the moons, including Earth's Moon and Jupiter's moon Ganymede (shown here to scale).

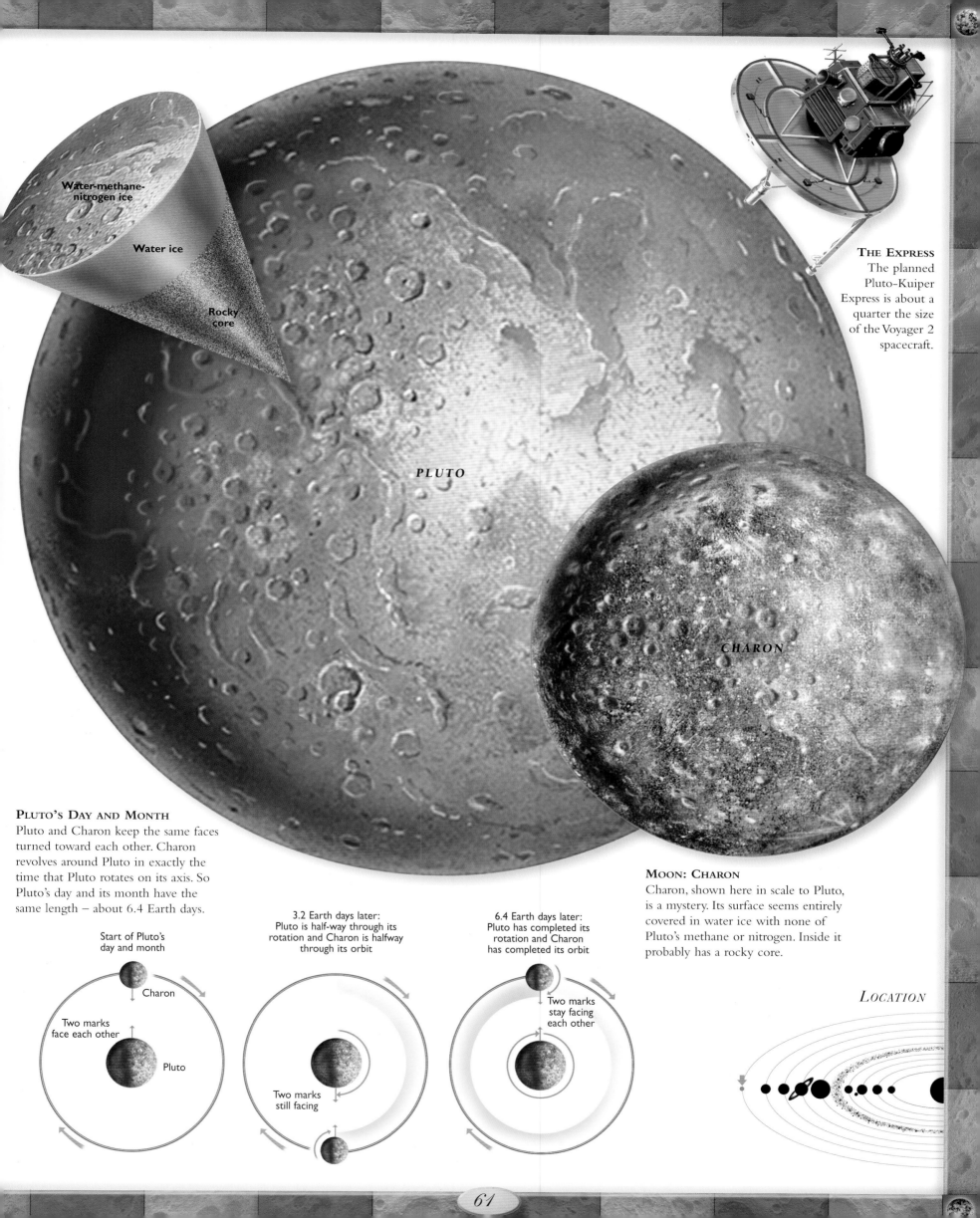

Water-methane-
nitrogen ice

Water ice

Rocky
core

PLUTO

CHARON

THE EXPRESS
The planned
Pluto-Kuiper
Express is about a
quarter the size
of the Voyager 2
spacecraft.

PLUTO'S DAY AND MONTH
Pluto and Charon keep the same faces
turned toward each other. Charon
revolves around Pluto in exactly the
time that Pluto rotates on its axis. So
Pluto's day and its month have the
same length – about 6.4 Earth days.

MOON: CHARON
Charon, shown here in scale to Pluto,
is a mystery. Its surface seems entirely
covered in water ice with none of
Pluto's methane or nitrogen. Inside it
probably has a rocky core.

Start of Pluto's
day and month

Charon

Two marks
face each other

Pluto

3.2 Earth days later:
Pluto is half-way through its
rotation and Charon is halfway
through its orbit

Two marks
still facing

6.4 Earth days later:
Pluto has completed its
rotation and Charon
has completed its orbit

Two marks
stay facing
each other

LOCATION

Comets

MOST COMETS EXIST in the icy-cold regions beyond Neptune. Here they are loosely packed lumps of frozen water and other ices mixed with dust. Many are only the size of a house, but others measure about 20 kilometres (12 mi) or more across. Sometimes one of these lumps is pulled by gravity or pushed by a collision towards the centre of the Solar System. As the comet approaches the Sun, its ices grow warm and begin to boil away, forming a cloud of dusty gas called a coma. The coma can be thousands of kilometres wide, much bigger than the nucleus (core) of the comet. Sunlight and solar radiation pressing on the coma drive its dust and gas into two separate tails, which may be millions of kilometres long. The tail of gas is bluish and always points away from the Sun. The dust tail is yellowish or white. It looks smooth and is often curved.

Comets sometimes meet dramatic ends. Satellites have seen more than 60 small comets evaporate as they approached the Sun. In 1994, 20 or so pieces of comet Shoemaker-Levy 9 struck Jupiter, causing bright explosions. Jupiter wore dusty marks in its clouds for months afterwards.

Scientists think that comets are left-overs from the formation of the Solar System and that they contain a frozen record of this time. Space probes such as Giotto, which flew past Halley's Comet in 1986, have provided close-up views of comets. The Stardust probe is on the way to comet Wild 2 to snatch a sample of dust and bring it back to Earth in 2006.

COMET ORBITS

Short-period comets such as Halley and Encke orbit the Sun in 200 years or less and travel among the planets. Comets that take longer than 200 years are long-period comets. Comet Hale-Bopp will return in 2,400 years.

Uranus

ORIGIN OF NAME
COMET IS FROM THE GREEK WORDS FOR 'HAIRY STAR'.

SIZE OF NUCLEUS
COMET NUCLEI RANGE FROM ABOUT 100 M TO 40 KM (300 FT TO 25 MI) IN DIAMETER.

LENGTH OF TAIL
CAN BE 160 MILLION KM (100 MILLION MI) LONG

COMPOSITION
FROZEN WATER AND OTHER ICES, WITH DUST RICH IN CARBON AND SILICATES

NUMBER OF COMETS IN THE SOLAR SYSTEM
UNKNOWN – PROBABLY IN THE BILLIONS

COMET HALE-BOPP
Comet Hale-Bopp was a striking sight in early 1997. This photograph clearly shows the comet's broad, white dust tail and bluish gas tail.

◆ LOOK AGAIN ◆

- Which comet tail always points away from the Sun?
- If you melted a comet, what would you have?
- Where do most comets come from?

WHERE COMETS COME FROM
The Oort Cloud is an enormous region surrounding the Solar System. It contains billions of icy objects and is the source of long-period comets (ones that take more than 200 years to orbit the Sun). Short-period comets come from the Kuiper Belt, an inner region that begins near the orbit of Neptune.

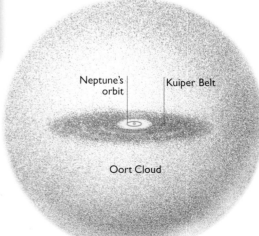

Neptune's orbit

Kuiper Belt

Oort Cloud

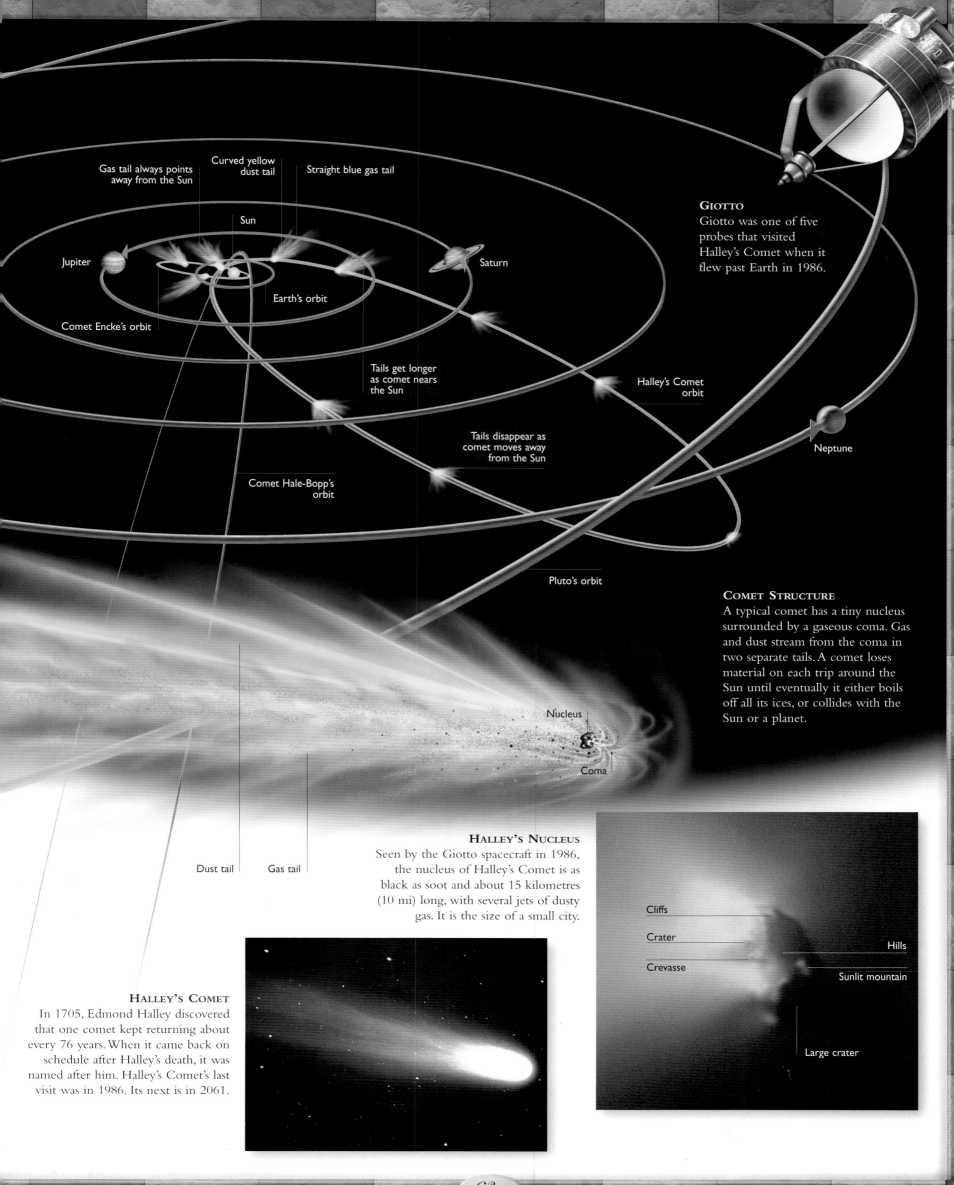

Gas tail always points away from the Sun

Curved yellow dust tail

Straight blue gas tail

Sun

Jupiter

Earth's orbit

Comet Encke's orbit

Saturn

Tails get longer as comet nears the Sun

Halley's Comet orbit

Tails disappear as comet moves away from the Sun

Comet Hale-Bopp's orbit

Neptune

Pluto's orbit

GIOTTO
Giotto was one of five probes that visited Halley's Comet when it flew past Earth in 1986.

COMET STRUCTURE
A typical comet has a tiny nucleus surrounded by a gaseous coma. Gas and dust stream from the coma in two separate tails. A comet loses material on each trip around the Sun until eventually it either boils off all its ices, or collides with the Sun or a planet.

Nucleus

Coma

Dust tail

Gas tail

HALLEY'S NUCLEUS
Seen by the Giotto spacecraft in 1986, the nucleus of Halley's Comet is as black as soot and about 15 kilometres (10 mi) long, with several jets of dusty gas. It is the size of a small city.

Cliffs

Crater

Crevasse

Hills

Sunlit mountain

Large crater

HALLEY'S COMET
In 1705, Edmond Halley discovered that one comet kept returning about every 76 years. When it came back on schedule after Halley's death, it was named after him. Halley's Comet's last visit was in 1986. Its next is in 2061.

Deep Space

BIG AS IT SEEMS TO US, the Solar System is just Earth's backyard. Beyond lies the rest of the universe – deep space. There are stars and other solar systems in deep space, but that's not all. Even though space looks dark and empty, astronomers have discovered that gas and dust drift through it. This interstellar matter is normally invisible, but it can be detected if a bright star lies behind it.

Some interstellar matter collects in thick clouds of dust and gas called nebulas. These are places where stars (and planets) are born. Typically, a large nebula creates an open cluster of several hundred stars. Another kind of cluster is the globular cluster, containing up to a million stars. Larger in scale are the galaxies, usually vast assemblies of billions of stars. Galaxies take different forms such as spiral, elliptical and irregular. On the largest scales, galaxies themselves cluster into groups.

Distances in deep space are much greater than within the Solar System, so astronomers use the light-year, the distance that light travels in one year – roughly 10 billion kilometres (6 billion mi). This is an enormous distance. If the distance between Earth and the Sun were 2.5 cm (1 in), a light-year would be 1.6 kilometres (1 mi). The star nearest the Sun, Alpha Centauri, is about 4.3 light-years away, while the most distant galaxy detected is 12 to 15 thousand million light-years away.

SMALLEST STAR KNOWN
GLIESE 623B, ONLY 10% AS LARGE AS THE SUN

LARGEST STAR KNOWN
ETA CARINAE, ABOUT 150 TIMES AS LARGE AS THE SUN

SMALLEST GALAXY KNOWN
PEGASUS II, A DWARF ELLIPTICAL GALAXY WITH PERHAPS 10 MILLION STARS

LARGEST GALAXY KNOWN
M87, A GIANT ELLIPTICAL GALAXY WITH ABOUT 800,000 MILLION STARS

A TOUR OF DEEP SPACE

Beyond our Solar System, there are nebulas where stars are born (below left), stars of all sizes, clusters of stars, galaxies of various shapes and clusters of galaxies. Astronomers use giant telescopes on Earth and orbiting telescopes in space to study these spectacular objects.

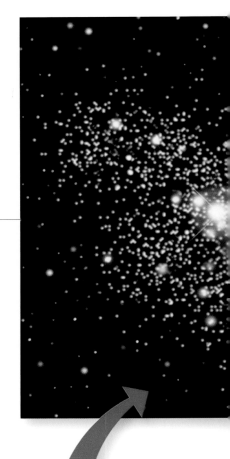

Star Cluster
Star clusters such as the Jewel Box are common in deep space. When clouds of gas and dust collapse, they make clusters of stars. The stars have different masses and age at various speeds, the largest ageing fastest.

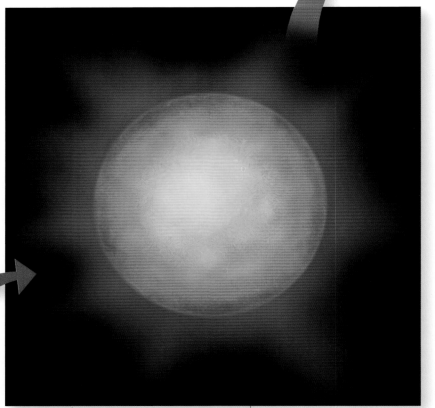

Star
After shining for millions of years, stars like the Sun start to run out of their hydrogen fuel supply. They grow larger and redder, becoming red giants or super-giants such as Betelgeuse (pictured).

Nebula
Stars are born in giant clouds of dust and hydrogen gas such as the Lagoon nebula (shown here). This giant cloud may produce thousands of stars.

ROSAT
The ROSAT space telescope detected the X-ray energy coming from stars, nebulas and galaxies.

Spiral Galaxy
Spiral galaxies have a nucleus of older yellow and reddish stars, and a spiral-armed disk with dusty gas clouds where new stars emerge.

◆ **LOOK AGAIN** ◆

- Where are stars born?
- What kinds of stars age fastest?
- How far away is the most distant known galaxy?

◆ **AMAZING FACT** ◆

If you could travel to the nearest star – Alpha Centauri – in a space shuttle at 8 kilometres (5 mi) per second, the journey would take you roughly 162,000 years.

Galaxy Cluster
Like stars, galaxies gather in groups known as clusters. Astronomers are studying whether galaxies form in a cluster first or whether the clusters grow from galaxies that are born separately.

HORSEHEAD NEBULA
This dark nebula gets its name from its shape. It can be seen outlined against a cloud of red hydrogen.

STARRY SKY
The stars you can see with the naked eye all lie relatively close to Earth. Binoculars or a telescope will show you more, such as the dense star field pictured here.

Nebulas

Clouds of dust and gas in space are known as nebulas, from the Latin word for 'cloud'. In some nebulas, gravity packs the dust and gas so tightly that parts of the nebula condense into stars. By studying these star-making 'factories', astronomers have caught stars in the act of being born.

Nebulas are usually cold and do not shine, so they can be hard to see. But a nebula that lies near a hot star absorbs energy from the star and its gases glow like a vivid red fluorescent light. This is called an emission nebula. Because they are bright, emission nebulas can be seen for great distances. For example, astronomers have detected emission nebulas in the Andromeda galaxy, some 2.5 million light-years away.

Another kind of nebula is made of tiny dust grains. These are just the right size to reflect starlight, so this nebula shines by reflecting the light of nearby stars. Reflection nebulas often appear blue because the dust grains reflect blue starlight especially well. Some dark dust nebulas are visible only because we see them against a bright background. The Horsehead nebula, for example, is a big cloud of dusty gas thick enough to block the light from the emission nebula behind it (see page 65).

While many nebulas are the birthplace of stars, others represent a star's final stages. When stars like the Sun grow old, they throw off their outer layers. The layers become a glowing shell of gas that expands into space, lit by the hot core of the star. These gas clouds are called planetary nebulas, but they have no relation to planets. They just looked like planets to the 19th century astronomers who came up with the name.

EMISSION NEBULA
The Orion nebula is a beautiful example of an emission nebula. It can be seen faintly with the naked eye, but looks best through a telescope. Astronomers have detected dozens of newborn stars within it.

REFLECTION NEBULA
Starlight reflecting from tiny dust grains produces this reflection nebula, seen in the constellation of Corona Australis. The bluish colour comes from the light of the hot stars inside the nebula, and also from the dust grains, which reflect blue light especially well.

EAGLE NEBULA (main image)
Type: emission; Distance: 7,000 light-years; Diameter: 315 light-years

ORION NEBULA (page 66, top)
Type: emission; Distance: 1,500 light-years; Diameter: 40 light-years

REFLECTION NEBULA IN CORONA AUSTRALIS (page 66, middle)
Type: reflection; Distance: 445 light-years; Diameter: 0.13 light-years

CONE NEBULA (page 67, bottom centre)
Type: dark; Distance: 3,000 light-years; Length: 50 light-years

HELIX NEBULA (page 67, lower right)
Type: planetary; Distance: 600 light-years; Diameter: 2 light-years

◆ Amazing Fact ◆

Only about 0.1 per cent of a nebula ends up making stars (and their planets, if they have any). The rest gets blown back into space, where it will eventually end up in another nebula.

Nebula

Star forming

A STARRY EAGLE

The Eagle nebula is an emission nebula surrounding a cluster of stars. It is 7,000 light-years away and appears in the constellation of Serpens. This photo taken through a telescope on Earth (right) shows dust clouds and gas being lit up by the light from hot, young stars. Our Sun and planets formed out of a similar nebula about 4.6 thousand million years ago.

PLANETARY NEBULA

The Helix nebula in the constellation of Aquarius is the closest planetary nebula to the Sun. It is only about 10,000 years old. Eventually the gas cloud will drift away and disappear, leaving just the white-hot central star.

PILLARS OF DUST AND GAS

The Hubble Space Telescope peered into the Eagle nebula and revealed pillars of dust and gas. The left-hand pillar (above) is about one light-year high. The light from newborn stars is eroding the gas in the pillars, much as wind moves dust on Earth. Little spikes emerging from the pillars (left) are denser globules of dusty gas. Each is about the size of the Solar System.

DARK NEBULA

The Cone nebula in the constellation of Monoceros is a cloud of dense dust visible against a bright emission nebula.

Stars

EVERY STAR IS A BIG BALL of extremely hot gases. Stars are mostly hydrogen (about 90 per cent) and helium (roughly 10 per cent), with tiny amounts of other gases. At its core, a true star must be hot enough – at least 6 million degrees Celsius (11 million degrees Fahrenheit) – to have nuclear reactions. These reactions fuse hydrogen into helium and release energy. The outward push of energy keeps the star from collapsing under its own weight. As each bit of energy reaches the surface, it flies into space – and the star shines.

The smallest true stars have about 10 per cent of the Sun's mass. Smaller than these are the brown dwarfs, star-like bodies that never became hot enough to fuse hydrogen into helium. They give off a little heat but they cannot shine like a true star. The largest stars known seem to have about 150 times the Sun's mass. Astronomers think that if a star larger than this tried to form, the cloud that gave birth to it would probably break apart and produce two or more stars.

Many common stars, in fact, are really two stars that orbit each other. The nearest star to the Sun is a triple-star system known as Alpha Centauri, with two stars, each about the Sun's size – Alpha Centauri A and B – and a much smaller third star – Proxima Centauri. The brightest star system in the sky, Sirius, is made up of two stars – Sirius A, also known as the Dog Star, and Sirius B, the Pup. Astronomers can estimate the mass of multiple stars by closely observing how they orbit one another.

SUN
TYPE: YELLOW MAIN SEQUENCE; DISTANCE: 8 LIGHT-MINUTES; DIAMETER: 1,392,000 KM (865,000 MI)

ALPHA CENTAURI
TYPE: YELLOW MAIN SEQUENCE; DISTANCE: 4.3 LIGHT-YEARS; DIAMETER: 1 X THE SUN'S DIAMETER

SIRIUS
TYPE: WHITE MAIN SEQUENCE; DISTANCE: 8.6 LIGHT-YEARS; DIAMETER: 2.4 X THE SUN'S DIAMETER

BETELGEUSE
TYPE: RED SUPER-GIANT; DISTANCE: 427 LIGHT-YEARS; DIAMETER: 800 X THE SUN'S DIAMETER

AN ORDINARY LIFE
From dust to dust – a star is born from a lump of dusty gas in a nebula. And at the end of its life, many millions of years later, it will throw some of its material back into space. The bigger a star is, the hotter it becomes and the faster its life runs. This sequence shows the life cycle of an average-sized star like the Sun.

Red Giant Star
After another 10,000 million years, the star runs low on hydrogen fuel. It swells into a red giant that starts to pulsate. If the star has planets, the innermost ones are destroyed.

Main Sequence Star
About 40 million years later, the star is fully formed and living a normal existence, perhaps with a system of planets.

Starbirth Nebula
An ordinary star like the Sun is born in a nebula when a cloud of gas and dust starts to collapse and grow hotter.

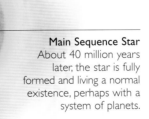

Common centre of gravity

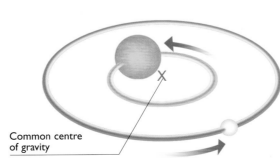

DOUBLE-STAR SYSTEM
The two stars in the Sirius system orbit each other every 50 years. When astronomers computed the mass of each star, they found that the smaller star, Sirius B, was very massive for its size. It was the first white dwarf star ever found.

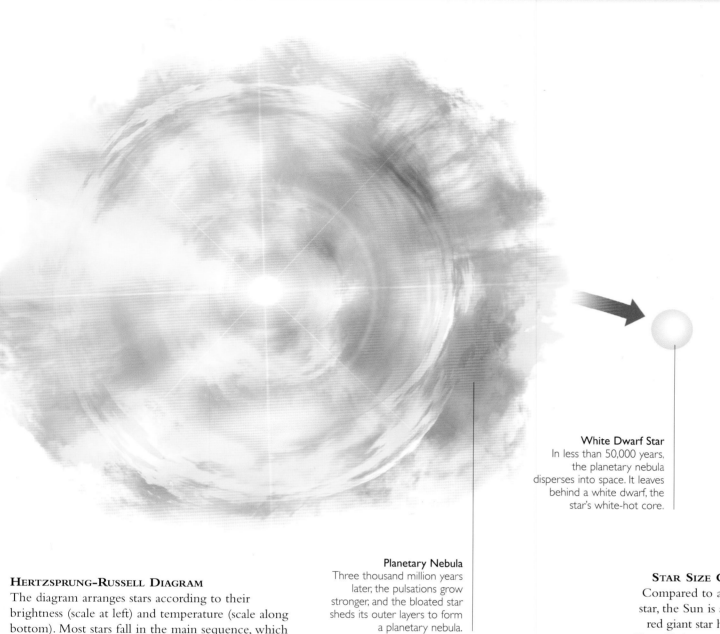

HERTZSPRUNG–RUSSELL DIAGRAM

The diagram arranges stars according to their brightness (scale at left) and temperature (scale along bottom). Most stars fall in the main sequence, which runs from top left to bottom right. Not surprisingly, most stars that are hotter are also brighter. In the upper right are red super-giants – cool but very bright because of their great size. White dwarfs, near the bottom, can be hot but still very dim.

Planetary Nebula
Three thousand million years later, the pulsations grow stronger, and the bloated star sheds its outer layers to form a planetary nebula.

White Dwarf Star
In less than 50,000 years, the planetary nebula disperses into space. It leaves behind a white dwarf, the star's white-hot core.

STAR SIZE COMPARISON
Compared to a white dwarf star, the Sun is a giant. But a red giant star has a diameter 20 to 40 times greater than the Sun's, and a red super-giant is roughly 800 times larger.

Red super-giant

Red giant

Sun

White dwarf

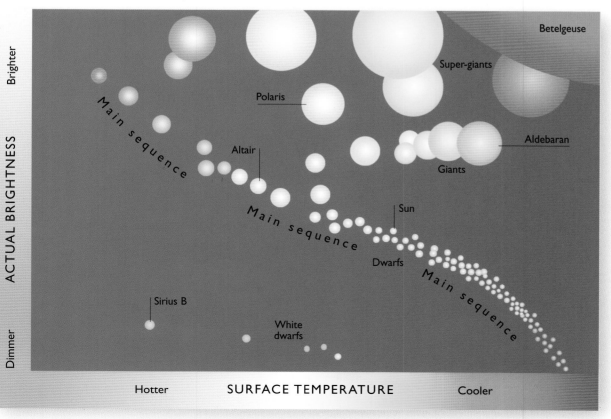

Brighter

Dimmer

ACTUAL BRIGHTNESS

Main sequence

Main sequence

Main sequence

Betelgeuse

Super-giants

Polaris

Altair

Aldebaran

Giants

Sun

Dwarfs

Sirius B

White dwarfs

Hotter

SURFACE TEMPERATURE

Cooler

Variable Stars

WHILE MANY STARS SHINE STEADILY year after year, others seem to change in brightness. One kind of variable star is called an eclipsing binary. It is really a double-star system in which one star passes in front of the other. When the two are side by side, they are at their brightest. When one is in front of the other, the system appears dimmer. These stars' actual brightness remains the same, but they appear dimmer because they eclipse each other.

Some stars do change their actual brightness. Giants and super-giants regularly grow larger and smaller, changing colour and brightness. They are called pulsating variables and are classified by how much their brightness changes and by their period – how long they take to go from bright to dim to bright again.

The Cepheids are a group of pulsating stars that change in brightness over periods ranging from 1 day to 70 days. Any two Cepheids with the same period have the same actual brightness. The longer a Cepheid's period, the brighter the star is. In the 1920s, American astronomer Edwin Hubble found Cepheids in the Andromeda galaxy. By measuring their period, he could tell their actual brightness. Then, by comparing their apparent brightness to their actual brightness, he could estimate how far away they are. He proved that the Cepheids and Andromeda are too far away to be part of the Milky Way – and that the universe is larger than anyone had expected.

Some variables change dramatically. In a double-star system, the star with stronger gravity may pull so much gas from its companion that it sets off an explosion known as a nova. The system suddenly brightens enormously and then fades slowly. The explosions can happen again and again.

NOVA EXPLOSION

In a double-star system, things can get complicated. As one star ages, it swells into a red giant and some of its gas may be captured by its companion star, a white dwarf. When the captured material crashes on to the white dwarf, the gas can become hot enough to touch off a nuclear explosion. The resulting blast of energy is called a nova. If the bloated red giant keeps feeding gas to the white dwarf, the nova will erupt repeatedly.

Red giant

Gas streamimg to white dwarf

ALGOL
TYPE: ECLIPSING BINARY; MAGNITUDE: VARIES FROM 2.1 TO 3.4; PERIOD: 2 DAYS 20 HOURS 49 MINUTES

MIRA
TYPE: PULSATING VARIABLE; MAGNITUDE: VARIES FROM 3.4 TO 9.3; PERIOD: 332 DAYS

ETA CARINAE
TYPE: IRREGULAR VARIABLE; MAGNITUDE: WAS 2ND MAGNITUDE IN THE 1840S, THEN DIMMED GREATLY, BUT IS NOW BRIGHTENING AGAIN

White dwarf

ECLIPSING BINARY

In eclipsing binaries such as Algol, two stars orbit each other. If the orbit is tipped just right, when one star passes behind the other, its light is blocked and the total light from the pair dims.

Bright white star blocks some light from orange star – medium brightness

White star beside orange star – maximum brightness

CATACLYSMIC VARIABLE

In 1841, the star known as Eta Carinae suffered a violent outburst and blew off two giant clouds of gas. Since then, the clouds have been expanding. This strange cataclysmic variable recently doubled in brightness. It will explode as a supernova (see page 72) sometime in the next few thousand years.

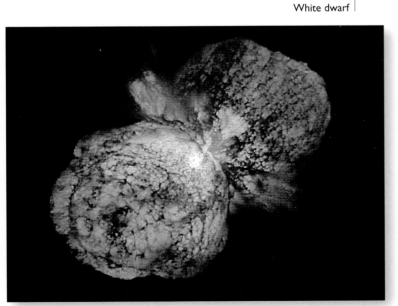

Orange star blocks all light from white star – minimum brightness

PULSATING VARIABLE

A pulsating variable star expands and contracts regularly. As it swells, the star's surface becomes cooler, redder and dimmer. The reverse happens when it shrinks. The time it takes for one complete cycle of swelling and shrinking is called the period, and it may last hours or months.

◆ AMAZING FACT ◆

One of the most spectacular novas ever observed was nova Cygni 1975. Before it erupted, it was too faint to be seen. At its peak, on 31 August, 1975, it had an apparent magnitude of 1.8. Astronomers calculated that its actual brightness must have increased by at least 20 million times, making it 1 million times more luminous than the Sun.

MAGNITUDE SCALE

Astronomers measure star brightness in magnitudes. Lower numbers mean a brighter star. The brightest stars use negative numbers – Sirius is −1.4 magnitude. The faintest stars your eyes can see are 6th magnitude.

| −1 | 0 | 1 | 2 | 3 | 4 | 5 | 6 | 7 | 8 |

APPARENT BRIGHTNESS

In the constellation of Orion, red Betelgeuse (upper left) and blue Rigel (lower right) appear nearly the same brightness. But Rigel lies almost twice as far away, so in reality it is much brighter. Astronomers compare stars' actual brightness by measuring how each would appear at a standard distance of 32.6 light-years.

◆ PROJECT: *Follow a Variable* ◆

Follow a star's brightness as it changes. A good star to observe in the Northern Hemisphere is Algol in the constellation of Perseus – observe it every night for a week if you can. In the Southern Hemisphere, try looking at Mira in Cetus once every two weeks for a couple of months.

❶ Locate the star on one of the star maps in this book (see pages 94–109), then find it in the night sky. Note how bright it looks compared with the stars around it. Draw a picture of the stars, indicating whether the variable is brighter or dimmer than each of the nearby stars.

❷ When you next observe, compare the variable with the nearby stars and note whether its brightness has changed.

Supernovas

A SUPERNOVA IS THE EXPLOSION of a massive star. In a supernova, a single star can briefly outshine all the rest of its galaxy. There are two types of star that can become a supernova. The first is a white dwarf in a double-star system (see diagram, below). If the white dwarf's companion swells to become a red giant, some of its gas can be captured by the white dwarf. As this material falls on the white dwarf, it steadily adds mass. If the white dwarf grows to be 1.4 times more massive than the Sun, it becomes unstable. Runaway nuclear reactions cause the white dwarf to explode, producing a supernova that destroys the stars.

The second star that can become a supernova is a massive star at least eight times larger than the Sun (see diagram, right). Such stars are very hot and have short, intense lives. The end comes when the star runs out of fuel and its nuclear reactions stop. In a second, the core collapses and sends a shock wave through the outer layers. When the shock wave reaches the surface, the supernova explodes. In this kind of supernova, the star's core survives as a neutron star – a very dense, city-size sphere – or collapses further to become a black hole – an infinitely dense object with such powerful gravity that even light cannot escape.

Each supernova throws off a supernova remnant – a cloud of gas and dust that will help to make new stars. Earth contains elements created in hot stars that died before the Sun was born. When the stars exploded as supernovas, these elements were tossed back into the Milky Way, where some of them formed the Solar System. We are literally made of recycled star debris.

SUPERNOVA 1987A
SEEN EXPLODING: 23 FEBRUARY, 1987; NOW: A YOUNG SUPERNOVA REMNANT; DISTANCE: 179,000 LIGHT-YEARS; DIAMETER: 0.2 LIGHT-YEAR

CRAB NEBULA
SEEN EXPLODING: 1054; NOW: A SUPERNOVA REMNANT;
DISTANCE: 6,520 LIGHT-YEARS; SIZE: 8.8 BY 13.7 LIGHT-YEARS

SAX J1808.4-3658
SEEN EXPLODING: IN PRE-HISTORIC TIMES; NOW: A PULSAR;
DISTANCE: 13,000 LIGHT-YEARS

MASSIVE-STAR SUPERNOVA

One type of supernova signals the explosive death of a massive star. Such stars have at least eight times the Sun's mass. Their high temperatures cause them to race through their fuel supplies and then explode. They leave behind either a neutron star or, if the original star was very massive, a black hole.

Ordinary Star
A star with at least eight times the Sun's mass evolves quickly. It shines as an ordinary star for only about 30 million years.

Super-giant Star
The massive star swells to become a super-giant star and begins to pulsate. This pulsating stage may last for 70 million years.

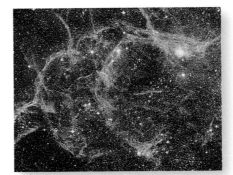

SUPERNOVA REMNANT

About 120,000 years ago, a massive star exploded in the constellation of Vela. By now, the expanding wisps of gas look almost like a spiderwebs. Supernova explosions return gas and dust to space, where they will help to build new stars.

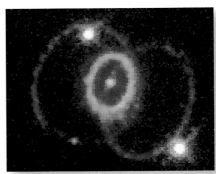

A RECENT SUPERNOVA

In 1987, a massive star known as supernova 1987A was seen exploding in the Large Magellanic Cloud. The expanding bubble of gas is still small, but eventually it will look like the Vela remnant.

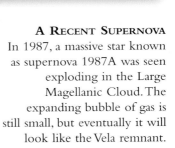

Mass Transfer
A white dwarf star attracts gas from its red giant companion.

Unstable Dwarf
The white dwarf grows in mass and becomes unstable.

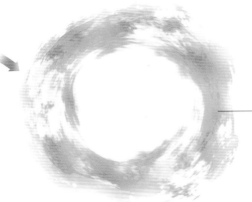

DOUBLE-STAR SUPERNOVA

A supernova can occur in some kinds of double-star system. Here the gas flows from one star to its companion. Made unstable by the extra mass, the companion star explodes. Both stars are destroyed in the explosion and all that is left of them is a supernova remnant – a shell of hot gas.

Supernova Explosion
Eventually, the white dwarf explodes as a supernova.

Supernova Remnant
The explosion destroys the stars, leaving a shell of hot, expanding gas.

Supernova Explosion

The star runs out of fuel and no longer has nuclear reactions to support its upper layers. The star explodes as a supernova.

Black Hole

If the original star had much more than 10 times the Sun's mass, its surviving core collapses into a black hole. This is so compact that even light can't escape. The hole is surrounded by a supernova remnant of gas and dust.

Neutron Star

A star that began with a mass up to 10 times greater than the Sun's leaves behind a neutron star. Surrounding the neutron star is a supernova remnant – an expanding shell of hot gas.

PULSARS

A neutron star, the collapsed core of a supernova, is only a few kilometres across but it spins very rapidly and turns some of its momentum into beams of energy. If Earth lies in the beam, we see a signal that repeats like a light from a lighthouse. The pulses of energy give neutron stars their other name – pulsars.

Pulsar

Pulsar

Pulsar

Earth

Earth

Earth

◆ AMAZING FACT ◆

A huge supernova in AD 1054 was seen in many parts of the world. The starburst (bottom left) was scratched into stone by Native Americans in present-day New Mexico soon after. It is believed to be a record of the exploding star in the night sky.

Other Solar Systems

THE SUN ISN'T THE ONLY STAR with planets. In October 1995, astronomers discovered that a star called 51 Pegasi has a planet with about half the mass of Jupiter orbiting close to it. Since then, more than 20 other planetary systems have been confirmed. Astronomers think they will eventually find that lots of stars have their own families of planets.

The search is difficult because it is impossible to see these planets directly. Viewed from Earth, the planets appear close to their star, so they are lost in its glare. To find the planets, astronomers look for tiny movements of the star, indicated by subtle changes in the colour of the star's light produced by the Doppler shift (see page 19). These changes occur because, when a planet orbits a star, its gravity causes the star to move back and forth a little. Current telescopes limit how small a shift can be detected. So far, astronomers have found only massive planets with strong gravity orbiting fairly close to their star. These are Jupiter-sized planets. When equipment improves, Earth-sized planets may be discovered too.

A look at the other planetary systems shows that they are built differently from the Sun's. Our Solar System has small-mass planets, such as Earth, orbiting near the Sun, while the big planets, such as Jupiter, orbit much further out. But the other solar systems have big planets close to their star. Perhaps as these solar systems were forming, something happened that moved the large planets inwards. In any case, astronomers expect that other solar systems will have small planets as well. Earth-sized planets would be the most likely places to look for alien life.

NUMBER OF OTHER SOLAR SYSTEMS DISCOVERED
MORE THAN 20 CONFIRMED (11 MORE HAVE BROWN DWARFS INSTEAD OF PLANETS)

ESTIMATED NUMBER OF OTHER SOLAR SYSTEMS
MOST STARS THAT ARE SINGLE (RATHER THAN MULTIPLE) PROBABLY HAVE PLANETS.

SMALLEST PLANET FOUND OUTSIDE THE SOLAR SYSTEM
A PLANET WITH 0.4 X JUPITER'S MASS THAT ORBITS THE STAR HD 75289

LARGEST PLANET FOUND OUTSIDE THE SOLAR SYSTEM
A PLANET WITH 11 X JUPITER'S MASS THAT ORBITS THE STAR HD 114762

◆ AMAZING FACT ◆

If you lived on a planet that orbited a double star, you would see two suns in the sky at least part of the time. Everyday objects would have two shadows when both suns were visible. And if the suns were very different from each other, the shadows might have different colours.

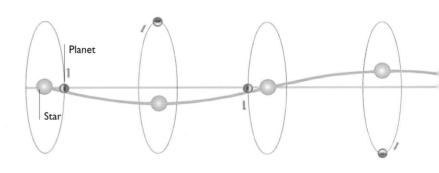

Planet

Star

COROT

The French space telescope named COROT will be launched in 2003. Its main purpose is to study small pulsations in stars, but it will also search for planets.

KEPLER

The proposed Kepler space telescope will search for Earth-sized planets by looking for a slight dimming of the star as a planet moves in front of it.

◆ PROJECT: *Making a Solar System* ◆

For this project, you need several sheets of paper, crayons or coloured pencils and the information contained in the Planet Comparison chart on the facing page.

❶ Pick one of the other planetary systems in the chart.

❷ Draw what you think its planets would look like if you approached them in a spaceship. Keep in mind that big planets will probably have thick atmospheres like Jupiter's. Each planetary system probably also has undiscovered planets the size of Earth.

❸ For comparison, draw in some members of our Solar System, such as Mercury, Earth and Jupiter.

◆ LOOK AGAIN ◆

- Why have astronomers found only massive planets so far?
- How do astronomers discover planets they can't see?
- How do other solar systems differ from ours?

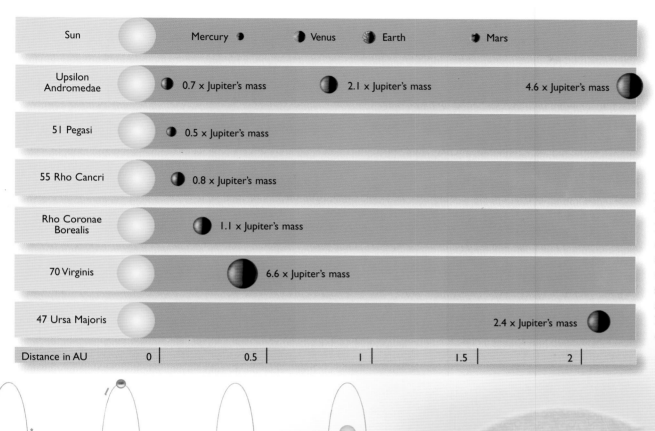

Sun		Mercury	Venus	Earth	Mars
Upsilon Andromedae		0.7 x Jupiter's mass	2.1 x Jupiter's mass	4.6 x Jupiter's mass
51 Pegasi		0.5 x Jupiter's mass		
55 Rho Cancri		0.8 x Jupiter's mass		
Rho Coronae Borealis		1.1 x Jupiter's mass		
70 Virginis		6.6 x Jupiter's mass		
47 Ursa Majoris				2.4 x Jupiter's mass

Distance in AU   0   0.5   1   1.5   2

PLANET COMPARISON

This chart shows some of the other known planetary systems, along with our inner Solar System. The differences are striking – the star 70 Virginis, for example, has a planet with more than six times Jupiter's mass orbiting about as close as Mercury orbits the Sun. Perhaps these other systems formed in a different way than the Sun's planets did.

ANOTHER SOLAR SYSTEM

What would an alien planet system look like? So far, all the planets found around other stars are large bodies with masses roughly similar to Jupiter's. Astronomers believe that such planets would probably resemble Jupiter and have cloud belts and swirling storms.

WOBBLING STAR

When careful observation reveals a slight wobble in a star's path, this suggests that a planet is orbiting the star – even if the planet is too small to see. If the planet is massive or close to its star, the effect is greater.

Star Clusters

MOST STARS OCCUR IN GROUPS, which astronomers call associations or clusters. The group with the smallest number of stars is the stellar association. An association has up to a hundred young stars scattered across hundreds of light-years. The brightest members are hot, blue-white stars, each more massive than the Sun. Some associations, however, contain mostly smaller stars that are still forming. The bright stars of the constellation Perseus belong to three associations. No association is more than a few million years old.

Open clusters have many more stars than an association – several hundred to a thousand. They cluster in a much smaller space than an association – only tens of light-years instead of hundreds. Two open clusters near our Solar System are the Pleiades and Hyades. The Sun is also part of an open cluster, but the cluster is hard to identify because it is all around us. Some of our fellow cluster members are stars in the Big Dipper. Open clusters can be as much as 500 million years old.

The giants of the star-cluster kingdom are the globular clusters. They can have up to a million stars concentrated in a region smaller than that taken up by a hundred stars in an association. Stars in a globular cluster are old and well evolved, and include many red giants and white dwarfs. Because the red giants are so much brighter than white dwarfs, they are the most visible stars in a globular cluster.

OMEGA CENTAURI
Omega Centauri is the largest globular star cluster known. Astronomers estimate that it contains about a million stars. Imagine what the night sky would look like from a planet near its centre.

Pleione

Atlas

STELLAR ASSOCIATIONS IN MILKY WAY
ABOUT 70 ARE KNOWN

SIZE OF THE LARGEST ASSOCIATION IN PERSEUS
LESS THAN 100 STARS; ABOUT 800 LIGHT-YEARS IN DIAMETER

OPEN CLUSTERS IN MILKY WAY
ABOUT 1,000 ARE KNOWN

SIZE OF PLEIADES OPEN CLUSTER
SEVERAL HUNDRED STARS; ABOUT 13 LIGHT-YEARS IN DIAMETER

GLOBULAR CLUSTERS IN MILKY WAY
ABOUT 125 ARE KNOWN

SIZE OF OMEGA CENTAURI GLOBULAR CLUSTER
ABOUT 1 MILLION STARS; ABOUT 180 LIGHT-YEARS IN DIAMETER

◆ PROJECT: *Collecting Clusters* ◆

You can collect star clusters. All you need is the star maps on pages 94–109 and a pair of binoculars.

1. Find the right star maps for the season and your part of the world.

2. Look for the globular and open cluster symbols on the maps. Make a list of all the clusters that should be visible tonight.

3. Go outside with the star map and try to locate the clusters on your list. (Start with the easy, bright ones!) Tick them off when you find them.

4. Sketch what you see and label the sketch with the date and time.

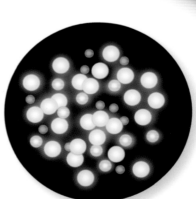

A young globular cluster has many white-hot stars, plus yellow stars like the Sun and dim red dwarfs.

GLOBULAR CLUSTERS
Because they have so much mass and gravity, globular clusters hold onto most of their stars for a long time. A few stars are ejected, however, when cluster stars move randomly and almost collide.

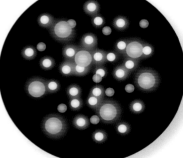

In an old globular, the stars in the original population have evolved, becoming red giants and white dwarfs.

Asterope

Maia

Taygeta

OPEN CLUSTERS
When an open cluster forms, it is less than about 30 light-years in diameter and has a broad range of stars, with many being hotter and more massive than the Sun.

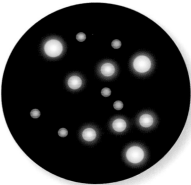

In time, the members of the open cluster drift apart as the gravity of the rest of the galaxy pulls on them.

Celaeno

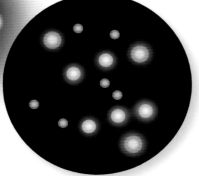

The cluster members evolve as all stars do, with the more massive stars becoming red giants.

Electra

Merope

*L*OOK *A*GAIN

- Which cluster type is the oldest?
- How large is the Pleiades cluster?
- What is the most massive globular cluster?

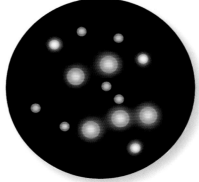

As the open cluster becomes fainter and more scattered, its red giants become white dwarfs and its yellow stars become the new red giants.

THE PLEIADES
The Pleiades is a beautiful open cluster in the constellation of Taurus. It lies 375 light-years away and contains several hundred stars. The cluster is dominated by young, hot blue stars, and surrounded by a blue reflection nebula. Although you can see the Pleiades easily with the naked eye, it looks especially beautiful in binoculars.

Alcyone

CLUSTERS IN THE MILKY WAY
In this side-on view of the Milky Way, open clusters lie in or near the disk of the galaxy. Globular clusters, on the other hand, orbit the Milky Way's central bulge like a cloud of moons.

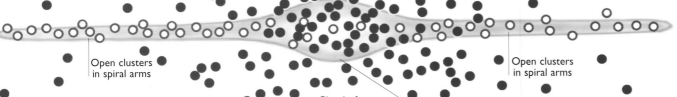

Cloud of globular clusters

Open clusters in spiral arms

Cloud of globular clusters

Central bulge of Milky Way

Open clusters in spiral arms

Eventually, the cluster becomes hard to tell apart from the rest of the galaxy's stars. Its smallest stars will hardly have changed.

The Milky Way

If the Solar System is like a neighbourhood, the Milky Way galaxy is like a gigantic city. In fact, it is larger than most galaxies astronomers have found. Our galaxy's name comes from how it appears in the night sky. Ancient people saw a smooth band dividing the sky like a milky stream and wondered what it was made of. About 400 years ago, Galileo studied the band with his telescope and saw that it contained countless tiny stars, just like the ones you can see with the naked eye, but fainter.

It took astronomers hundreds of years to work out the actual shape and size of the Milky Way galaxy – and many details are still unclear. Because the Solar System lies within the Milky Way, surveying the galaxy is like studying a big, grassy field while lying down in it. In the 1930s, astronomers found the Sun was not at the galaxy's centre, but about two-thirds of the way towards one edge. Later, radio telescopes peered through the galaxy's dust clouds to reveal that the Milky Way has several spiral arms. The Sun lies in the Orion arm, part of which is what we see in the sky. The Perseus arm is in front of Orion, while the Sagittarius arm is behind. Stars, clusters and gas clouds all orbit the centre of the galaxy. Our star takes 226 million years to complete one orbit around the Milky Way.

At the centre of the Milky Way lies a massive black hole, probably containing a million times more material than the Sun. Around this swirls the galactic bulge, a huge collection of older red and yellow stars. Surrounding the bulge like a wide collar is the many-armed disk, which is turning slowly. Recent studies show the disk may be warped like a hat-brim, although astronomers don't yet know why. Floating above both bulge and disk is the galactic halo, sparsely populated by old red stars and globular clusters. These probably formed at the same time as the galaxy itself.

SIZE OF MILKY WAY
100,000 light-years in diameter

STARS IN MILKY WAY
About 200 billion

STAR CLUSTERS IN MILKY WAY
About 125 globular clusters and roughly 1,000 open clusters are known.

DUST AND GAS IN MILKY WAY
About 5% of the Milky Way's visible matter is gas and dust.

BETELGEUSE
Aged red stars like Betelgeuse are more common in the Milky Way's central bulge than in the spiral arms.

ORION NEBULA
The Orion nebula is part of a giant cloud of gas and dust – a 'star factory' that has been at work for the last 12 million years.

THE PLEIADES
Open clusters such as the Pleiades are slowly being pulled apart by the tug of gravity from other stars and clouds of dust and gas.

OMEGA CENTAURI
Globular clusters such as Omega Centauri formed along with the Milky Way's first stars. Both are now millions of years old.

EAGLE NEBULA
Clouds of gas and new stars such as the Eagle nebula are found only in the galaxy's central bulge and spiral arms.

• Amazing Fact •

If you were to leave Earth on a space shuttle, travelling at 8 kilometres (5 mi) per second, it would you take 1.2 billion years to reach the centre of the galaxy. That's about one-tenth the age of the universe.

SIDE-ON GALAXY
If we could see the Milky Way in profile, its disk would look much thinner than its central bulge. Above and below the disk is a halo made of globular clusters and old red stars.

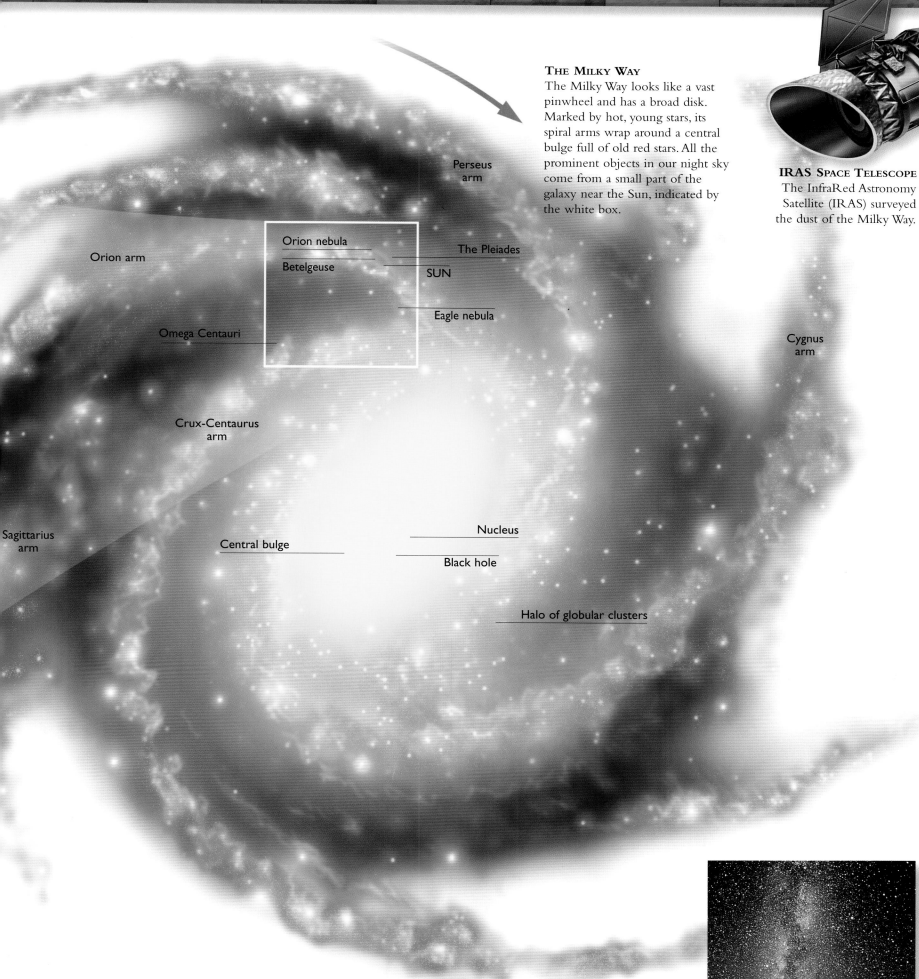

THE MILKY WAY

The Milky Way looks like a vast pinwheel and has a broad disk. Marked by hot, young stars, its spiral arms wrap around a central bulge full of old red stars. All the prominent objects in our night sky come from a small part of the galaxy near the Sun, indicated by the white box.

IRAS SPACE TELESCOPE
The InfraRed Astronomy Satellite (IRAS) surveyed the dust of the Milky Way.

Perseus arm

Orion arm

Orion nebula

Betelgeuse

The Pleiades

SUN

Eagle nebula

Omega Centauri

Crux-Centaurus arm

Cygnus arm

Sagittarius arm

Central bulge

Nucleus

Black hole

Halo of globular clusters

INFRARED MILKY WAY
This infrared image highlights the warmest areas of the Milky Way. The infrared radiation comes mostly from the dust that lies all through the disk. The dust glows with the heat of starlight, and clumps of dust contain new stars.

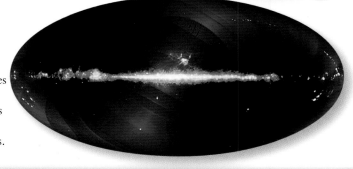

A BAND OF STARS
The Milky Way in the sky is not completely smooth to the eye. The darker patches are places where vast clouds of dust block the light of faraway stars.

Galaxies

GALAXIES VARY IN APPEARANCE, size and shape. Astronomers, however, fit them into three basic patterns – spirals, ellipticals and irregulars. Spiral galaxies are easy to identify with their sweeping arms, which contain gas and dust that make new stars. An important subclass of the spirals are barred spirals. These have a roughly oblong-shaped centre and may be ordinary spiral galaxies that have collided with or devoured smaller galaxies. Astronomers believe that the Milky Way has absorbed several small galaxies already, and that its central bulge may be bar-like in shape. It could be that we live in a barred spiral galaxy.

Elliptical galaxies contain mostly older stars and little or no gas to make new ones. These ball- or oval-shaped galaxies may have formed early in the universe's history and stopped making new stars when they ran out of gas. A subclass, the dwarf elliptical, may be the most numerous of all galaxies. But because these small galaxies of dim stars are more difficult to see than larger, brighter galaxies, we have discovered only a few of them.

Irregular galaxies are small and shapeless, but many are still actively making stars. The Small Magellanic Cloud is an irregular galaxy that is being distorted by the Large Magellanic Cloud and the Milky Way.

Galaxies gather in clusters, just as stars do. Here, they often collide or interact, pulling one another out of shape. When a galaxy's dust and gas clouds are disturbed by a collision, bright new stars may be born, leading to a spectacular fireworks display.

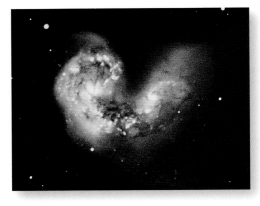

COLLIDING GALAXIES
When galaxies collide, they pass right through each other because their stars lie far apart. But the gravitational pull of such a collision usually trigger each galaxy's gas clouds to begin making new stars. The Antennae galaxies, which began colliding 500 million years ago, feature bright areas of young stars.

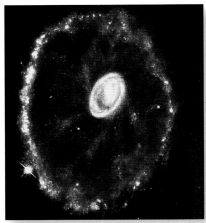

RING OF STARS
When a small galaxy collided with the larger Cartwheel galaxy, a wave of star formation – the blue ring – spread outwards through the Cartwheel's disk. The ring of young stars is now big enough to encircle the whole Milky Way.

POPULATIONS OF KNOWN GALAXIES
SPIRAL GALAXIES: 63%; BARRED SPIRAL GALAXIES: 15%; ELLIPTICAL GALAXIES: 18%; IRREGULAR GALAXIES: 4%

WHIRLPOOL/M51 (page 80)
TYPE: SPIRAL; DISTANCE: 15 MILLION LIGHT-YEARS; DIAMETER: 50,000 LIGHT-YEARS

GREAT BARRED SPIRAL/NGC 1365 (page 81)
TYPE: barred spiral; DISTANCE: 55 MILLION LIGHT-YEARS; DIAMETER: 157,800 LIGHT-YEARS

M87 (page 81, top)
TYPE: GIANT ELLIPTICAL; DISTANCE: 55 MILLION LIGHT-YEARS; DIAMETER: 147,000 LIGHT-YEARS

SMALL MAGELLANIC CLOUD (page 81, right)
TYPE: IRREGULAR; DISTANCE: 210,000 LIGHT YEARS; DIAMETER: 17,000 LIGHT-YEARS

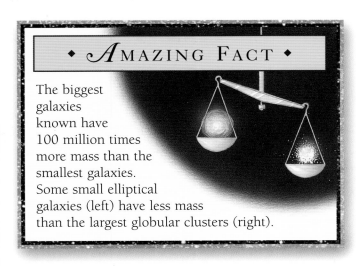

• *A*MAZING FACT •

The biggest galaxies known have 100 million times more mass than the smallest galaxies. Some small elliptical galaxies (left) have less mass than the largest globular clusters (right).

ELLIPTICAL GALAXY

As you can see in this illustration of M87, an elliptical galaxy looks like the central bulge of a spiral galaxy. Ellipticals can be more massive than the Milky Way, but range down to tiny dwarf ellipticals, which can be smaller than the largest globular star cluster.

IRREGULAR GALAXY

Like many other irregular galaxies, the Small Magellanic Cloud is small but contains many bright nebulas and hot, young stars. Astronomers think most irregular galaxies will eventually be absorbed by larger galaxies.

BARRED SPIRAL GALAXY

A regular spiral galaxy has a circular bulge at its centre, but the centre of a barred spiral is longer than it is wide. Obvious barred spirals, such as the Great Barred Spiral (NGC 1365) shown here, make up only a fraction of all spirals, but many ordinary spirals seem to have weak bars.

SPIRAL GALAXY

The Whirlpool (M51) is a spectacular spiral galaxy. All spiral galaxies feature the trademark arms, but some have tightly wound arms, while others are more open. Spiral galaxies also differ in how much dust and gas they contain.

Spirals

Ellipticals

Barred spirals

GALAXY CLASSIFICATION

Edwin Hubble developed this scheme for classifying galaxies by shape, which is still used. Hubble thought ellipticals evolved to become spirals, but today's astronomers think most spirals are born that way.

◆ PROJECT: *Pie Dish Spiral* ◆

You need a round glass or aluminium pie dish, a coin and a sprinkle of dots from a hole-punch.

1 Place the coin under the centre of the pie dish on a kitchen worktop, so the dish turns easily.

2 Pour about 1 centimetre (½ in) of tap water into the dish.

3 Carefully sprinkle the hole-punch dots in the centre of the dish.

4 Spin the dish slowly. Notice how the dots stream into spiral arms.

The Local Group

THE LOCAL GROUP IS THE NAME Edwin Hubble gave to the galaxies nearest the Milky Way. Today, astronomers know of about 35 Local Group galaxies spread across roughly 8 million light-years of space. This is not a random collection of galaxies that just happen to lie nearby. Linked by the pull of gravity, the Local Group members form a cluster of galaxies, just as the Pleiades forms a cluster of stars.

Two big galaxies dominate the Local Group – the Milky Way and the Andromeda galaxy, which is slightly larger. Each has attracted a collection of smaller Local Group galaxies. Belonging to the Andromeda galaxy are M32, NGC 147, NGC 185, NGC 205 and four dwarf galaxies. The Pinwheel (M33), the third-largest galaxy in the group, also lies near Andromeda. The Milky Way's satellite galaxies are the Large and Small Magellanic Clouds and several dwarf galaxies. The rest of the Local Group galaxies appear to stand alone.

Because the Local Group is our local cluster, astronomers can study it in detail. They have found 3 spiral galaxies, 4 ellipticals, 14 irregulars and about 14 dwarf ellipticals. Several of the smaller member-galaxies were discovered only recently. An unsolved question is whether the Local Group has a bigger share of small galaxies than the universe as a whole. If the Local Group is typical, then the universe has a great many more small galaxies waiting to be discovered.

Several other 'local groups' surround ours, each cluster held together by its own gravity. The largest galaxy cluster near us lies in the constellation of Virgo. Together with many other clusters, the Local Group and Virgo cluster form a bigger group called the Local Supercluster, some 60 million light-years across.

SIZE OF LOCAL GROUP
ABOUT 8 MILLION LIGHT-YEARS IN DIAMETER, WITH ABOUT 35 MEMBERS

MAGELLANIC CLOUDS
LARGE CLOUD – DISTANCE: 179,000 LIGHT-YEARS; DIAMETER: 34,000 LIGHT-YEARS
SMALL CLOUD – DISTANCE: 210,000 LIGHT-YEARS; DIAMETER: 17,000 LIGHT-YEARS

ANDROMEDA GALAXY (M31)
DISTANCE: 2.5 MILLION LIGHT-YEARS; DIAMETER: 128,000 LIGHT-YEARS

PINWHEEL GALAXY (M33)
DISTANCE: 2.6 MILLION LIGHT-YEARS; DIAMETER: 50,000 LIGHT-YEARS

SCULPTOR DWARF
DISTANCE: 284,000 LIGHT-YEARS; DIAMETER: 1,400 LIGHT-YEARS

FORNAX CLUSTER
In the same constellation as the Fornax dwarf galaxy, the Fornax cluster of galaxies is hundreds of times further away. Like the Local Group, it is an immense area of empty space dotted with galaxies clustered in strings and sheets.

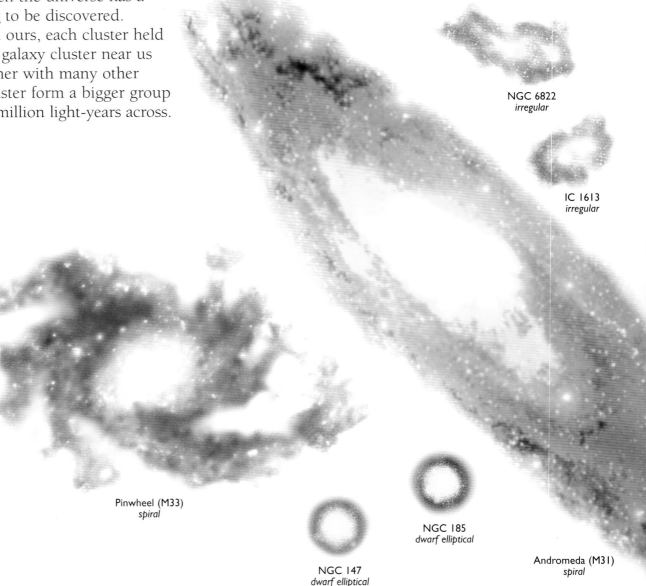

NGC 6822
irregular

IC 1613
irregular

GALACTIC NEIGHBOURS
The Local Group has a few big, bright member-galaxies and a lot of small ones. The 17 largest members of the cluster are illustrated here. To be a Local Group member, a galaxy must lie nearby and must not be moving so fast that it can escape the cluster's gravity.

M32
elliptical

Pinwheel (M33)
spiral

NGC 147
dwarf elliptical

NGC 185
dwarf elliptical

Andromeda (M31)
spiral

◆ LOOK AGAIN ◆

- How many galaxies does the Local Group contain?
- What is the most common type of galaxy in the Group?
- What does the Local Group belong to?

SMALL MAGELLANIC CLOUD
The Small Magellanic Cloud is the
second-largest satellite galaxy of the
Milky Way. Studying its irregular shape,
astronomers found that it has been
distorted by the gravity of the Milky
Way and the Large Magellanic Cloud.

VIRGO CLUSTER
The Local Group sits on the edge
of a large supercluster of galaxies that
surrounds the Virgo cluster (shown
here). The Virgo cluster contains the
giant elliptical galaxy M87, which is
a powerful radio and X-ray source.

ANDROMEDA GALAXY
The Andromeda galaxy is the most
distant object we can see with the naked
eye, some 2.5 million light-years away.
Like the Milky Way, it is a spiral, but it
is more massive than the Milky Way.

NGC 205
elliptical

Leo I
dwarf elliptical

Draco dwarf
dwarf elliptical

Sculptor dwarf
irregular

Leo II
dwarf elliptical

Ursa Minor dwarf
dwarf elliptical

Fornax dwarf
dwarf elliptical

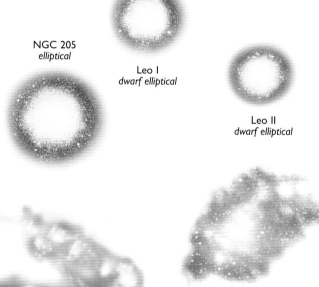

Small Magellanic Cloud
dwarf irregular

Large Magellanic Cloud
irregular

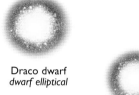

Milky Way
spiral

✦ AMAZING FACT ✦

The life of a small galaxy in a cluster of galaxies
isn't easy. The biggest galaxies
attract and devour
the smaller ones,
usually by
pulling them
apart and
absorbing
their stars.

Black Holes

SOME GALAXIES HAVE SMALL, BRIGHT CENTRES that emit lots of energy. These are known as active galaxies, and astronomers believe their energy is generated by a small but extremely large object, most likely a black hole. Black holes are so dense that they swallow everything that comes near them – even light cannot escape their incredible gravity. A stellar black hole, one that forms after a supernova, has about the mass of a star (see page 73), but a galactic black hole in the heart of a galaxy can be as big as a billion Suns.

Since black holes pull in light, astronomers can't see them directly. Instead, they pinpoint black holes by looking for the effects of extremely strong gravity. An active galaxy's energy comes not from inside the black hole, but from the region just outside. Swirling around a black hole like water going down a drain is a disk of material made from torn-apart stars and clouds of gas. The black hole's powerful gravity squeezes this disk with extreme force, heating it to hundreds of thousands of degrees. Before the matter is sucked into the black hole, it radiates X-rays, radio waves and lots of visible energy.

Astronomers have found several kinds of active galaxies that harbour a black hole in their centre. The activity differs depending on how compressed the gas is near the black hole and whether we are looking at the disk from one side or from above. In some active galaxies, the disk around the black hole is very thick. This lets energy and hot gas shoot out from the disk, producing enormous jets that can stretch thousands of light-years.

DIAMETER OF A STELLAR BLACK HOLE
A BLACK HOLE WITH AS MUCH MASS AS THE SUN WOULD BE 6 KM (3.6 MI) ACROSS.

DIAMETER OF A GALACTIC BLACK HOLE
A BLACK HOLE WITH AS MUCH MASS AS 1 MILLION SUNS WOULD BE 6 MILLION KM (3.6 MILLION MI) ACROSS.

QUASAR PKS 0637-752 (page 84, top)
DISTANCE: 6,000 MILLION LIGHT-YEARS; DIAMETER: UNKNOWN

EINSTEIN CROSS (page 84, centre right)
DISTANCE: 10 BILLION LIGHT-YEARS; DIAMETER: UNKNOWN

CENTAURUS A/NGC 5128 (page 84, centre left)
DISTANCE: 26 MILLION LIGHT-YEARS; DIAMETER: 138,000 LIGHT-YEARS

SEYFERT NGC 1275 (page 84, bottom)
DISTANCE: 230 MILLION LIGHT-YEARS; DIAMETER: 175,000 LIGHT-YEARS

♦ PROJECT: *Gravitational Lens* ♦

A gravitational lens works because strong gravity can bend and focus light. For this project, you need a simple lens (such as one from a magnifying glass) that you can hold in your hand. It works better if the lens isn't perfect.

❶ Hold the lens about 2 or 3 centimetres (1 in) above a sheet of newspaper. Move it back and forth slowly.

❷ The distortions you see are what astronomers see (in very slow motion.) as a black hole or a massive galaxy moves in front of a more distant object.

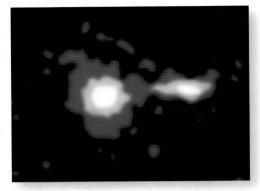

QUASAR
The bright cores of active galaxies that vary in brightness over weeks or days are known as quasars, short for quasi-stellar object. Quasar PKS 0637-752 gives off the energy of 10 billion Suns. This X-ray image shows a powerful jet thousands of light-years long.

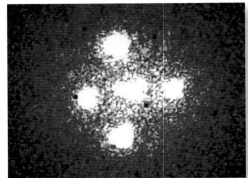

GRAVITATIONAL LENS
In the Einstein Cross, the four outside objects are all images of the same quasar. In the middle is a massive galaxy whose gravity works like a lens to bend the quasar's light, creating four images instead of one (see diagram, facing page). The galaxy lies 20 times closer to us than the quasar does.

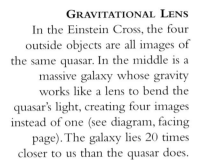

RADIO GALAXY
Centaurus A (NGC 5128) is the nearest active galaxy to Earth. Here the optical image at the centre shows it as a large elliptical galaxy. The colourful radio image shows two enormous lobes of radio energy, flowing north and south from the central galaxy.

SEYFERT GALAXY
NGC 1275, shown here in an X-ray image, is a type of active galaxy called a Seyfert galaxy, after the astronomer who first discovered them. Seyfert galaxies have star-like centres and show evidence of hot gas moving at high speeds.

SHOOTING JETS
Radio astronomers long ago detected enormous jets of hot gas and energy shooting from some galaxies. But the jets remained a mystery until theorists worked out how a black hole at the centre of a galaxy could produce them.

Earth

Path of light

Image of distant galaxy

Path of light

Active galaxy with black hole at centre

Path of light

Actual position of distant galaxy

Path of light

Image of distant galaxy

MULTIPLE IMAGES

A black hole is so powerful that it can bend light travelling near it. Here a galaxy with a black hole bends light from a distant galaxy, creating the optical illusion of a double galaxy for observers on Earth. In some cases, such as the Einstein Cross (see facing page), this effect produces four images of the distant object.

GALACTIC BLACK HOLE

Active galaxies produce a huge amount of energy in a very small space. Astronomers believe such galaxies contain a black hole devouring a disk of gas. As the gas falls into the black hole, it becomes extremely hot and emits lots of energy.

◆ LOOK AGAIN ◆

- How does a black hole 'shine'?
- Can galaxies make optical illusions?
- Why do some active galaxies produce jets?

The Universe

THE UNIVERSE WAS BORN SOME 12 to 15 billion years ago in a gigantic explosion that astronomers call the Big Bang. It began as a super-hot, super-compressed speck containing all the matter in the universe today. This churning, seething soup of particles had a temperature of more than a billion degrees.

As the universe expanded, it cooled and more familiar kinds of matter, such as protons, electrons and neutrons, began to appear. As time continued, these particles merged to make simple chemical elements – first hydrogen, then helium. The earliest stars and galaxies took shape from these elements. Once stars formed, their nuclear reactions began creating more complex elements, such as oxygen, carbon, lead and gold. These included the elements that would later form the Sun and the Solar System – and us! In the meantime, stars clumped together to form galaxies, and galaxies merged into clusters and superclusters.

The Big Bang created a universe that is expanding along with space itself. Wherever they look, astronomers find that the further away a galaxy is, the faster it is moving away from us. Will this expansion continue forever? That depends on how much matter the universe has within it, which is very hard to determine. Astronomers make estimates from the light given off by stars and nebulas. This shows only one-tenth of the mass needed to stop the expansion, so many believe the universe will expand forever. But astronomers are also looking for 'dark matter' – stars too dim to see, black holes and strange particles. If there's enough dark matter, gravity will halt the expansion and someday the universe will fall back on itself, producing a Big Crunch. Most astronomers now think this is unlikely, but some believe there might be enough extra matter to slow down the expansion so that the universe eventually stabilizes.

DISTANCE TO THE EDGE OF UNIVERSE
12 TO 15 BILLION LIGHT-YEARS

AGE OF UNIVERSE
12 TO 15 BILLION YEARS

FAINTEST GALAXIES DETECTED
30TH MAGNITUDE – 4 BILLION TIMES FAINTER THAN YOU CAN SEE

TEMPERATURE OF BIG BANG'S FADING GLOW
–270°C (–455°F)

◆ LOOK AGAIN ◆

- Will the Big Bang's expansion ever stop?
- How long ago was the universe born?
- What does the fading glow of the Big Bang look like?

First stars and galaxies form

Atoms (hydrogen and helium) form

Matter (electrons, protons and neutrons) forms

Time and space begin with the Big Bang

ANCIENT GALAXIES
In 1995, the Hubble Space Telescope took a long look into deep space and photographed the oldest galaxies ever seen. Astronomers are studying these ancient galaxies to see how today's galaxies formed and evolved.

WALLS OF GALAXIES
The universe shows structure even on very large scales. Astronomers are studying whether galaxies formed first and then merged into clusters – or whether vast chains and sheets of matter appeared before turning into galaxies.

◆ AMAZING FACT ◆

As the universe expands, the galaxies are all moving away from one another – just as galaxies drawn on a balloon get further apart as you blow up the balloon. Unlike the balloon, however, the universe is not expanding into anything. There is no 'outside' because the universe contains everything there is, including space itself.

Void

Void

Great Wall of Galaxies

450

450

300

300

Millions of light-years

150

150

Local Supercluster

Today's universe
has perhaps
50 billion galaxies

THE BIG CRUNCH

A cramped fate awaits the universe if it contains enough matter to stop the expansion altogether. As the universe implodes, galaxies squeeze together and time may flow backwards. In the end, everything crunches into a black hole. Recent evidence, however, indicates that this Big Crunch fate is unlikely.

THE BIG BANG

The Big Bang explains how matter and energy combined to make the stars and galaxies of today. The universe is still expanding and its future depends on how much matter it contains. There might be enough matter to slow down the expansion, so that the universe eventually stabilizes. But if the universe keeps expanding at the same rate, galaxies will drift further apart, stars will eventually burn out, and ordinary matter will disintegrate, leaving a boundless 'sea' of particles.

FADING GLOW

This map by the COBE satellite shows ripples in the cosmic background radiation – the fading glow of the Big Bang. The blue regions, which are slightly denser, became the first stars and galaxies.

COSMIC EXPLORER

The Cosmic Background Explorer (COBE) satellite was launched to study the radiation left over from the Big Bang. The map it produced (above) revealed ripples in this radiation.

Stargazing

STARGAZING IS EASY – you can start in your own garden this evening if the sky is clear. Many skywatchers, however, choose a spot that has an uninterrupted view of the sky, such as a park or a school playground. Find a safe, dark place (and make sure someone knows where you are!) away from distractions such as streetlights and lights from houses. Then pick the best star map from pages 94 to 109 for your location and season.

Before you begin stargazing, give your eyes at least 15 minutes to adjust to the dark. You will need a small torch to see the star map. White light will take away your night vision, so cover the torch lens with red cellophane. Once your eyes have adjusted, try to match the bright stars in the sky with those on the star map. After you locate the brighter stars, find dimmer ones by drawing imaginary lines to them on the map and then looking for the same pattern in the sky.

The naked eye is ideal for finding constellations and observing meteor showers. If you want to see more, use binoculars. These give a better view than most cheap telescopes do. The Milky Way becomes thousands of individual stars. Big star clusters such as the Pleiades look best through binoculars, and brighter galaxies show as patches of fuzzy light.

The next step is a good telescope. This will show craters on the Moon, the rings of Saturn, glowing nebulas and more. Buying a telescope is a big decision – it calls for careful research to avoid wasting money. If you don't already own a telescope, check whether a local astronomy club, observatory or science centre will let you look through theirs.

With the star maps in this book, you can find your way around the sky. Once you've mastered this, you may want to consult a star atlas that shows even more stars and objects. Star atlases are like road maps for a journey through space that you can follow for the rest of your life.

NAKED-EYE PLANETS
Just as in ancient times, five of the planets can be easily seen with the unaided eye – Mercury, Venus, Mars, Jupiter and Saturn. This evening sky shows the crescent Moon with Venus above it, near the top of the photo and Jupiter below.

LIGHT POLLUTION
The glow from streetlights and other outdoor lighting washes out stars and makes it impossible to see faint objects in the night sky. Your best view of the night sky will be in the countryside on clear, moonless nights.

NIGHT-SKY EVENTS
Some special events in the night sky can be predicted. Lunar eclipses usually occur at least once a year (see page 113 for dates). This time-exposure photo shows the Moon before, during and after an eclipse.

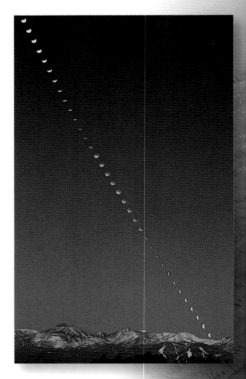

A GOOD TELESCOPE
The most important quality in a telescope – much more important than how much it magnifies – is a sturdy, shake-free mount.

◆ PROJECT: *Daytime Stars* ◆

Stars shine day and night but we can see them only at night. During the day, the atmosphere catches the bright light of the Sun and makes a brilliant blue sky that hides the stars. To see how this works, try a simple experiment.

❶ Use a hole-punch to make holes in a piece of card to represent the stars. You can copy your favourite constellation.

❷ Put the card inside an ordinary white envelope.

❸ In a dark room, shine a light on the front of the envelope. The envelope reflects the light so you can't see the 'stars'.

❹ Now shine the light from behind the envelope. When the envelope is dark, the 'stars' can shine through.

PREPARING FOR STARGAZING

You'll see more in the sky if you are comfortable. Depending on the season, comfort may mean wearing thermal underwear and a hat – or using insect repellent. (But even summer nights can become chilly, so be prepared.) A deckchair lets you relax and makes holding binoculars easier. And a flask of hot tea or soup tastes great when you've been outside for a while.

♦ *A*MAZING FACT ♦

Under a dark sky in the countryside, you can't really see 'millions' of stars, although it might look like it. Instead, under good conditions, the naked eye is able to spot about 2,000 stars.

Constellations

CONSTELLATIONS DIVIDE THE SKY into easy-to-remember pieces. In ancient times, when few people could read, constellations were like heavenly storybooks. They helped people remember important tales about the gods. Astronomers now recognize a total of 88 constellations.

The major constellations come from Greek and Roman civilization, more than 2,000 years ago. But even then, some constellations were already old, having been created in ancient Mesopotamia (today's Iraq). Astronomers think that Taurus the Bull, Leo the Lion and Scorpius the Scorpion may have been among the very first constellations. They marked where the Sun appeared during important seasons for crops.

Stars have been named in various ways. Ptolemy named stars after their place in the constellation. Rigel, a star in the constellation of Orion the Hunter, means 'foot' in Arabic. (The name is Arabic because Ptolemy's names came to us in the Middle Ages through an Arabic translation.) Somewhat later, astronomers began to identify stars using Greek letters, with Alpha being the brightest star in a constellation, Beta the second-brightest and so on. Other astronomers gave stars numbers.

Star clusters, galaxies and nebulas usually have names like M35 or NGC 1365. M-numbers were assigned by Charles Messier, who lived in the late 1700s and discovered many of these objects. NGC-numbers come from the *New General Catalogue,* a giant list of discoveries collected in the late 1800s. Astronomical names sometimes seem complicated, but this is because they combine the efforts of countless skywatchers, working together over thousands of years.

• AMAZING FACT •

Other cultures have grouped the same stars in different ways. For example, where the Americans see the Big Dipper, the Europeans named these stars the Plough – and the Sioux Indians of North America saw a skunk!

MOVING STARS

Stars are always moving, but because distances in space are so enormous, the stars in a constellation appear fixed in place. Gradually, however, their movements will make today's constellations unrecognizable.

The Plough
100,000
years ago

The Plough
today

The Plough
100,000 years
from now

ORION THE HUNTER

The oldest constellations, such as Orion, were created using stars that can be seen with the naked eye. In skylore, Orion was a mighty hunter shaking a lion-skin shield towards Taurus, whilst holding a club over his head. The row of three stars in the middle forms the hunter's belt.

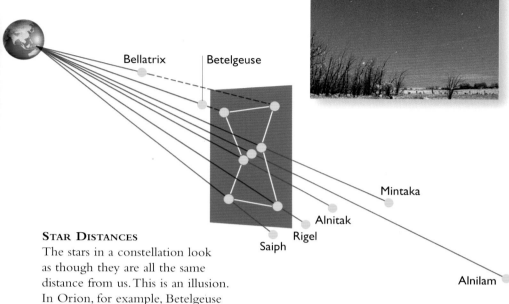

Bellatrix   Betelgeuse

Mintaka

Alnitak

Saiph   Rigel

Alnilam

STAR DISTANCES

The stars in a constellation look as though they are all the same distance from us. This is an illusion. In Orion, for example, Betelgeuse lies 427 light-years away, while Rigel is 773 light-years away.

INDIAN STAR CHART

This beautiful star chart was commissioned by an Indian monarch in 1840. It is decorated with Indian and Islamic patterns, but features many of the constellations we use today. How many can you pick out?

MYTHOLOGICAL FIGURES

Many old star maps combine carefully plotted stars with colourful figures from mythology. The constellations illustrated on this map include Gemini the Twins, Orion the Hunter, Taurus the Bull and Eridanus the River.

◆ PROJECT: *Constellation Figures* ◆

Just as different cultures have seen different figures in the stars, you can make your own pictures from the constellations.

1. Pick one of the mythological constellation figures illustrated on pages 94 to 109.

2. Find the constellation on the star map and copy its stars.

3. Copy the drawing of the mythological constellation figure.

4. What other pictures can you make out of the star pattern? Draw as many as you can imagine.

Our example shows two different figures based on the constellation of Orion.

Using a Star Map

THE FOLLOWING PAGES SHOW STAR MAPS for the Northern and Southern hemispheres and for each of the four seasons in the year. Just turn to the page that shows the current season for the hemisphere where you live. The two maps on each spread show the stars and constellations of the evening sky that you'll see when looking north or south. The maps also wrap around to the east and west points on the horizon, so together they show the entire sky.

Star maps change with the seasons because constellations move in and out of view as Earth travels around the Sun. For example, the stars visible on a March evening are different from those you see on a September evening. As Earth travels its orbit through the year, we look out at different stellar backgrounds. The change from one night to the next isn't much, but it adds up. After a month has passed, any constellation or star is rising and setting two hours earlier. This means that when you use a star map for a given season, you may find that the constellations do not lie exactly as shown on the map. Early in the season they may lie more to the east, while late in the season they will be towards the west. (Similarly, if you observe late at night, try the next season's chart.)

The maps show stars, the Milky Way, clusters, nebulas and even galaxies. Planets and objects such as comets are not shown because these are constantly moving. Constellations always return to view every year at the same season, but planets don't. To find where to look for a given planet, check with an astronomy magazine, newspaper or web sites.

OVER ONE HOUR
Earth's rotation makes the sky appear to move from east to west – over an hour, you can see Orion shift westwards. If you are looking south, as shown here, the movement is from left to right. Looking north, it is from right to left.

OVER TWO WEEKS
Earth's movement around the Sun has the same effect as its rotation – if you look south at Orion at the same time of night two weeks apart, you'll see a similar shift to the one shown here, with Orion appearing further west.

STAR MAPS
Each half-circular star map shows half of the sky that is visible at a given season. The horizon runs along the bottom with either north or south in the centre. East and west are marked, and overhead is at the top. Turn the map to match the compass direction you are facing.

Open star clusters use this symbol, and are identified by name.

This is the name of a star.

Thin lines connect the brighter stars in major constellations to help you trace the patterns.

The Milky Way is shown in light blue.

STAR TRAILS
As Earth rotates, stars around the celestial pole appear to travel in a circle. This time-exposure photo captures the movement.

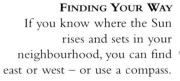

FINDING YOUR WAY
If you know where the Sun rises and sets in your neighbourhood, you can find east or west – or use a compass.

URSA

LYNX

Pollux

Castor

GEMINI   *AURIGA*   *CAMELO*

M35   *Capella*

ORION   *PERSEUS*

Betelgeuse   *TAURUS*   *Algol*

WEST

KEY TO MAP SYMBOLS
Sky maps show star brightness using dots sized according to their magnitude. Fainter stars have higher magnitude numbers, while the brightest stars have negative magnitudes. Objects such as clusters, nebulas and galaxies are plotted using special symbols.

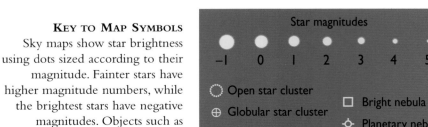

Star magnitudes

–1   0   1   2   3   4   5

○ Open star cluster
⊕ Globular star cluster
▭ Bright nebula
◇ Planetary nebula
⬯ Galaxy

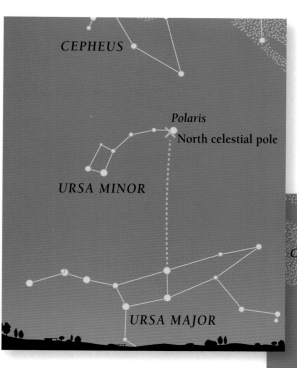

CEPHEUS

Polaris
North celestial pole

URSA MINOR

URSA MAJOR

FINDING NORTH

In the Northern Hemisphere, use the Plough to find the north celestial pole, which is near the star Polaris in Ursa Minor. First locate the Plough using the correct map from pages 94 to 101 for your location and season. Then draw an imaginary line along the handle of the Plough to Polaris.

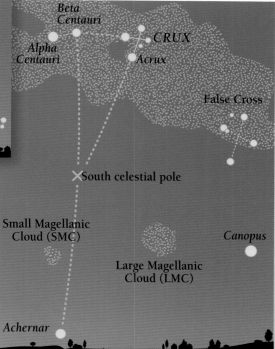

Beta Centauri

Alpha Centauri

CRUX

Acrux

False Cross

South celestial pole

Small Magellanic Cloud (SMC)

Large Magellanic Cloud (LMC)

Canopus

Achernar

FINDING SOUTH

In the Southern Hemisphere, the south celestial pole is not marked by a star like Polaris, but Crux (the Southern Cross) makes a good guide. First find Crux using the correct map from pages 102 to 109. Then draw imaginary lines between the other bright stars marked here to find your way to the pole.

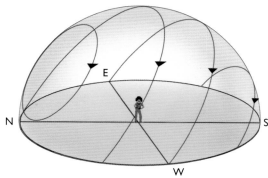

At the North Pole (90°N)

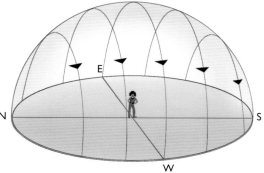

At the northern middle latitudes (40°N)

At the Equator (0°)

DIFFERENT PATHS

The paths that stars appear to follow across the sky are different depending on your latitude – the distance north or south of the Equator. Most people live in the middle latitudes north and south.

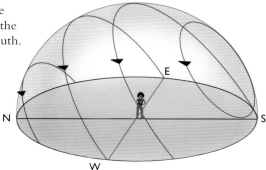

At the southern middle latitudes (40°S)

Galaxies use this symbol, and are identified by name.

Globular star clusters use this symbol, and are identified by name.

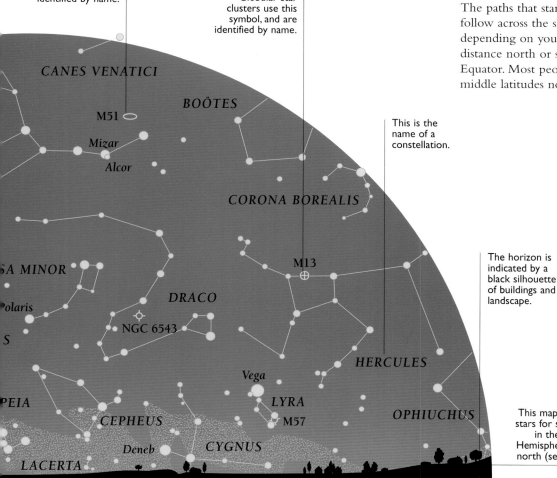

CANES VENATICI

BOÖTES

M51

Mizar

Alcor

CORONA BOREALIS

SA MINOR

Polaris

DRACO

NGC 6543

M13

HERCULES

Vega

PEIA

CEPHEUS

LYRA

M57

OPHIUCHUS

Deneb

CYGNUS

LACERTA

EAST

This is the name of a constellation.

The horizon is indicated by a black silhouette of buildings and landscape.

This map shows the stars for spring skies in the Northern Hemisphere, looking north (see page 96).

┌─────────────────────────────┐
│   ♦ LOOK AGAIN ♦   │
│   │
│ ● Which of the paths above do │
│   stars follow in your night sky? │
│   │
│ ● How would you find north   │
│   or south?   │
│   │
│ ● If Orion rises tonight at 9 PM, │
│   when will it rise in a month? │
└─────────────────────────────┘

Winter Stars of the Northern Skies

LOOKING NORTH   Many people can recognize the Plough (known as the Big Dipper in the U.S.A.). The Plough is made from the seven bright stars that mark out the back and tail of Ursa Major, the Big Bear. This evening, the Plough seems to be standing on its handle in the north-east. An imaginary line pointing left from the two top stars of the Plough leads to Polaris in Ursa Minor, the Little Bear. As the Plough rises, Cassiopeia the Queen sinks in the north-west. Cassiopeia is shaped like the letter M. Nearby are Cassiopeia's mythological companions: Cepheus the King (her husband), Andromeda (her daughter), Perseus (Andromeda's hero and rescuer) and Pegasus (Perseus' horse). Cetus the Sea Monster, who was about to eat Andromeda when Perseus saved her, is setting in the south-west (see Looking South map, facing page). Use the naked eye or binoculars to look for the Andromeda galaxy (M31) in Andromeda. Under dark skies it looks like an oval smudge of light.

WHERE YOU CAN SEE THIS SKY
NORTHERN HEMISPHERE AREAS SUCH AS EUROPE, UNITED STATES, CANADA AND JAPAN

WHEN YOU CAN BEST SEE THIS SKY
JANUARY TILL MARCH

BEST NAKED-EYE SIGHTS
ALGOL IN PERSEUS, BIG DIPPER IN URSA MAJOR, POLARIS IN URSA MINOR

BEST BINOCULAR SIGHTS
DOUBLE CLUSTER IN PERSEUS, DOUBLE STAR MIZAR AND ALCOR AND GALAXY M81 IN URSA MAJOR

BEST TELESCOPE SIGHTS
ANDROMEDA GALAXY (M31) IN ANDROMEDA, WHIRLPOOL GALAXY (M51) IN CANES VENATICI

DOUBLE CLUSTER
Lying close together in space, these two open star clusters can just be seen by eye between the constellations of Perseus and Cassiopeia.

URSA MAJOR
The Big Bear includes more than just the Plough, but you need dark skies to see the entire figure.

◆ LOOK AGAIN ◆

● Which star is the night sky's brightest?

● The Plough is part of what constellation?

● Who did Perseus rescue? From whom?

PERSEUS THE HERO
According to legend, the hero Perseus married Andromeda after rescuing her from the sea monster Cetus.

THE PLOUGH
The Plough took its name from the old wooden ploughs drawn by oxen to till the fields. It is also known as the Big Dipper because it is shaped like a saucepan.

N

WEST

AURIGA
Capella
Algol
LYNX
ARIES
PERSEUS
TRIANGULUM
M33
CAMELOPARDALIS
LEO MINOR
Double Cluster
M81
URSA MAJOR
CASSIOPEIA
LEO
M31
Polaris
ANDROMEDA
URSA MINOR
PISCES
M66
CEPHEUS
CANES VENATICI
M65
PEGASUS
LACERTA
Alcor Mizar
North America nebula
NGC 6543
M51
COMA BERENICES
Deneb
CYGNUS
DRACO

EAST

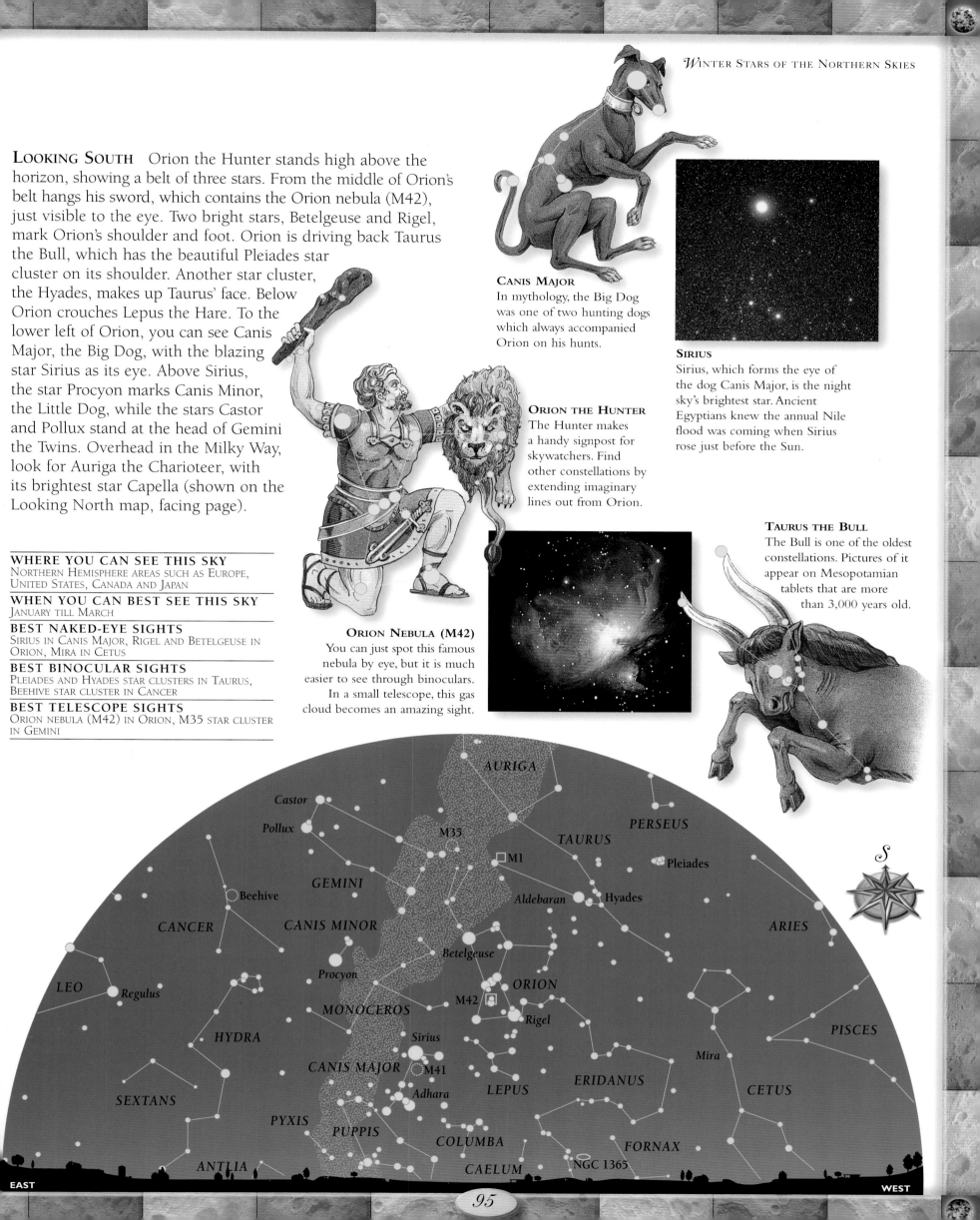

LOOKING SOUTH   Orion the Hunter stands high above the horizon, showing a belt of three stars. From the middle of Orion's belt hangs his sword, which contains the Orion nebula (M42), just visible to the eye. Two bright stars, Betelgeuse and Rigel, mark Orion's shoulder and foot. Orion is driving back Taurus the Bull, which has the beautiful Pleiades star cluster on its shoulder. Another star cluster, the Hyades, makes up Taurus' face. Below Orion crouches Lepus the Hare. To the lower left of Orion, you can see Canis Major, the Big Dog, with the blazing star Sirius as its eye. Above Sirius, the star Procyon marks Canis Minor, the Little Dog, while the stars Castor and Pollux stand at the head of Gemini the Twins. Overhead in the Milky Way, look for Auriga the Charioteer, with its brightest star Capella (shown on the Looking North map, facing page).

WHERE YOU CAN SEE THIS SKY
NORTHERN HEMISPHERE AREAS SUCH AS EUROPE, UNITED STATES, CANADA AND JAPAN

WHEN YOU CAN BEST SEE THIS SKY
JANUARY TILL MARCH

BEST NAKED-EYE SIGHTS
SIRIUS IN CANIS MAJOR, RIGEL AND BETELGEUSE IN ORION, MIRA IN CETUS

BEST BINOCULAR SIGHTS
PLEIADES AND HYADES STAR CLUSTERS IN TAURUS, BEEHIVE STAR CLUSTER IN CANCER

BEST TELESCOPE SIGHTS
ORION NEBULA (M42) IN ORION, M35 STAR CLUSTER IN GEMINI

CANIS MAJOR
In mythology, the Big Dog was one of two hunting dogs which always accompanied Orion on his hunts.

SIRIUS
Sirius, which forms the eye of the dog Canis Major, is the night sky's brightest star. Ancient Egyptians knew the annual Nile flood was coming when Sirius rose just before the Sun.

ORION THE HUNTER
The Hunter makes a handy signpost for skywatchers. Find other constellations by extending imaginary lines out from Orion.

TAURUS THE BULL
The Bull is one of the oldest constellations. Pictures of it appear on Mesopotamian tablets that are more than 3,000 years old.

ORION NEBULA (M42)
You can just spot this famous nebula by eye, but it is much easier to see through binoculars. In a small telescope, this gas cloud becomes an amazing sight.

EAST

WEST

Spring Stars of the Northern Skies

LOOKING NORTH   Tonight the Plough (part of Ursa Major, the Big Bear) is upside down high in the northern sky. The left-hand stars of the Plough point down to Polaris, the Pole Star, of the constellation of Ursa Minor, the Little Bear. Between the Plough and Polaris winds the snaky form of Draco the Dragon. Below the Pole Star, the W shape of Cassiopeia the Queen sits just above the trees. Setting in the north-west are Gemini the Twins, with the stars Castor and Pollux. Rising in the north-east, the bright star Vega marks Lyra, which represents a lyre (a stringed musical instrument). Above Lyra, look for Hercules. In mythology, Hercules was the half-mortal son of Jupiter, the ruler of the gods. Finally, follow the curved handle of the Plough as it 'arcs to Arcturus', the brightest star in Boötes the Herdsman, high in the south-east (see Looking South map, facing page).

HERCULES CLUSTER (M13)
This globular star cluster is just visible by eye on a dark night, and is easy to see through binoculars.

WHERE YOU CAN SEE THIS SKY
NORTHERN HEMISPHERE AREAS SUCH AS EUROPE, UNITED STATES, CANADA AND JAPAN

WHEN YOU CAN BEST SEE THIS SKY
APRIL TILL JUNE

BEST NAKED-EYE SIGHTS
VEGA IN LYRA, CASTOR AND POLLUX IN GEMINI

BEST BINOCULAR SIGHTS
HERCULES CLUSTER (M13) IN HERCULES, DOUBLE STAR MIZAR AND ALCOR IN URSA MAJOR

BEST TELESCOPE SIGHTS
GALAXY M81 IN URSA MAJOR, WHIRLPOOL GALAXY (M51) IN CANES VENATICI

WHIRLPOOL GALAXY (M51)
The Whirlpool galaxy (near the Plough's handle) has its spiral arms distorted by the passage of a smaller galaxy nearby.

HERCULES
In mythology, Hercules was famed for his feats of strength. Among them was cleaning out the stables where the Sun god's horses lived!

• AMAZING FACT •

In 1845, William Parsons, the Earl of Rosse, used his giant telescope to discover that the Whirlpool galaxy (M51) had a spiral shape. It was the first time a galaxy had been seen as a spiral.

URSA MINOR
The Little Bear is also called the Little Dipper. Find Polaris, then the two stars of the small bowl – the rest lie in between.

N

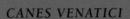

CANES VENATICI

BOÖTES

URSA MAJOR

M51

Mizar

Alcor

CORONA BOREALIS

LYNX

M81

URSA MINOR

M13

DRACO

Pollux

Castor

Polaris

NGC 6543

HERCULES

GEMINI

AURIGA

CAMELOPARDALIS

Vega

M35

Capella

LYRA

M57

OPHIUCHUS

CASSIOPEIA

ORION

PERSEUS

CEPHEUS

Betelgeuse

TAURUS

Algol

Double Cluster

Deneb

CYGNUS

LACERTA

LOOKING SOUTH With the Milky Way wrapped around the horizon, where it is hard to see, spring skies are relatively dark. Yet four bright stars light the southern half of the sky. Arcturus in Boötes the Herdsman stands high in the south-east, while Spica in Virgo the Maiden lies in the south. In the south-west, look for Regulus in Leo the Lion, and setting in the west you'll find Procyon in Canis Minor, the Little Dog. Leo also contains two spiral galaxies, M65 and M66, which you can spot through binoculars or a telescope. Below Leo and Virgo stretches the figure of Hydra the Sea Serpent, the sky's longest constellation. Hydra's stars are dim, so it is a difficult constellation to find except on dark, moonless nights. Between Virgo and the tail of Leo lies the Virgo cluster of galaxies, a nearby group of spiral and elliptical galaxies about 55 million light-years away.

LEO THE LION
The Lion is one of the oldest constellations known. The Sumerians of nearly 6,000 years ago showed it in pictures of the zodiac.

WHERE YOU CAN SEE THIS SKY
NORTHERN HEMISPHERE AREAS SUCH AS EUROPE, UNITED STATES, CANADA AND JAPAN
WHEN YOU CAN BEST SEE THIS SKY
APRIL TILL JUNE
BEST NAKED-EYE SIGHTS
ARCTURUS IN BOÖTES, SPICA IN VIRGO, REGULUS IN LEO, PROCYON IN CANIS MINOR
BEST BINOCULAR SIGHTS
Beehive star cluster in Cancer
BEST TELESCOPE SIGHTS
GALAXIES M65 AND M66 IN LEO, VIRGO CLUSTER OF GALAXIES

BEEHIVE CLUSTER
Ancient skylore said that when Cancer's Beehive star cluster disappeared from the sky, rain would follow in a day or two.

◆ LOOK AGAIN ◆
- Where would you look to find a cluster of galaxies?
- How do you find the Pole Star using the Plough?
- What constellation does the star Capella belong to?

CANCER THE CRAB
The Crab is hard to see in city skies. Try looking half-way between Regulus in Leo (on this map), and Castor and Pollux in Gemini (in the west on the Looking North map, facing page).

HYDRA
Hydra the Sea Serpent winds its way across the sky. In mythology, Hercules had to kill a nine-headed Hydra.

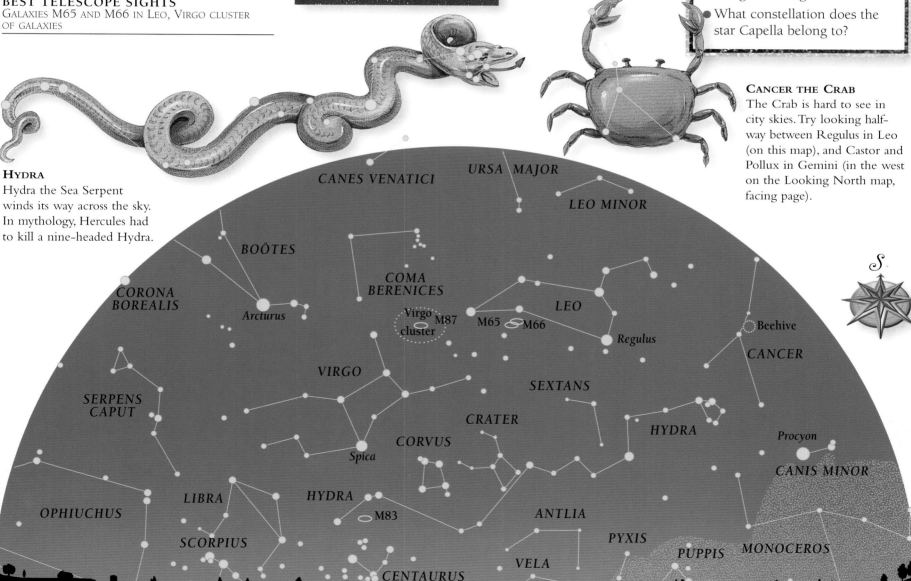

Summer Stars of the Northern Skies

LOOKING NORTH This evening, the Plough (in Ursa Major, the Big Bear) lies to the left of Polaris, the Pole Star, opposite Cassiopeia the Queen, which is rising on the right. Ursa Minor, the Little Bear, curves upwards from Polaris. Above Ursa Minor, the dim form of Draco the Dragon wraps around the Pole Star. This is the best time of year to see the Milky Way in the Northern Hemisphere. If the night is moonless and dark, look for the Milky Way crossing the sky from north-east to south. It passes from Cassiopeia, through her husband, Cepheus the King, to Cygnus the Swan overhead. The stars of Cygnus continue onto the Looking South map (see facing page) and form a cross that resembles a bird flying south along the Milky Way. This constellation is sometimes called the Northern Cross.

WHERE YOU CAN SEE THIS SKY
NORTHERN HEMISPHERE AREAS SUCH AS EUROPE, UNITED STATES, CANADA AND JAPAN

WHEN YOU CAN BEST SEE THIS SKY
JULY TILL SEPTEMBER

BEST NAKED-EYE SIGHTS
SUMMER TRIANGLE (MADE UP OF THREE STARS: DENEB IN CYGNUS, VEGA IN LYRA AND ALTAIR IN AQUILA)

BEST BINOCULAR SIGHTS
MILKY WAY FROM CASSIOPEIA THROUGH CYGNUS, GALAXY M81 IN URSA MAJOR

BEST TELESCOPE SIGHTS
ANDROMEDA GALAXY (M31) IN ANDROMEDA, PLANETARY NEBULA NGC 6543 IN DRACO

CEPHEUS THE KING
A mythical king of Ethiopia, Cepheus saw his daughter Andromeda rescued by the hero Perseus from the sea monster Cetus.

DRACO THE DRAGON
In Greek mythology, the Dragon was defeated by Hercules. Some old star charts show Draco under one of Hercules' feet.

CYGNUS THE SWAN
The Swan's shape has suggested a bird in flight to many cultures. Our figure comes from Greek mythology.

ANDROMEDA GALAXY (M31)
The Andromeda galaxy is a spiral much like the Milky Way. The nearest major galaxy to us, it can just be seen with the naked eye, but looks better through binoculars or a telescope.

M81
Seen as a smudge of light with binoculars, this spiral galaxy in Ursa Major has about as many stars as the Milky Way.

Vega
LYRA
HERCULES
CYGNUS
Deneb
North America nebula
BOÖTES
DRACO
NGC 6543
CEPHEUS
M51
Alcor
Mizar
URSA MINOR
LACERTA
COMA BERENICES
CANES VENATICI
Polaris
M31
M81
CAMELOPARDALIS
CASSIOPEIA
PEGASUS
URSA MAJOR
Double Cluster
PISCES
LEO
PERSEUS
ANDROMEDA
LEO MINOR
LYNX
PISCES

WEST

EAST

LOOKING SOUTH The brightest part of the Milky Way parades across the southern sky on summer nights. The most star-rich constellations are Scorpius the Scorpion and Sagittarius the Archer. Behind their stars lies the centre of the Milky Way galaxy. More than 30,000 light-years of dusty gas hide it from view. To the right of the Milky Way, look for the large but faint constellation of Ophiuchus the Serpent Carrier. In Greek legend, Ophiuchus learnt about the healing powers of plants from a serpent. He appears in the sky with the constellation Serpens the Serpent. If you look further north, you'll see that the Milky Way divides in two near Aquila the Eagle and Cygnus the Swan. The dark rift is caused by a cloud of dust near the Sun that obscures the distant Milky Way stars. Three bright stars make up the Summer Triangle – Deneb in Cygnus (see Looking North map, facing page), Vega in Lyra and Altair in Aquila.

WHERE YOU CAN SEE THIS SKY
NORTHERN HEMISPHERE AREAS SUCH AS EUROPE, UNITED STATES, CANADA AND JAPAN

WHEN YOU CAN BEST SEE THIS SKY
JULY TILL SEPTEMBER

BEST NAKED-EYE SIGHTS
DARK RIFT IN THE MILKY WAY, ANTARES IN SCORPIUS

BEST BINOCULAR SIGHTS
STAR CLOUDS IN SCORPIUS AND SAGITTARIUS

BEST TELESCOPE SIGHTS
LAGOON (M8) AND TRIFID (M20) NEBULAS IN SAGITTARIUS, EAGLE NEBULA (M16) IN SERPENS, DUMB-BELL NEBULA (M27) IN VULPECULA

OPHIUCHUS
Ophiuchus the Serpent Carrier appears between the two halves of the constellation Serpens the Serpent – Serpens Cauda and Serpens Caput.

LAGOON NEBULA (M8)
The Lagoon nebula (in the Milky Way near the horizon) can be seen with binoculars and makes a beautiful sight in a small telescope. Stars are being born inside its dusty gas clouds.

AQUILA THE EAGLE
In ancient myth, the Eagle was sent by the chief of the gods to rescue people – or to punish them.

DUMB-BELL NEBULA (M27)
The constellation of Vulpecula, the Little Fox, is home to the Dumb-bell nebula, a cloud of gas thrown off by an old star.

◆ LOOK AGAIN ◆

- What three stars make up the Summer Triangle?
- How far away is the centre of the Milky Way?
- What did a serpent teach Ophiuchus?

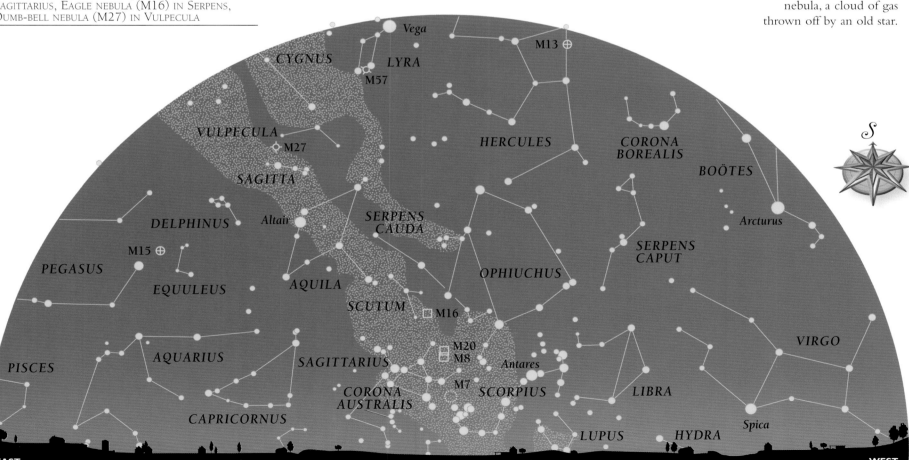

Autumn Stars of the Northern Skies

LOOKING NORTH On autumn evenings, the Plough (in Ursa Major, the Big Bear) lies on the northern horizon below Polaris, the Pole Star. Polaris is part of Ursa Minor, the Little Bear. Above Polaris, you can see Cassiopeia the Queen, which resembles a slightly bent M. Cepheus the King lies to the lower left of Cassiopeia. Auriga the Charioteer is rising in the north-east, dominated by a bright yellowish star, Capella. Above Auriga, Perseus the Hero lies in the band of the Milky Way. Perseus' bright star Algol is a famous variable. Over in the west, the Summer Triangle of the stars Deneb in Cygnus, Vega in Lyra and Altair in Aquila (which is shown on the Looking South map, facing page) is setting. Cassiopeia's daughter, Andromeda, stands overhead, with the Andromeda galaxy (M31) visible to the naked eye as a small oval patch of light. This spiral galaxy is the most distant object we can see with the naked eye. It is similar in size to our own Milky Way galaxy.

WHERE YOU CAN SEE THIS SKY
NORTHERN HEMISPHERE AREAS SUCH AS EUROPE, UNITED STATES, CANADA AND JAPAN

WHEN YOU CAN BEST SEE THIS SKY
OCTOBER TILL DECEMBER

BEST NAKED-EYE SIGHTS
VARIABLE STAR ALGOL IN PERSEUS, SUMMER TRIANGLE (MADE UP OF THREE STARS: DENEB IN CYGNUS, VEGA IN LYRA AND ALTAIR IN AQUILA)

BEST BINOCULAR SIGHTS
DOUBLE CLUSTER IN PERSEUS, NORTH AMERICA NEBULA IN CYGNUS

BEST TELESCOPE SIGHTS
ANDROMEDA GALAXY (M31) IN ANDROMEDA, RING NEBULA (M57) IN LYRA

> ### ◆ LOOK AGAIN ◆
> - Two Local Group galaxies are visible tonight. What are they?
> - Which nebula can be seen near the star Deneb?
> - Who was Cassiopeia's daughter?

LYRA THE LYRE
This small constellation is easy to spot because it has a bright star, Vega, and a distinct shape.

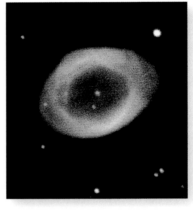

RING NEBULA (M57)
The Ring nebula in Lyra is a planetary nebula – a shell of gas surrounding a white dwarf star. A similar fate awaits the Sun.

AURIGA THE CHARIOTEER
Combining several legendary figures, Auriga is shown holding a baby goat while driving a chariot.

NORTH AMERICA NEBULA
This cloud of hydrogen gas in Cygnus the Swan got its name because it resembles a map of North America.

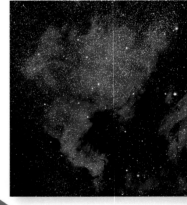

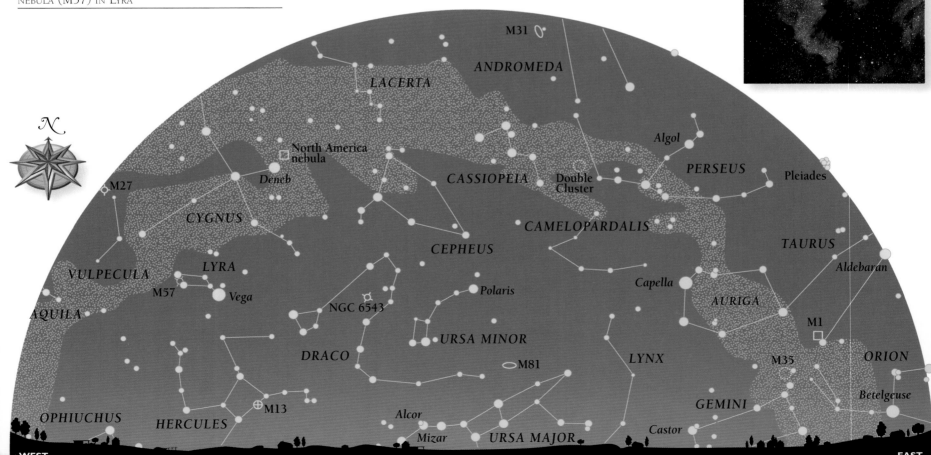

LOOKING SOUTH High in the southern sky, the Great Square of Pegasus, with a bright star at each corner, makes a signpost to other constellations. In mythology, Pegasus is the Flying Horse ridden by Perseus the Hero. The horse sprang from the blood of Medusa, a snake-haired monster whom Perseus decapitated. In tonight's sky, the constellation appears upside down, with the stars to the lower right of the Square marking the horse's neck. Pegasus reaches west towards the star Altair in Aquila the Eagle, which lies in the Milky Way. Nearby is tiny Delphinus the Dolphin, a small group of faint stars that looks like a kite. Below the Square lie several other 'watery' constellations: Aquarius (the Water Carrier), Piscis Austrinus (the Southern Fish), Pisces (the Fishes) and Cetus (the Sea Monster). You can spot Piscis Austrinus by looking for the bright star Fomalhaut, but the other figures lack bright stars and can be difficult to trace. Cetus has the famed variable star Mira in its neck. In the east, Taurus the Bull is rising, followed by winter's Orion the Hunter, which is still half below the horizon.

WHERE YOU CAN SEE THIS SKY
NORTHERN HEMISPHERE AREAS SUCH AS EUROPE, UNITED STATES, CANADA AND JAPAN

WHEN YOU CAN BEST SEE THIS SKY
OCTOBER TILL DECEMBER

BEST NAKED-EYE SIGHTS
FOMALHAUT IN PISCIS AUSTRINUS, VARIABLE STAR MIRA IN CETUS

BEST BINOCULAR SIGHTS
HYADES STAR CLUSTER IN TAURUS, HELIX NEBULA IN AQUARIUS, PINWHEEL GALAXY (M33) IN TRIANGULUM

BEST TELESCOPE SIGHTS
GLOBULAR CLUSTER M15 IN PEGASUS

PINWHEEL GALAXY (M33)
Like the Andromeda galaxy (M31) and our own Milky Way, the Pinwheel in Triangulum (high in the south-east sky) is a spiral galaxy in the Local Group.

AQUARIUS
In old star atlases, Aquarius the Water Carrier is usually shown pouring a jug of water into the mouth of the Southern Fish.

PISCES THE FISHES
Pisces is one of the 12 zodiac constellations. Since it is relatively dim, it is easiest to spot on a dark, moonless night.

HYADES
This loose open star cluster in Taurus (in the eastern sky) lies only about 150 light-years away.

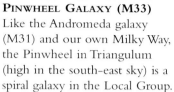

Winter Stars of the Southern Skies

LOOKING NORTH Three bright stars are visible, two of them low in the sky. In the north-west, yellowish Arcturus is setting along with Boötes the Herdsman. Lying due north near the horizon is white Vega, the brightest star in Lyra the Lyre, a small but distinct constellation. In the north-east and higher up is the white star Altair in Aquila the Eagle. It lies close to a great rift in the Milky Way that runs from Cygnus the Swan up to Serpens Cauda. The rift is caused by a huge cloud of dust. To Vega's lower right, you may be able to find Deneb in Cygnus, almost on the horizon. If you look to the left of Vega, you'll see Hercules and the curve of stars that marks Corona Borealis, the Northern Crown. High in the western sky, you might spot the faint stars of Libra the Scales, one of the zodiac constellations. Overhead, near Sagittarius the Archer, the Milky Way widens because that is where the centre of our galaxy lies. This region contains beautiful dense star clouds.

WHERE YOU CAN SEE THIS SKY
SOUTHERN HEMISPHERE AREAS SUCH AS AUSTRALIA, NEW ZEALAND, SOUTH AMERICA AND SOUTH AFRICA

WHEN YOU CAN BEST SEE THIS SKY
JULY TILL SEPTEMBER

BEST NAKED-EYE SIGHTS
DARK RIFT IN MILKY WAY FROM CYGNUS TO SERPENS CAUDA AND SCUTUM

BEST BINOCULAR SIGHTS
STAR CLOUDS IN SCORPIUS AND SAGITTARIUS

BEST TELESCOPE SIGHTS
LAGOON (M8) AND TRIFID (M20) NEBULAS IN SAGITTARIUS, EAGLE NEBULA (M16) IN SERPENS, DUMB-BELL NEBULA (M27) IN VULPECULA, HERCULES CLUSTER (M13) IN HERCULES

LIBRA THE SCALES
Libra's stars once formed the claws of Scorpius the Scorpion. But around 50 BC, astronomers made them into a separate constellation.

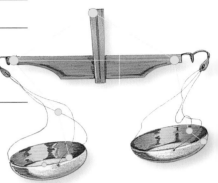

SAGITTARIUS THE ARCHER
The half-man, half-horse Sagittarius is one of two centaurs in the sky (the other is Centaurus). Its brightest stars actually look a bit like a teapot.

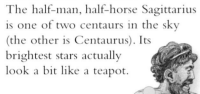

TRIFID NEBULA (M20)
The Trifid nebula in Sagittarius features dark dust lanes that split it into three parts.

EAGLE NEBULA (M16)
The Eagle nebula lies in Serpens at the edge of the Milky Way. Seen through a telescope, this cloud of gas resembles a crouching bird.

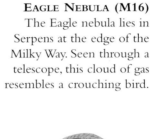

SERPENS THE SERPENT
Serpens the Serpent is the only constellation in two halves (Caput, which means 'head' in Latin, and Cauda, which means 'tail'). It is divided by Ophiuchus the Serpent Carrier (see page 99).

Antares · M8 · M20 · SAGITTARIUS · SCORPIUS · CAPRICORNUS · M16 · SCUTUM · LIBRA · OPHIUCHUS · SERPENS CAUDA · AQUILA · Altair · EQUULEUS · Spica · SERPENS CAPUT · SAGITTA · DELPHINUS · AQUARIUS · HERCULES · M27 · VULPECULA · M15 · CORONA BOREALIS · M57 · Arcturus · LYRA · M13 · Vega · CYGNUS · PEGASUS · PISCES · VIRGO · BOÖTES · Deneb · COMA BERENICES · DRACO

N

LOOKING SOUTH The Milky Way is setting in the south-west. Along with it go a number of bright stars. Crux, the Southern Cross, is easy to identify by its shape. Next to it lies the dark Coalsack nebula, a large patch of interstellar dust that you can see with the naked eye. In the south, to the left of Crux, the Small Magellanic Cloud (SMC) looks like a piece of detached Milky Way. Curving above Crux is Centaurus the Centaur, a mythical half-man, half-horse creature. The stars Alpha and Beta Centauri mark the Centaur's forelegs. Above the Centaur lies Lupus the Wolf, and above the Wolf is a stretch of Milky Way that runs up to Scorpius the Scorpion, at the very top of the map. Here, and in nearby Sagittarius the Archer (who is also a centaur), lie many of the Milky Way's greatest sights. They are perfect for exploring with binoculars or a telescope on a moonless night.

WHERE YOU CAN SEE THIS SKY
SOUTHERN HEMISPHERE AREAS SUCH AS AUSTRALIA, NEW ZEALAND, SOUTH AMERICA AND SOUTH AFRICA

WHEN YOU CAN BEST SEE THIS SKY
JULY TILL SEPTEMBER

BEST NAKED-EYE SIGHTS
ALPHA AND BETA CENTAURI IN CENTAURUS

BEST BINOCULAR SIGHTS
OPEN CLUSTER M7 IN SCORPIUS, GLOBULAR CLUSTERS 47 TUCANAE (47 TUC) IN THE SMALL MAGELLANIC CLOUD AND OMEGA CENTAURI IN CENTAURUS, SMALL MAGELLANIC CLOUD (SMC)

BEST TELESCOPE SIGHTS
JEWEL BOX CLUSTER IN CRUX

CORONA AUSTRALIS
The Southern Crown (below Sagittarius on the map) originally represented a crown of leaves.

◆ LOOK AGAIN ◆

● Which constellation is in two pieces?

● Why does the Milky Way look wider in Sagittarius and Scorpius?

● Can you see the Northern and Southern Crowns at the same time?

47 TUCANAE (47 TUC)
This splendid globular cluster near the Small Magellanic Cloud (SMC) looks beautiful in binoculars or a telescope. It lies 16,000 light-years away.

LUPUS THE WOLF
In Greek mythology, the Wolf was speared by the Centaur (Centaurus) and placed on the Altar (Ara) as a sacrifice.

MILKY WAY
Seeing the Milky Way in binoculars on a moonless night away from city lights is a sight no one forgets.

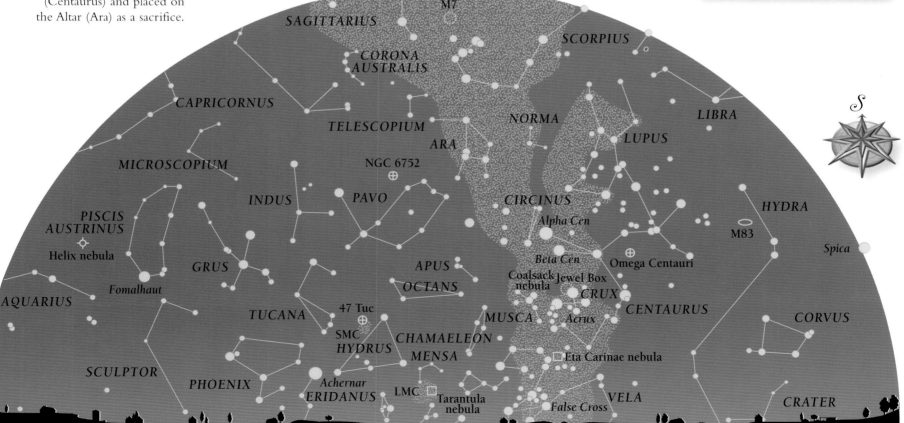

SAGITTARIUS M7
SCORPIUS
CORONA AUSTRALIS
CAPRICORNUS
NORMA
LIBRA
TELESCOPIUM
LUPUS
ARA
MICROSCOPIUM
NGC 6752
CIRCINUS
HYDRA
INDUS
PAVO
Alpha Cen
M83
PISCIS AUSTRINUS
Helix nebula
APUS
Beta Cen
Omega Centauri
Spica
GRUS
OCTANS
Coalsack Jewel Box
nebula
CRUX
CENTAURUS
Fomalhaut
CORVUS
AQUARIUS
47 Tuc
MUSCA
Acrux
TUCANA
SMC
CHAMAELEON
Eta Carinae nebula
SCULPTOR
HYDRUS
MENSA
VELA
PHOENIX
Achernar
LMC
CRATER
ERIDANUS
Tarantula
nebula
False Cross

Spring Stars of the Southern Skies

LOOKING NORTH The Great Square of Pegasus, the Flying Horse, makes a signpost tonight as it 'gallops' west across the northern horizon. The two lower stars in the Square point left towards the bright white star Altair in Aquila the Eagle. The two stars on the left side of the Square point upwards to Fomalhaut in Piscis Austrinus, the Southern Fish, which is high overhead. Between Pegasus and Fomalhaut lie three dim constellations with watery themes: Pisces the Fishes, Cetus the Sea Monster and Aquarius the Water Carrier. These are seen most easily on moonless nights, preferably well away from city lights. Rising in the east is the bright star Aldebaran, which forms the eye of Taurus the Bull. To the left of Aldebaran is the pretty Pleiades star cluster, also known as the Seven Sisters. Orion the Hunter is on the eastern horizon, half-risen into view.

• AMAZING FACT •

The Magellanic Clouds (shown on the facing page) are named after explorer Ferdinand Magellan, whose sailors probably saw the galaxies on their round-the-world voyage in the early 1500s.

WHERE YOU CAN SEE THIS SKY
SOUTHERN HEMISPHERE AREAS SUCH AS AUSTRALIA, NEW ZEALAND, SOUTH AMERICA AND SOUTH AFRICA

WHEN YOU CAN BEST SEE THIS SKY
OCTOBER TILL DECEMBER

BEST NAKED-EYE SIGHTS
GREAT SQUARE OF PEGASUS, FOMALHAUT IN PISCIS AUSTRINUS, VARIABLE STAR MIRA IN CETUS

BEST BINOCULAR SIGHTS
PLEIADES AND HYADES STAR CLUSTERS IN TAURUS

BEST TELESCOPE SIGHTS
GLOBULAR CLUSTER M15 IN PEGASUS, ANDROMEDA GALAXY (M31) IN ANDROMEDA

CETUS
In the neck of Cetus the Sea Monster lies the variable star Mira, which brightens and fades from view every 11 months.

FOMALHAUT
In ancient mythology, the star Fomalhaut was seen as a bright bubble in the mouth of the Southern Fish.

SQUARE OF PEGASUS
If you find the Great Square and extend imaginary lines drawn between its four stars, you can locate many of tonight's constellations.

PEGASUS
In Greek mythology, Pegasus the Flying Horse grew from the blood of a monster slain by the hero Perseus.

Fomalhaut

PISCIS AUSTRINUS

SCULPTOR

Helix nebula

CAPRICORNUS

AQUARIUS

CETUS

ERIDANUS

Mira

EQUULEUS

PISCES

N

AQUILA

DELPHINUS

M15

PEGASUS

ARIES

ANDROMEDA

M33

TAURUS

Altair

SCUTUM

SAGITTA

M27

LACERTA

M31

TRIANGULUM

Pleiades

ORION

SERPENS CAUDA

VULPECULA

CYGNUS

CASSIOPEIA

PERSEUS

Algol

Hyades

Aldebaran

Deneb

LOOKING SOUTH In this sky, two bright stars catch your eye, one high in the south, the other low in the south-east. The higher star is Achernar in Eridanus the River. This is a long, winding figure that runs from Achernar at one end over to the eastern horizon, where Orion is rising. The star low in the south-east is Canopus in Carina the Keel. Canopus is the sky's second-brightest star, after Sirius. Between Canopus and Achernar lies the Large Magellanic Cloud (LMC), with the Small Magellanic Cloud (SMC) to its upper right. Both are satellite galaxies of the Milky Way and, in the night sky, look like stray Milky Way pieces. Several celestial birds flock here. Phoenix the Firebird is above Achernar, and Grus the Crane stands to the right of Phoenix. Tucana the Toucan and Pavo the Peacock crouch below both. The setting Milky Way lies on the western horizon.

WHERE YOU CAN SEE THIS SKY
SOUTHERN HEMISPHERE AREAS SUCH AS AUSTRALIA, NEW ZEALAND, SOUTH AMERICA AND SOUTH AFRICA

WHEN YOU CAN BEST SEE THIS SKY
OCTOBER TILL DECEMBER

BEST NAKED-EYE SIGHTS
CANOPUS IN CARINA, ACHERNAR IN ERIDANUS

BEST BINOCULAR SIGHTS
SMALL MAGELLANIC CLOUD (SMC), LARGE MAGELLANIC CLOUD (LMC)

BEST TELESCOPE SIGHTS
GLOBULAR CLUSTER 47 TUCANAE (47 TUC) IN THE SMALL MAGELLANIC CLOUD, GREAT BARRED SPIRAL (NGC 1365) IN FORNAX

TUCANA THE TOUCAN
This bird from the tropics of America was added to the list of constellations in the early 1600s.

GREAT BARRED SPIRAL (NGC 1365)
The Great Barred Spiral is one of the brightest of a cluster of galaxies in the constellation of Fornax the Furnace.

MAGELLANIC CLOUDS
These two satellite galaxies of the Milky Way will one day collide with our galaxy, which will then swallow up their stars.

GRUS THE CRANE
Like Tucana, the Crane is a 'new' constellation that does not date from ancient times. It was invented in 1603.

◆ LOOK AGAIN ◆

● Name at least three night-sky birds visible this evening.

● What is the second-brightest star in the whole night sky?

● Where will you find the variable star Mira?

SCULPTOR · Fomalhaut · PISCIS AUSTRINUS · PHOENIX · FORNAX · GRUS · MICROSCOPIUM · CAPRICORNUS · ERIDANUS · Achernar · NGC 1365 · HOROLOGIUM · TUCANA · INDUS · 47 Tuc · SMC · RETICULUM · HYDRUS · PAVO · CORONA AUSTRALIS · CAELUM · DORADO · NGC 6752 · LEPUS · Tarantula nebula · MENSA · OCTANS · TELESCOPIUM · SAGITTARIUS · PICTOR · LMC · CHAMAELEON · APUS · SCUTUM · Rigel · M42 · COLUMBA · Canopus · VOLANS · ARA · M7 · M8 · M16 · SERPENS CAUDA · ORION · CANIS MAJOR · PUPPIS · CARINA · MUSCA · CIRCINUS · SCORPIUS · M20 · OPHIUCHUS · Adhara · VELA · CRUX · NORMA

𝒮

EAST   **WEST**

Summer Stars of the Southern Skies

LOOKING NORTH To explore the sky this evening, use the tall figure of Orion the Hunter, standing high in the north. Notice how the colours of the stars Betelgeuse (a cool, red star) and Rigel (a hot, blue one) differ. A row of three dimmer stars in the middle of Orion makes up the Hunter's belt. Extending the belt down to the left points to Taurus the Bull, with the ruddy star Aldebaran and the Hyades and Pleiades star clusters. Aldebaran forms the Bull's angry eye and the Hyades form his face. Extend Orion's belt up to the right and it points to Sirius, the sky's brightest star, in Canis Major, the Big Dog. From Sirius, a line down to the north-east horizon passes Procyon in Canis Minor, the Little Dog, then reaches Regulus in Leo the Lion. Below Orion, the yellow star Capella arcs low in the north with Auriga the Charioteer. To its right stands Gemini the Twins, with the two bright stars Castor and Pollux. The highlight of Cancer the Crab is the Beehive star cluster, which can be seen just to the right of Pollux. This beautiful open cluster contains more than 200 stars and looks best through binoculars.

WHERE YOU CAN SEE THIS SKY
SOUTHERN HEMISPHERE AREAS SUCH AS AUSTRALIA, NEW ZEALAND, SOUTH AMERICA AND SOUTH AFRICA

WHEN YOU CAN BEST SEE THIS SKY
JANUARY TILL MARCH

BEST NAKED-EYE SIGHTS
SIRIUS IN CANIS MAJOR, ORION THE HUNTER

BEST BINOCULAR SIGHTS
BEEHIVE STAR CLUSTER IN CANCER, PLEIADES AND HYADES STAR CLUSTERS IN TAURUS

BEST TELESCOPE SIGHTS
OPEN STAR CLUSTERS M35 IN GEMINI AND M41 IN CANIS MAJOR, CRAB NEBULA (M1) IN TAURUS, ORION NEBULA (M42) IN ORION

GEMINI THE TWINS
Castor and Pollux, the two brightest stars in Gemini the Twins, were named after the twins in Greek mythology who hatched from an egg.

◆ AMAZING FACT ◆

Legend says the star Canopus was named after a famous navigator by the Greek king Menelaus. The star, used by sailors in the Mediterranean for centuries, is also used by rocket scientists today for guiding spacecraft.

MONOCEROS THE UNICORN
The Unicorn was created in the early 1600s, using dim stars. It appears upside down on the star map below.

PLEIADES
The Pleiades are sometimes called 'the Seven Sisters', but most people can see only six stars by eye. Those with sharp eyesight may see nine stars.

CRAB NEBULA (M1)
The Crab nebula in Taurus is the expanding cloud of hot gas left by a star that was seen exploding in AD 1054.

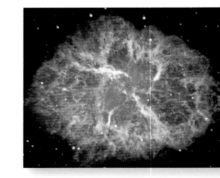

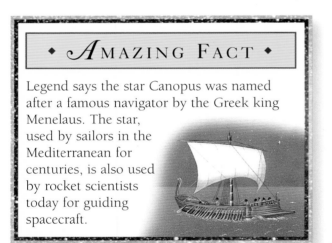

Adhara
CANIS MAJOR
M41
LEPUS
PUPPIS
Sirius
ERIDANUS
Rigel
M42
MONOCEROS
Betelgeuse
Mira
Procyon
HYDRA
ORION
TAURUS
Aldebaran
CANIS MINOR
CETUS
SEXTANS
Hyades
M1
M35
GEMINI
CANCER
Pleiades
Pollux
Beehive
ARIES
Castor
Regulus
AURIGA
PISCES
PERSEUS
LYNX
LEO
TRIANGULUM
Capella
M33
Algol
LEO MINOR

LOOKING SOUTH High in the south, the bright star Canopus marks the rudder of Carina the Keel. Carina is part of the mythical ship *Argo*. This ship was sailed by Jason and the Argonauts in their quest for the Golden Fleece, a ram's coat of gold kept in a dragon-guarded grove. Other parts of the *Argo* include Vela the Sails, Puppis the Stern and Pyxis the Compass, all of which lie in the Milky Way. Rising in the south-east below Vela is tiny Crux, the Southern Cross. Centaurus the Centaur partly wraps around it. In the south-western sky, you'll see a single bright star, Achernar. It marks the end of Eridanus the River, which begins at a point next to Rigel in Orion (see Looking North map, facing page). Look between Achernar and Canopus for a misty patch. This is the Large Magellanic Cloud (LMC), one of two satellite galaxies that orbit our own Milky Way galaxy. The other, the Small Magellanic Cloud (SMC), makes a triangle with Achernar and the Large Cloud.

WHERE YOU CAN SEE THIS SKY
SOUTHERN HEMISPHERE AREAS SUCH AS AUSTRALIA, NEW ZEALAND, SOUTH AMERICA AND SOUTH AFRICA

WHEN YOU CAN BEST SEE THIS SKY
JANUARY TILL MARCH

BEST NAKED-EYE SIGHTS
CANOPUS IN CARINA, CRUX (THE SOUTHERN CROSS)

BEST BINOCULAR SIGHTS
LARGE MAGELLANIC CLOUD (LMC), SMALL MAGELLANIC CLOUD (SMC)

BEST TELESCOPE SIGHTS
JEWEL BOX STAR CLUSTER IN CRUX, GLOBULAR CLUSTER 47 TUCANAE (47 TUC) IN THE SMALL MAGELLANIC CLOUD (SMC), TARANTULA NEBULA IN THE LARGE MAGELLANIC CLOUD (LMC)

ERIDANUS THE RIVER
The meandering celestial River commemorates Oceanus, a mythical stream once believed to circle the ancient world.

ETA CARINAE NEBULA
In the centre of this gas cloud in Carina lies the unstable star Eta Carinae. Astronomers expect to see the star explode any time in the next few thousand years.

LARGE MAGELLANIC CLOUD (LMC)
In 1987, astronomers saw a star explode in this small irregular galaxy. It was the first bright supernova seen since the telescope was invented about 400 years ago.

COLUMBA THE DOVE
The Dove, near the top of the map, was invented around 1600. It honours the biblical bird that Noah sent from the ark to look for land.

♦ LOOK AGAIN ♦
- What happened in 1987 in the Large Magellanic Cloud?
- Where is 'Oceanus' in tonight's sky?
- What is the Crab nebula?

Autumn Stars of the Southern Skies

LOOKING NORTH Four bright stars make easy jumping-off points for finding constellations this evening. Look for Procyon in Canis Minor, the Little Dog, setting in the north-west. In the north, Regulus marks the heart of Leo the Lion. Then over in the north-east at about the same height as Regulus, you'll see reddish Arcturus. It stands in the constellation of Boötes the Herdsman. Directly above Arcturus, and with a marked contrast in colour, is white Spica in Virgo the Maiden. The patch of sky between Leo and Virgo contains the Virgo cluster of galaxies. At about 55 million light-years away, this is the nearest large galaxy cluster to our own Local Group. The long figure of Hydra the Sea Serpent has his head near Procyon. His body weaves high overhead past Crater the Cup and Corvus the Crow, ending not far from Spica.

WHERE YOU CAN SEE THIS SKY	Southern Hemisphere areas such as Australia, New Zealand, South America and South Africa
WHEN YOU CAN BEST SEE THIS SKY	April till June
BEST NAKED-EYE SIGHTS	Regulus in Leo, Arcturus in Boötes, Spica in Virgo
BEST BINOCULAR SIGHTS	Beehive star cluster in Cancer
BEST TELESCOPE SIGHTS	Galaxies M65 and M66 in Leo, M83 in Hydra, M87 in Virgo, Virgo cluster of galaxies

VIRGO THE MAIDEN
Virgo is the only female figure to be found among the 12 constellations of the zodiac.

BOÖTES THE HERDSMAN
According to ancient legend, when Boötes invented the plough, the gods honoured him with a place in the heavens.

M87
An elliptical galaxy, M87 in Virgo is one of the most massive galaxies known. In a small telescope, it looks like a hazy patch of light.

◆ LOOK AGAIN ◆

- What ship has Vela for its sails?
- When did Crux become a separate constellation?
- How did Boötes earn his place in the night sky?

M83
M83 is a barred spiral galaxy that is turned so we see its disk face-on. You can observe it high in the north-eastern sky through binoculars.

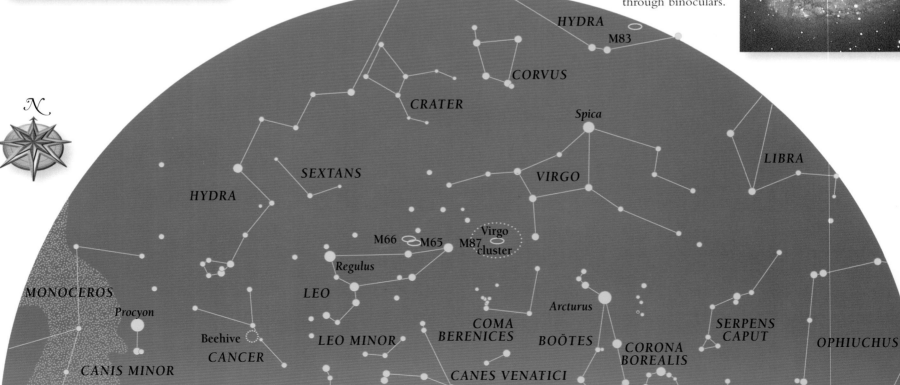

N

WEST

EAST

LOOKING SOUTH   To fully appreciate the glories of the Milky Way arching across the southern sky, try to get away from city lights on a moonless evening at this time of year. If you have a pair of binoculars or a small telescope, take the opportunity to sweep through the band of Milky Way stars. The band runs from the dazzling star Sirius in Canis Major, the Big Dog, which is setting in the west, to ruddy Antares in Scorpius the Scorpion, rising in the south-east. In the south-west, look above the bright star Canopus for Carina the Keel, Vela the Sails and Puppis the Stern – all constellations that were once part of Jason and the Argonauts' mythical ship *Argo*. To the left of these stand the bright stars of tiny Crux, the Southern Cross, which Centaurus the Centaur so nimbly hops over, his forefeet marked by Alpha and Beta Centauri.

SCORPIUS THE SCORPION
Greek mythology said that Scorpius killed Orion, which is why one is always setting as the other rises.

THE JEWEL BOX
Seen through a telescope, this small but rich open cluster near Crux shows stars of different colours. It lies about 6,800 light-years away.

WHERE YOU CAN SEE THIS SKY
SOUTHERN HEMISPHERE AREAS SUCH AS AUSTRALIA, NEW ZEALAND, SOUTH AMERICA AND SOUTH AFRICA

WHEN YOU CAN BEST SEE THIS SKY
APRIL TILL JUNE

BEST NAKED-EYE SIGHTS
MILKY WAY, CRUX, COALSACK NEBULA IN CRUX

BEST BINOCULAR SIGHTS
MILKY WAY, LARGE MAGELLANIC CLOUD (LMC)

BEST TELESCOPE SIGHTS
JEWEL BOX STAR CLUSTER IN CRUX, OMEGA CENTAURI GLOBULAR CLUSTER IN CENTAURUS, ETA CARINAE NEBULA IN CARINA, TARANTULA NEBULA IN LARGE MAGELLANIC CLOUD (LMC)

TARANTULA NEBULA
The Tarantula nebula got its name because its gas clouds look a bit like the hairy legs of a spider. You can find it to the left of the star Canopus.

CENTAURUS THE CENTAUR
Centaurs were half-man and half-horse. Centaurus honours Chiron, the wisest of these mythical beasts. Sagittarius the Archer is also a centaur.

CRUX
Crux, the Southern Cross, dates only from 1592. Before then, its stars were part of Centaurus.

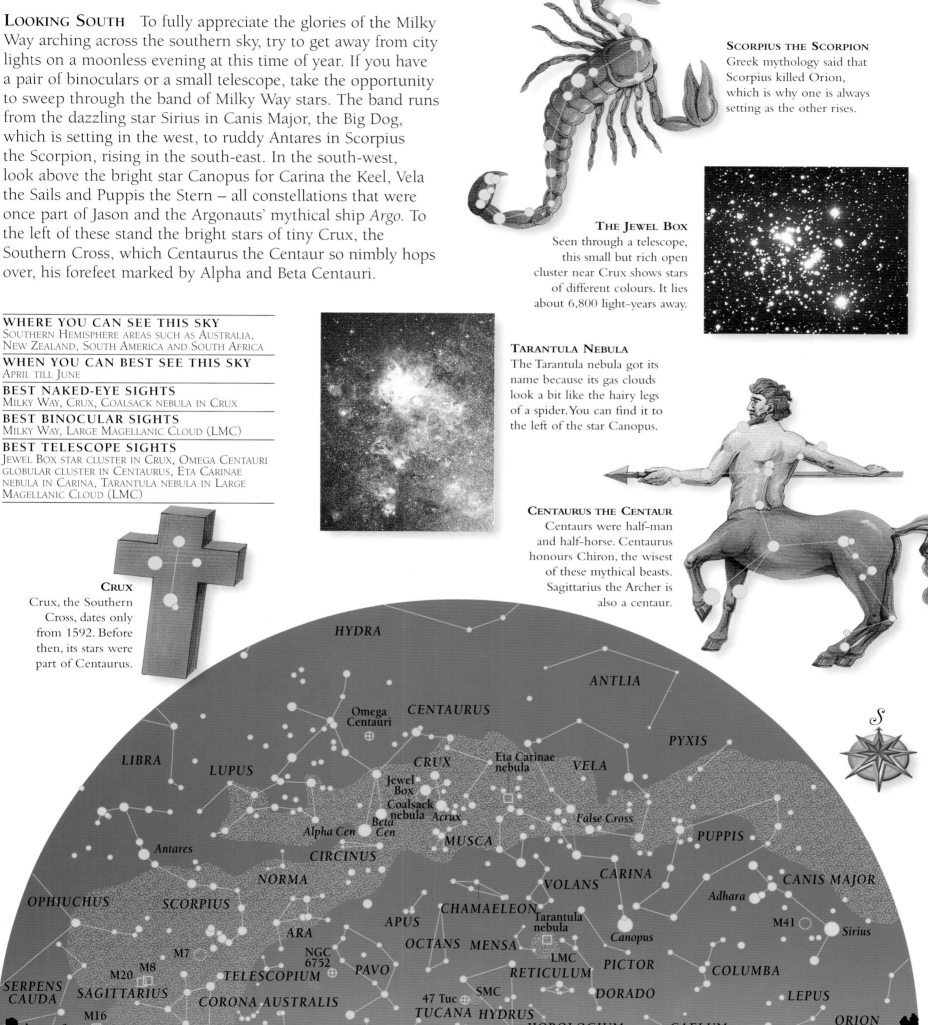

HYDRA

ANTLIA

CENTAURUS

Omega Centauri

PYXIS

LIBRA

LUPUS

CRUX

Eta Carinae nebula

VELA

Jewel Box

Coalsack nebula

Acrux

False Cross

PUPPIS

Alpha Cen

Beta Cen

MUSCA

Antares

CIRCINUS

CARINA

CANIS MAJOR

NORMA

VOLANS

Adhara

OPHIUCHUS

SCORPIUS

CHAMAELEON

M41

Sirius

APUS

Tarantula nebula

ARA

Canopus

M7

OCTANS   MENSA

NGC 6752

PAVO

LMC

PICTOR

COLUMBA

M20   M8

TELESCOPIUM

RETICULUM

DORADO

LEPUS

SERPENS CAUDA

SAGITTARIUS

CORONA AUSTRALIS

47 Tuc   SMC

TUCANA   HYDRUS

HOROLOGIUM

CAELUM

ORION

M16

INDUS

EAST

WEST

Universe Fact File

SUN FACTS

APPARENT MAGNITUDE: −26.8
ABSOLUTE (ACTUAL) MAGNITUDE: 4.8
ROTATION TIME: 25 Earth days at Equator, 34 Earth days near poles
DIAMETER: 1,392,000 km (865,000 mi)
MASS: 332,946 x Earth's
DENSITY: 1.4 x water's density
SURFACE GRAVITY: 27.9 x Earth's
COMPOSITION: 92.1% hydrogen, 7.8% helium, 1% other elements
SURFACE TEMPERATURE: 5,500°C (9,900°F)
CORE TEMPERATURE: 15,500,000°C (27,900,000°F)
MAGNETIC FIELD STRENGTH: up to 10,000 x Earth's

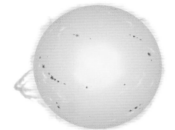

MERCURY FACTS

WHEN DISCOVERED: pre-historic
WHO DISCOVERED IT: unknown
HOW WE CAN SEE IT: naked eye
APPARENT MAGNITUDE: −2 to +3
DISTANCE FROM SUN: 0.4 AU, or 58 million km (36 million mi)
LENGTH OF YEAR: 88 Earth days
AVERAGE SPEED: 48 km (30 mi) per second
INCLINATION OF ORBIT: 7.0°
ECCENTRICITY OF ORBIT: 0.21
TILT OF AXIS: 0.5°
ROTATION TIME: 59 Earth days
SOLAR DAY: 176 Earth days
DIAMETER: 4,875 km (3,029 mi)
MASS: 55% x Earth's
DENSITY: 5.4 x water's density
SURFACE GRAVITY: 0.38 x Earth's
COMPOSITION: iron and rock
ATMOSPHERE: essentially none
AVERAGE TEMPERATURE: −173°C to 427°C (−280°F to 800°F)
MAGNETIC FIELD STRENGTH: 0.5% x Earth's
NUMBER OF MOONS: none
NUMBER OF RINGS: none
NUMBER OF PROBE VISITS: 1

VENUS FACTS

WHEN DISCOVERED: pre-historic
WHO DISCOVERED IT: unknown
HOW WE CAN SEE IT: naked eye
APPARENT MAGNITUDE: −4.0 to −4.6
DISTANCE FROM SUN: 0.7 AU, or 108 million km (67 million mi)
LENGTH OF YEAR: 225 Earth days
AVERAGE SPEED: 35 km (22 mi) per second
INCLINATION OF ORBIT: 3.4°
ECCENTRICITY OF ORBIT: 0.01
TILT OF AXIS: 177.4°
ROTATION TIME: 243 Earth days
SOLAR DAY: 117 Earth days
DIAMETER: 12,104 km (7,521 mi)
MASS: 82% x Earth's
DENSITY: 5.2 x water's density
SURFACE GRAVITY: 0.90 x Earth's
COMPOSITION: mostly rock
ATMOSPHERE: 97% carbon dioxide, 3% nitrogen
PRESSURE OF ATMOSPHERE: 96 x Earth's
AVERAGE TEMPERATURE: 470°C (880°F)
MAGNETIC FIELD STRENGTH: less than 0.05% x Earth's
NUMBER OF MOONS: none
NUMBER OF RINGS: none
NUMBER OF PROBE VISITS: 31

EARTH FACTS

WHEN DISCOVERED: pre-historic
WHO DISCOVERED IT: unknown
DISTANCE FROM SUN: 1.0 AU, or 150 million km (93 million mi)
LENGTH OF YEAR: 365.25 days
AVERAGE SPEED: 30 km (18.5 mi) per second
INCLINATION OF ORBIT: 0°
ECCENTRICITY OF ORBIT: 0.02
TILT OF AXIS: 23.5°
ROTATION TIME: 23 hours 56 minutes
SOLAR DAY: 24 hours
DIAMETER: 12,756 km (7,926 mi)
MASS: 5.5×10^{24} tonnes (6×10^{24} tons)
DENSITY: 5.5 x water's density
COMPOSITION: mostly rock
ATMOSPHERE: 78% nitrogen, 21% oxygen, plus water, argon, carbon dioxide
AVERAGE TEMPERATURE: 17°C (63°F)
NUMBER OF MOONS: 1
NUMBER OF RINGS: none

MARS FACTS

WHEN DISCOVERED: pre-historic
WHO DISCOVERED IT: unknown
HOW WE CAN SEE IT: naked eye
APPARENT MAGNITUDE: −2.6 to +1.8
DISTANCE FROM SUN: 1.5 AU, or 228 million km (142 million mi)
LENGTH OF YEAR: 687 Earth days
AVERAGE SPEED: 24 km (15 mi) per second
INCLINATION OF ORBIT: 1.9°
ECCENTRICITY OF ORBIT: 0.09
TILT OF AXIS: 25.2°
ROTATION TIME: 24 hours 37 minutes
SOLAR DAY: 24 hours 40 minutes
DIAMETER: 6,780 km (4,213 mi)
MASS: 64% x Earth's
DENSITY: 3.9 x water's density
SURFACE GRAVITY: 0.38 x Earth's
COMPOSITION: mostly rock
ATMOSPHERE: 95% carbon dioxide, 2.7% nitrogen, 1.6% argon, plus others
PRESSURE OF ATMOSPHERE: 0.6% x Earth's
AVERAGE TEMPERATURE: −59°C (−74°F)
MAGNETIC FIELD STRENGTH: less than 0.1% x Earth's
NUMBER OF MOONS: 2
NUMBER OF RINGS: none
NUMBER OF PROBE VISITS: 23

JUPITER FACTS

WHEN DISCOVERED: pre-historic
WHO DISCOVERED IT: unknown
HOW WE CAN SEE IT: naked eye
APPARENT MAGNITUDE: −2.5 to −1.2
DISTANCE FROM SUN: 5.2 AU, or 778 million km (483 million mi)
LENGTH OF YEAR: 11.9 Earth years
AVERAGE SPEED: 13 km (8 mi) per second
INCLINATION OF ORBIT: 1.3°
ECCENTRICITY OF ORBIT: 0.05
TILT OF AXIS: 3.1°
ROTATION TIME: 9 hours 55 minutes
SOLAR DAY: same as rotation time
DIAMETER: 142,984 km (88,846 mi)
MASS: 317.8 x Earth's mass
DENSITY: 1.3 x water's density
GRAVITY AT CLOUDTOPS: 2.6 x Earth's surface gravity
COMPOSITION: mostly gaseous
ATMOSPHERE: 86% hydrogen, 13.6% helium, plus methane, ammonia, water
AVERAGE TEMPERATURE AT CLOUDTOPS: −108°C (−162°F)
MAGNETIC FIELD STRENGTH: 7.1 x Earth's
NUMBER OF MOONS: 16
NUMBER OF RINGS: 3
NUMBER OF PROBE VISITS: 5

NOTES ON PLANET FACTS

APPARENT MAGNITUDE: How bright an object looks in the sky. Brighter objects have smaller numbers than dimmer ones.
DISTANCE FROM SUN: The planet's average distance from the Sun.
INCLINATION OF ORBIT: The angle of the planet's orbit relative to the plane of Earth's orbit.
ECCENTRICITY OF ORBIT: How elliptical the planet's orbit is. The larger the number, the more elliptical the orbit is.

NOTES ON ASTEROID FACTS

DISTANCE FROM SUN: The asteroid's average distance from the Sun.
ORBIT TIME: All years listed are Earth years.

NOTES ON COMET FACTS

NAME: Comets are named after their discoverers.
ORBIT TIME: All years listed are Earth years.
ORBIT INCLIN.: The inclination of the comet's orbit relative to the plane of Earth's orbit.
ORBIT ECCENT.: The eccentricity of the comet's orbit. The larger the number, the more elliptical the orbit is.

GENERAL NOTES

• 1 AU (astronomical unit) is the average distance between Earth and the Sun, about 150 million km (93 million mi).
• A tonne is equal to 1,000 kg (about 2,200 lb).

SATURN FACTS

WHEN DISCOVERED: pre-historic
WHO DISCOVERED IT: unknown
HOW WE CAN SEE IT: naked eye
APPARENT MAGNITUDE: 0.6 to 1.5
DISTANCE FROM SUN: 9.6 AU, or 1,432 million km (890 million mi)
LENGTH OF YEAR: 29.4 Earth years
AVERAGE SPEED: 10 km (6 mi) per second
INCLINATION OF ORBIT: 2.5°
ECCENTRICITY OF ORBIT: 0.05
TILT OF AXIS: 26.7°
ROTATION TIME: 10 hours 39 minutes
SOLAR DAY: same as rotation time
DIAMETER: 120,533 km (74,896 mi)
MASS: 95.2 x Earth's
DENSITY: 0.7 x water's density
GRAVITY AT CLOUDTOPS: 1.1 x Earth's surface gravity
COMPOSITION: mostly gaseous
ATMOSPHERE: 96% hydrogen, 3.3% helium, plus methane, ammonia and others
AVERAGE TEMPERATURE AT CLOUDTOPS: −139°C (−218°F)
MAGNETIC FIELD STRENGTH: 0.34 x Earth's
NUMBER OF MOONS: 18
NUMBER OF RINGS: 7
NUMBER OF PROBE VISITS: 4

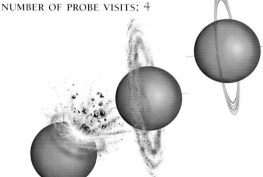

URANUS FACTS

WHEN DISCOVERED: March 1781
WHO DISCOVERED IT: William Herschel
HOW WE CAN SEE IT: barely visible to the naked eye, but easy to see with a telescope
APPARENT MAGNITUDE: 5.5 to 5.9
DISTANCE FROM SUN: 19.2 AU, or 2,871 million km (1,784 million mi)
LENGTH OF YEAR: 84.1 Earth years
AVERAGE SPEED: 7 km (4 mi) per second
INCLINATION OF ORBIT: 0.8°
ECCENTRICITY OF ORBIT: 0.04
TILT OF AXIS: 97.9°
ROTATION TIME: 17 hours 14 minutes
SOLAR DAY: same as rotation time
DIAMETER: 51,118 km (31,763 mi)
MASS: 14.5 x Earth's
DENSITY: 1.3 x water's density
GRAVITY AT CLOUDTOPS: 0.90 x Earth's surface gravity
COMPOSITION: mostly gaseous
ATMOSPHERE: 83% hydrogen, 15% helium, 2% methane
AVERAGE TEMPERATURE AT CLOUDTOPS: −197°C (−323°F)
MAGNETIC FIELD STRENGTH: 0.38 x Earth's
NUMBER OF MOONS: at least 20
NUMBER OF RINGS: 11
NUMBER OF PROBE VISITS: 1

PLANET FEATURES

The names of geological features on rocky planets and moons come from Latin and Greek.
Chasma: a deep, long depression with steep sides
Corona: an oval-shaped feature
Fossae: depressions that are long, narrow and shallow
Mons, montes: a mountain or range of mountains
Patera: an irregular crater
Planitia: a low plain
Planum: a plateau or high plain
Regio: a large area distinct from surrounding ones
Rupes: a long cliff caused by geological faulting
Terra: an extensive land mass
Tessera: terrain that is heavily broken up by faulting
Tholus: a small domed mountain or hill
Vallis, valles: a valley or set of connected valleys
Vastitas: an extensive plain

NEPTUNE

WHEN DISCOVERED: September 1846
WHO DISCOVERED IT: Urbain Leverrier, John Couch Adams, Johann Galle and Heinrich d'Arrest
HOW WE CAN SEE IT: telescope
APPARENT MAGNITUDE: 7.9
DISTANCE FROM SUN: 30.1 AU, or 4,498 million km (2,795 million mi)
LENGTH OF YEAR: 164.9 Earth years
AVERAGE SPEED: 5.5 km (3.5 mi) per second
INCLINATION OF ORBIT: 1.8°
ECCENTRICITY OF ORBIT: 0.01
TILT OF AXIS: 29.6°
ROTATION TIME: 16 hours 7 minutes
SOLAR DAY: same as rotation time
DIAMETER: 49,528 km (30,775 mi)
MASS: 17.2 x Earth's
DENSITY: 1.6 x water's density
GRAVITY AT CLOUDTOPS: 1.1 x Earth's surface gravity
COMPOSITION: mostly gaseous
ATMOSPHERE: 80% hydrogen, 19% helium, 1% methane
AVERAGE TEMPERATURE AT CLOUDTOPS: −201°C (−330°F)
MAGNETIC FIELD STRENGTH: 22% x Earth's
NUMBER OF MOONS: 8
NUMBER OF RINGS: 6
NUMBER OF PROBE VISITS: 1

PLUTO

WHEN DISCOVERED: February 1930
WHO DISCOVERED IT: Clyde Tombaugh
HOW WE CAN SEE IT: telescope
APPARENT MAGNITUDE: 13.7
DISTANCE FROM SUN: 39.5 AU, or 5,914 million km (3,675 million mi)
LENGTH OF YEAR: 248 Earth years
AVERAGE SPEED: 5 km (3 mi) per second
INCLINATION OF ORBIT: 17.1°
ECCENTRICITY OF ORBIT: 0.25
TILT OF AXIS: 122.5°
ROTATION TIME: 6.4 Earth days
SOLAR DAY: same as rotation time
DIAMETER: 2,304 km (1,432 mi)
MASS: 0.2% x Earth's
DENSITY: 2.1 x water's density
SURFACE GRAVITY: 0.065 x Earth's
COMPOSITION: rock and ice
ATMOSPHERE: methane, nitrogen
PRESSURE OF ATMOSPHERE: about 3 millionths x Earth's
AVERAGE TEMPERATURE: −233°C (−387°F)
MAGNETIC FIELD STRENGTH: unknown
NUMBER OF MOONS: 1
NUMBER OF RINGS: none
NUMBER OF PROBE VISITS: none

ASTEROID FACTS

NAME	DISCOVERY	DISTANCE FROM SUN	ORBIT TIME	ROTATION TIME	DIAMETER
1 Ceres	Piazzi, 1801	2.76 AU	4.6 yrs	9h 5m	913 km (567 mi)
2 Pallas	Olbers, 1802	2.77 AU	4.6 yrs	7h 49m	523 km (325 mi)
4 Vesta	Olbers, 1807	2.36 AU	3.6 yrs	5h 21m	520 km (323 mi)
10 Hygeia	De Gasparis, 1849	3.14 AU	5.6 yrs	27h 40m	429 km (267 mi)
511 Davida	Dugan, 1903	3.18 AU	5.7 yrs	5h 8m	337 km (209 mi)
704 Interamnia	Cerulli, 1910	3.06 AU	5.4 yrs	8h 44m	333 km (207 mi)
253 Mathilde	Palisa, 1885	2.65 AU	4.3 yrs	17h 24m	66 km (41 mi)
243 Ida	Palisa, 1884	2.86 AU	4.9 yrs	4h 38m	60 km (37 mi)
433 Eros	Witt & Charlois, 1898	1.46 AU	1.8 yrs	5h 18m	33 km (21 mi)
951 Gaspra	Neujmin, 1916	2.21 AU	3.3 yrs	7h 3m	18 km (11 mi)

COMET FACTS

NAME	FIRST RECORDED	FURTHEST FROM SUN	CLOSEST TO SUN	TYPE	ORBIT TIME	ORBIT INCLIN.	ORBIT ECCENT.
Encke	1786	4.1 AU	0.3 AU	short period	3.3 yrs	11.9°	0.85
Wirtanen	1954	5.1 AU	1.1 AU	short period	5.5 yrs	11.7°	0.65
Wild 2	1978	5.3 AU	1.6 AU	short period	6.4 yrs	3.2°	0.54
d'Arrest	1851	5.6 AU	1.4 AU	short period	6.5 yrs	19.5°	0.61
Tempel-Tuttle	1866	19.5 AU	1.0 AU	short period	32.9 yrs	163°	0.90
Halley	239 BC	35.0 AU	0.6 AU	short period	76.0 yrs	162°	0.97
Swift-Tuttle	1862	52.3 AU	1.0 AU	short period	137.3 yrs	113°	0.96
Bennett	1970	281.8 AU	0.5 AU	long period	1,678 yrs	90.0°	0.99
Donati	1858	311.6 AU	0.6 AU	long period	1,950 yrs	117°	0.99
Hale-Bopp	1995	370.6 AU	0.9 AU	long period	2,529 yrs	89.4°	0.99
Hyakutake	1996	2,006 AU	0.2 AU	long period	31,781 yrs	125°	0.99
Ikeya-Seki	1965	4,000 AU	0.01 AU	long period	89,443 yrs	129°	0.99

MOON FACTS

NAME	DISCOVERY	DISTANCE FROM PLANET IN KM (MI)	ORBIT TIME	DIAMETER IN KM (MI)	MASS IN TONNES (TONS)	SURFACE COMPOSITION
Earth						
the Moon	pre-historic	384,401 (238,856)	27.3 days	3,476 (2,160)	7.3×10^{19} (8.0×10^{19})	anorthosite & basalt rock, dust
Mars						
Phobos	Hall, 1877	9,378 (5,827)	0.3 day	27 (17)	9.6×10^{12} (1.1×10^{13})	carbon-rich rock, dust
Deimos	Hall, 1877	23,459 (14,577)	1.3 days	15 (9)	1.8×10^{12} (2.0×10^{12})	carbon-rich rock, dust
45 Eugenia						
S/1998(45)1	Merline, 1998	1,240 (771)?	4.7 days	10 (6)?	unknown	rock?
243 Ida						
Dactyl	Galileo spacecraft, 1993	90 (56)	unknown	1 (0.6)	3.7×10^{9} (4.1×10^{9})	carbon-rich rock, dust
Jupiter						
Metis	Synnott, 1979	127,960 (79,511)	0.3 day	40 (25)	9.5×10^{13} (1.0×10^{14})	rock
Adrastea	Jewitt & Danielson, 1979	128,980 (80,145)	0.3 day	25 (16)	1.9×10^{13} (2.1×10^{13})	rock
Amalthea	Barnard, 1892	181,300 (112,655)	0.5 day	270 (168)	7.2×10^{15} (7.9×10^{15})	rock, sulphur coating?
Thebe	Synnott, 1979	221,900 (137,882)	0.7 day	110 (68)	7.6×10^{14} (8.4×10^{14})	rock
Io	Galileo, 1610	421,600 (261,970)	1.8 days	3,643 (2,264)	8.9×10^{19} (9.8×10^{19})	rock
Europa	Galileo, 1610	670,900 (416,880)	3.5 days	3,120 (1,939)	4.8×10^{19} (5.3×10^{19})	rock
Ganymede	Galileo, 1610	1,070,000 (664,870)	7.2 days	5,268 (3,273)	1.5×10^{20} (1.7×10^{20})	rock
Callisto	Galileo, 1610	1,883,000 (1,170,000)	16.7 days	4,800 (2,983)	1.1×10^{20} (1.2×10^{20})	rock
Leda	Kowal, 1974	11,094,000 (6,893,500)	238.7 days	16 (10)	5.7×10^{12} (6.3×10^{12})	carbon-rich dirt, ice
Himalia	Perrine, 1904	11,480,000 (7,133,300)	250.6 days	186 (116)	9.5×10^{15} (1.0×10^{16})	carbon-rich dirt, ice
Lysithea	Nicholson, 1938	11,720,000 (7,282,500)	259.2 days	36 (22)	7.6×10^{13} (8.4×10^{13})	carbon-rich dirt, ice
Elara	Perrine, 1905	11,737,000 (7,293,000)	259.6 days	76 (47)	7.6×10^{14} (8.4×10^{14})	carbon-rich dirt, ice
Ananke	Nicholson, 1951	21,200,000 (13,173,100)	631 days	30 (19)	3.8×10^{13} (4.2×10^{13})	carbon-rich dirt, ice
Carme	Nicholson, 1938	22,600,000 (14,043,000)	692 days	40 (25)	9.5×10^{13} (1.0×10^{14})	carbon-rich dirt, ice
Pasiphae	Melotte, 1908	23,500,000 (14,602,200)	735 days	50 (31)	1.9×10^{14} (2.1×10^{14})	carbon-rich dirt, ice
Sinope	Nicholson, 1914	23,700,000 (14,726,500)	758 days	36 (22)	7.6×10^{13} (8.4×10^{13})	carbon-rich dirt, ice
Saturn						
Pan	Showalter, 1990	133,583 (83,005)	0.6 day	20 (12)	unknown	ice?
Atlas	Terrile, 1980	137,670 (85,544)	0.6 day	38 (24)	unknown	dirty ice?
Prometheus	Collins & others, 1980	139,353 (86,590)	0.6 day	140 (87)	1.4×10^{14} (1.5×10^{14})	ice?
Pandora	Collins & others, 1980	141,700 (88,048)	0.6 day	110 (68)	1.3×10^{14} (1.4×10^{14})	ice?
Epimetheus	Walker & others, 1966	151,422 (94,089)	0.7 day	140 (87)	5.5×10^{14} (6.0×10^{14})	dirty ice?
Janus	Dollfus, 1966	151,472 (94,120)	0.7 day	220 (137)	2.0×10^{15} (2.2×10^{15})	dirty ice?
Mimas	Herschel, 1789	185,520 (115,280)	0.9 day	392 (244)	3.8×10^{16} (4.2×10^{16})	ice
Enceladus	Herschel, 1789	238,020 (147,900)	1.4 days	500 (310)	8.0×10^{16} (8.8×10^{16})	ice
Tethys	Cassini, 1684	294,660 (183,090)	1.9 days	1,060 (659)	7.6×10^{17} (8.4×10^{17})	ice
Telesto	Smith & others, 1980	294,660 (183,090)	1.9 days	34 (21)	unknown	ice?
Calypso	Pascu & others, 1980	294,660 (183,090)	1.9 days	34 (21)	unknown	ice?
Dione	Cassini, 1684	377,400 (234,500)	2.7 days	1,120 (696)	1.1×10^{18} (1.2×10^{18})	dirty ice
Helene	Laques & Lecacheux, 1980	377,400 (234,500)	2.7 days	36 (22)	unknown	dirty ice?
Rhea	Cassini, 1672	527,040 (327,490)	4.5 days	1,528 (950)	2.5×10^{18} (2.8×10^{18})	ice
Titan	Huygens, 1655	1,221,830 (759,210)	16 days	5,150 (3,200)	1.4×10^{20} (1.5×10^{20})	liquid methane, ice
Hyperion	Bond, 1848	1,481,100 (920,310)	21.3 days	350 (218)	1.7×10^{16} (1.9×10^{16})	dirty ice?
Iapetus	Cassini, 1671	3,561,300 (2,212,900)	79.3 days	1,436 (892)	1.9×10^{18} (2.1×10^{18})	ice, carbon-rich dirt
Phoebe	Pickering, 1898	12,952,000 (8,048,000)	550.5 days	230 (143)	4.0×10^{14} (4.4×10^{14})	ice, carbon-rich dirt?
Uranus						
Cordelia	Voyager 2, 1986	49,770 (30,926)	0.3 day	26 (16)	unknown	carbon-rich dirt, ice?
Ophelia	Voyager 2, 1986	53,790 (33,424)	0.4 day	30 (19)	unknown	carbon-rich dirt, ice?
Bianca	Voyager 2, 1986	59,166 (36,764)	0.4 day	42 (26)	unknown	carbon-rich dirt, ice?
Cressida	Voyager 2, 1986	61,780 (38,388)	0.5 day	62 (39)	unknown	carbon-rich dirt, ice?
Desdemona	Voyager 2, 1986	62,680 (38,948)	0.5 day	54 (34)	unknown	carbon-rich dirt, ice?
Juliet	Voyager 2, 1986	64,350 (39,985)	0.5 day	84 (52)	unknown	carbon-rich dirt, ice?
Portia	Voyager 2, 1986	66,090 (41,066)	0.5 day	108 (67)	unknown	carbon-rich dirt, ice?
Rosalind	Voyager 2, 1986	69,940 (43,459)	0.6 day	54 (34)	unknown	carbon-rich dirt, ice?
Belinda	Voyager 2, 1986	75,256 (46,762)	0.6 day	66 (41)	unknown	carbon-rich dirt, ice?
S/1986 U10	Karkoshka, 1999	76,416 (47,483)	0.6 day	40 (25)?	unknown	unknown
Puck	Voyager 2, 1986	86,010 (53,444)	0.8 day	154 (96)	unknown	carbon-rich dirt, ice?
Miranda	Kuiper, 1948	129,390 (80,399)	1.4 days	484 (301)	6.9×10^{16} (7.6×10^{16})	ice
Ariel	Lassell, 1851	191,020 (118,694)	2.5 days	1,158 (720)	1.4×10^{18} (1.5×10^{18})	ice
Umbriel	Lassell, 1851	266,300 (165,471)	4.1 days	1,172 (728)	1.2×10^{18} (1.3×10^{18})	ice
Titania	Herschel, 1787	435,910 (270,862)	8.7 days	1,580 (982)	3.5×10^{18} (3.9×10^{18})	ice
Oberon	Herschel, 1787	583,520 (362,583)	13.5 days	1,524 (947)	3.0×10^{18} (3.3×10^{18})	ice
Caliban	Gladman & others, 1997	7,169,000 (4,455,000)	579 days	60 (37)	unknown	unknown
S/1999 U1	Gladman & others, 1999	10,000,000 (6,200,000)?	unknown	20 (12)?	unknown	unknown
Sycorax	Nicholson & others, 1997	12,214,000 (7,589,000)	1,289 days	160 (100)	unknown	unknown
S/1999 U2	Gladman & others, 1999	25,000,000 (15,500,000)?	unknown	20 (12)?	unknown	unknown

NAME	DISCOVERY	DISTANCE FROM PLANET IN KM (MI)	ORBIT TIME	DIAMETER IN KM (MI)	MASS IN TONNES (TONS)	SURFACE COMPOSITION
Neptune						
Naiad	Voyager 2, 1989	48,227 (29,967)	0.3 day	58 (36)	unknown	carbon-rich dirt, ice?
Thalassa	Voyager 2, 1989	50,070 (31,112)	0.3 day	80 (50)	unknown	carbon-rich dirt, ice?
Despina	Voyager 2, 1989	52,526 (32,638)	0.3 day	148 (92)	unknown	carbon-rich dirt, ice?
Galatea	Voyager 2, 1989	61,953 (38,496)	0.4 day	158 (98)	unknown	carbon-rich dirt, ice?
Larissa	Reitsma & Voyager 2, 1989	73,548 (45,701)	0.6 day	208 (129)	unknown	carbon-rich dirt, ice?
Proteus	Voyager 2, 1989	117,647 (73,103)	1.1 days	436 (271)	unknown	carbon-rich dirt, ice?
Triton	Lassell, 1846	354,760 (220,438)	5.9 days	2,706 (1,681)	2.2×10^{19} (2.4×10^{19})	nitrogen & methane ice
Nereid	Kuiper, 1949	5,513,400 (3,425,900)	360.1 days	340 (211)	unknown	carbon-rich dirt, ice?
Pluto						
Charon	Christy, 1978	19,636 (12,201)	6.4 days	1,186 (737)	1.9×10^{18} (2.1×10^{18})	ice

NOTES ON MOON FACTS

NAME: 45 Eugenia and 243 Ida are asteroids with moons of their own.

ORBIT TIME: All days are Earth days.

MASS: The very large numbers measuring mass are given in scientific notation, such as 3.7×10^9. The little number after the 10 is the number of zeros that comes after the 1. Thus, 10^9 is 1,000,000,000 and 3.7×10^9 is 3,700,000,000 or 3,700 million.

- A tonne is equal to 1,000 kg (about 2,200 lb).
- A question mark indicates that the value is an unconfirmed estimate.

METEOR SHOWERS

Dates may vary slightly

SHOWER	CONSTELLATION	DATE	PER HOUR	PARENT OBJECT
Quadrantids	Boötes	3 Jan	40 meteors	unknown
Lyrids	Lyra	22 Apr	15 meteors	comet Thatcher
Eta Aquarids	Aquarius	5 May	20 meteors	Halley's Comet
Delta Aquarids	Aquarius	28 July	20 meteors	unknown
Perseids	Perseus	12 Aug	50 meteors	comet Swift-Tuttle
Orionids	Orion	22 Oct	25 meteors	Halley's Comet
Taurids	Taurus	3 Nov	15 meteors	comet Encke
Leonids	Leo	17 Nov	15 meteors	comet Tempel-Tuttle
Geminids	Gemini	14 Dec	50 meteors	asteroid 3200 Phaethon
Ursids	Ursa Minor	23 Dec	20 meteors	comet Tuttle

SOLAR ECLIPSES

DATE	TYPE	BEST SEEN FROM
5 Feb, 2000	partial	Antarctica
1 July, 2000	partial	south-east Pacific Ocean, Chile, Argentina
31 July, 2000	partial	Siberia, Arctic Ocean, north-west U.S.A. & Canada
25 Dec, 2000	partial	North and Central America
21 June, 2001	total	south Africa
14 Dec, 2001	partial	Pacific Ocean, Nicaragua
10 June, 2002	partial	Pacific Ocean
4 Dec, 2002	total	south Africa, Pacific Ocean & Australia
31 May, 2003	partial	central and east Europe, Asia
23 Nov, 2003	total	Antarctica
19 Apr, 2004	partial	south Africa
14 Oct, 2004	partial	north-east Asia, north Pacific Ocean
8 Apr, 2005	total	east Pacific Ocean, Colombia, Venezuela
3 Oct, 2005	partial	Spain, north and central Africa
29 Mar, 2006	total	west and north Africa, Turkey, south Russia
22 Sept, 2006	partial	Atlantic Ocean
19 Mar, 2007	partial	east Asia, Alaska
11 Sept, 2007	partial	South America, Antarctica
7 Feb, 2008	partial	Antarctica, east Australia, New Zealand
1 Aug, 2008	total	north Canada, Greenland, Siberia, Mongolia, China
26 Jan, 2009	partial	south Africa, Antarctica, south-east Asia, Australia
22 July, 2009	total	India, Nepal, China, central Pacific Ocean
15 Jan, 2010	partial	central Africa, India, Burma, China
11 July, 2010	total	south Pacific Ocean, Easter Island, Chile, Argentina
4 Jan , 2011	partial	Europe, north Africa, central Asia
1 June, 2011	partial	east Asia, Alaska, north Canada, Iceland
1 July, 2011	partial	south Indian Ocean
25 Nov, 2011	partial	south Africa, Antarctica, Tasmania, New Zealand
20 May, 2012	partial	China, Japan, Pacific Ocean, west U.S.A.
13 Nov, 2012	total	north Australia, south Pacific Ocean
10 May, 2013	partial	north Australia, Solomon Islands, Pacific Ocean
3 Nov, 2013	total	Atlantic Ocean, central Africa
29 Apr, 2014	partial	south Indian Ocean, Australia, Antarctica
23 Oct, 2014	partial	north Pacific Ocean, North America
20 Mar, 2015	total	north-east Atlantic Ocean
13 Sept, 2015	partial	south Africa, south Indian Ocean, Antarctica

LUNAR ECLIPSES

DATE	TYPE	BEST SEEN FROM
21 Jan, 2000	total	North & South America
16 July, 2000	total	Australia, west Pacific Ocean
9 Jan, 2001	total	west Asia, Africa, Europe
5 July, 2001	partial	Australia, west Pacific Ocean
16 May, 2003	total	North & South America
9 Nov, 2003	total	Europe, west Africa, North & South America
4 May, 2004	total	west Asia, Africa, Europe
28 Oct, 2004	total	North & South America
17 Oct, 2005	partial	central Pacific Ocean
7 Sept, 2006	partial	Indian Ocean, Asia, east Africa
3 Mar, 2007	total	Africa, Europe
28 Aug, 2007	total	central Pacific, west North & South America
21 Feb, 2008	total	North & South America, west Europe
16 Aug, 2008	partial	west Asia, Europe, Africa
21 Dec, 2009	partial	Asia, Indian Ocean, Africa, Europe
26 June, 2010	partial	central Pacific Ocean, west North & South America
21 Dec, 2010	total	North America, west South America
15 June, 2011	total	south-west Asia, Africa, Indian Ocean
10 Dec, 2011	total	western Pacific Ocean, east Asia, Alaska, Yukon
4 June, 2012	partial	central Pacific Ocean, west North & South America
15 Apr, 2014	total	North America, west South America, Pacific Ocean
8 Oct, 2014	total	Pacific Ocean, west North & South America
4 Apr, 2015	total	Pacific Ocean, west North & South America
28 Sept, 2015	total	west Europe & Africa, North & South America

MANNED MISSIONS TO THE MOON

* The names of the astronauts who landed on the Moon are in italics.

NAME	CREW	LAUNCH DATE	ARRIVAL DATE	LANDING SITE	SAMPLES RETURNED
Apollo 8	Frank Borman, James Lovell, William Anders	21 Dec, 1968	24 Dec, 1968	no landing	no samples
Apollo 10	Thomas Stafford, John Young, Eugene Cernan	18 May, 1969	22 May, 1969	no landing	no samples
Apollo 11	*Neil Armstrong, Edwin Aldrin,* Michael Collins	16 July, 1969	20 July, 1969	Mare Tranquillitatis	22 kg (49 lb)
Apollo 12	*Charles Conrad, Alan Bean,* Richard Gordon	14 Nov, 1969	19 Nov, 1969	Oceanus Procellarum	34 kg (76 lb)
Apollo 13	James Lovell, John Swigert, Fred Haise	11 Apr, 1970	14 Apr, 1970	no landing	no samples
Apollo 14	*Alan Shepard, Edgar Mitchell,* Stuart Roosa	31 Jan, 1971	5 Feb, 1971	Fra Mauro highlands	42 kg (93 lb)
Apollo 15	*David Scott, James Irwin,* Alfred Worden	26 July, 1971	30 July, 1971	Hadley Rille	77 kg (171 lb)
Apollo 16	*John Young, Charles Duke,* Thomas Mattingly	16 Apr, 1972	21 Apr, 1972	Descartes highlands	96 kg (213 lb)
Apollo 17	*Eugene Cernan, Harrison Schmitt,* Ronald Evans	7 Dec, 1972	11 Dec, 1972	Taurus-Littrow valley	111 kg (247 lb)

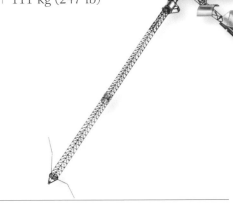

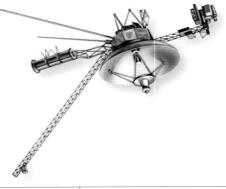

IMPORTANT ROBOT MISSIONS IN THE SOLAR SYSTEM

MISSION	COUNTRY	TYPE	LAUNCH DATE	ARRIVAL DATE	ACHIEVEMENTS
Moon					
Luna 2	Soviet Union	impact	12 Sept, 1959	13 Sept, 1959	first impact
Luna 3	Soviet Union	fly-by	4 Oct, 1959	7 Oct, 1959	first far side images show terrain is mostly highlands
Ranger 7	U.S.A.	impact	28 July, 1964	31 July, 1964	images surface until impact, finds many small craters
Ranger 8	U.S.A.	impact	17 Feb, 1965	20 Feb, 1965	impacts in Mare Tranquillitatis, takes more than 7,000 photos
Ranger 9	U.S.A.	impact	21 Mar, 1965	24 Mar, 1965	impacts in Alphonsus crater, finds volcanic vents
Zond 3	Soviet Union	fly-by	18 July, 1965	20 July, 1965	photographs lunar far side
Luna 9	Soviet Union	lander	31 Jan, 1966	3 Feb, 1966	first soft landing, panoramic photos of surface
Luna 10	Soviet Union	orbiter	31 Mar, 1966	3 Apr, 1966	first spacecraft to orbit the Moon
Surveyor 1	U.S.A.	lander	30 May, 1966	2 June, 1966	first lander to make chemical measurements of surface
Lunar Orbiter 1	U.S.A.	orbiter	10 Aug, 1966	14 Aug, 1966	photo-survey of potential Apollo landing sites
Luna 11	Soviet Union	orbiter	24 Aug, 1966	28 Aug, 1966	photographs surface
Luna 12	Soviet Union	orbiter	22 Oct, 1966	25 Oct, 1966	photographs surface
Lunar Orbiter 2	U.S.A.	orbiter	6 Nov, 1966	10 Nov, 1966	photo-survey of potential Apollo landing sites
Luna 13	Soviet Union	lander	21 Dec, 1966	24 Dec, 1966	panoramic photos, mechanical soil probe
Lunar Orbiter 3	U.S.A.	orbiter	5 Feb, 1967	8 Feb, 1967	photo-survey of potential Apollo landing sites
Surveyor 3	U.S.A.	lander	17 Apr, 1967	20 Apr, 1967	takes more than 6,000 photos, Apollo 12 later lands at site
Lunar Orbiter 4	U.S.A.	orbiter	4 May, 1967	8 May, 1967	photo-survey of entire nearside hemisphere
Lunar Orbiter 5	U.S.A.	orbiter	1 Aug, 1967	5 Aug, 1967	photo-survey of geologically interesting areas
Surveyor 5	U.S.A.	lander	8 Sept, 1967	11 Sept, 1967	analyses surface properties, takes more than 6,300 surface photos
Surveyor 6	U.S.A.	lander	7 Nov, 1967	10 Nov, 1967	takes almost 30,000 surface photos
Surveyor 7	U.S.A.	lander	7 Jan, 1968	10 Jan, 1968	lands near rim of Tycho crater, analyses surface properties
Zond 5	Soviet Union	fly-by	15 Sept, 1968	18 Sept, 1968	flies around Moon, returns to Earth 21 Sept
Zond 6	Soviet Union	fly-by	10 Nov, 1968	14 Nov, 1968	flies around Moon, returns to Earth 17 Nov
Zond 7	Soviet Union	fly-by	7 Aug, 1969	11 Aug, 1969	flies around Moon, returns to Earth 14 Aug
Luna 16	Soviet Union	lander	12 Sept, 1970	20 Sept, 1970	collects rock sample and returns it to Earth
Zond 8	Soviet Union	fly-by	20 Oct, 1970	24 Oct, 1970	flies around Moon, returns to Earth 27 Oct
Luna 17	Soviet Union	rover	10 Nov, 1970	17 Nov, 1970	first robotic rover, drives 10 km (6 mi) on surface
Luna 20	Soviet Union	lander	14 Feb, 1972	21 Feb, 1972	automatic sample return
Luna 21	Soviet Union	rover	8 Jan, 1973	15 Jan, 1973	explores Posidonius crater, drives 37 km (23 mi)
Luna 22	Soviet Union	orbiter	29 May, 1974	2 June, 1974	photo-survey from orbit
Luna 24	Soviet Union	lander	9 Aug, 1976	14 Aug, 1976	lands in Mare Crisium, returns sample to Earth
Hiten (Muses-A)	Japan	fly-by & orbiter	24 Jan, 1990	19 Mar, 1990	flies past Moon and releases satellite
Clementine	U.S.A.	orbiter	25 Jan, 1994	21 Feb, 1994	surveys surface mineralogy at high resolution
Lunar Prospector	U.S.A.	orbiter	7 Jan, 1998	11 Jan, 1998	surveys composition, finds ice in polar craters
Mercury					
Mariner 10	U.S.A.	fly-by	3 Nov, 1973	29 Mar, 1974	first close-up images show cratered surface, detects large iron core
Venus					
Mariner 2	U.S.A.	fly-by	27 Aug, 1962	14 Dec, 1962	first fly-by finds heavy atmosphere, hot surface
Venera 4	Soviet Union	lander	12 June, 1967	18 Oct, 1967	measures atmosphere, fails on descent
Mariner 5	U.S.A.	fly-by	14 June, 1967	19 Oct, 1967	improves measurements of atmospheric pressure and temperature
Venera 5	Soviet Union	lander	5 Jan, 1969	16 May, 1969	studies atmosphere

MISSION	COUNTRY	TYPE	LAUNCH DATE	ARRIVAL DATE	ACHIEVEMENTS
Venus (continued)					
Venera 6	Soviet Union	lander	10 Jan, 1969	17 May, 1969	studies atmosphere
Venera 8	Soviet Union	lander	27 Mar, 1972	22 July, 1972	sends back first data from surface
Mariner 10	U.S.A.	fly-by	4 Nov, 1973	5 Feb, 1974	flies past on way to Mercury, photographs swirling clouds
Venera 9	Soviet Union	orbiter & lander	8 June, 1975	22 Oct, 1975	first images of surface show volcanic rocks
Venera 10	Soviet Union	orbiter & lander	14 June, 1975	25 Oct, 1975	photographs surface rocks and dirt
Pioneer Venus Orbiter	U.S.A.	orbiter	20 May, 1978	4 Dec, 1978	first global radar map of landscape, studies clouds
Pioneer Venus Probes	U.S.A.	entry probes	8 Aug, 1978	9 Dec, 1978	five probes sample atmosphere
Venera 11	Soviet Union	orbiter & lander	9 Sept, 1978	25 Dec, 1978	photographs surface, analyses atmosphere
Venera 12	Soviet Union	orbiter & lander	14 Sept, 1978	21 Dec, 1978	photographs surface, analyses atmosphere
Venera 13	Soviet Union	orbiter & lander	30 Oct, 1981	1 Mar, 1982	photographs surface, analyses atmosphere
Venera 14	Soviet Union	orbiter & lander	4 Nov, 1981	5 Mar, 1982	photographs surface, analyses atmosphere
Venera 15	Soviet Union	orbiter	2 June, 1983	10 Oct, 1983	radar mapping of northern hemisphere
Venera 16	Soviet Union	orbiter	7 June, 1983	14 Oct, 1983	radar mapping of northern hemisphere
Vega 1	Soviet Union	lander & balloon	15 Dec, 1984	11 June, 1985	surveys atmosphere and winds with balloon
Vega 2	Soviet Union	lander & balloon	21 Dec, 1984	16 June, 1985	surveys atmosphere and winds with balloon
Magellan	U.S.A.	orbiter	4 May, 1989	10 Aug, 1990	surveys geology over most of Venus using radar
Galileo	U.S.A.	fly-by	18 Oct, 1989	10 Feb, 1990	flies past on way to Jupiter, studies clouds
Cassini	U.S.A.	fly-by	15 Oct, 1997	26 Apr, 1998	flies past on way to Saturn, studies clouds
Cassini	U.S.A.	fly-by	15 Oct, 1997	24 June, 1999	second Venus fly-by, studies clouds
Mars					
Mariner 4	U.S.A.	fly-by	28 Nov, 1965	14 July, 1965	first close-up images show many craters, thin atmosphere
Mariner 6	U.S.A.	fly-by	24 Feb, 1969	31 July, 1969	returns 75 photos, increases geological knowledge
Mariner 7	U.S.A.	fly-by	27 Mar, 1969	5 Aug, 1969	returns 126 photos, increases geological knowledge
Mars 3	Soviet Union	orbiter & lander	28 May, 1971	3 Dec, 1971	some data and few photos
Mariner 9	U.S.A.	orbiter	30 May, 1971	12 Nov, 1971	first survey of entire surface, finds water channels, big volcanoes
Mars 5	Soviet Union	orbiter	25 July, 1973	12 Feb, 1974	lasts a few days
Mars 6	Soviet Union	orbiter & lander	5 Aug, 1973	12 Mar, 1974	little data returned
Mars 7	Soviet Union	orbiter & lander	9 Aug, 1973	9 Mar, 1974	little data returned
Viking 1	U.S.A.	orbiter & lander	20 Aug, 1975	19 June, 1976	geological survey from orbit, unsuccessful search for life on surface
Viking 2	U.S.A.	orbiter & lander	9 Sept, 1975	7 Aug, 1976	geological survey from orbit, unsuccessful search for life on surface
Mars Global Surveyor	U.S.A.	orbiter	7 Nov, 1996	12 Sept, 1997	maps entire planet at high resolution
Mars Pathfinder	U.S.A.	lander & rover	2 Dec, 1996	4 July, 1997	explores geology of a once-flooded landscape
Nozomi (Planet-B)	Japan	orbiter	J4 July, 1998	Dec, 2003	studies upper atmosphere, magnetosphere, solar wind
Mars Climate Orbiter	U.S.A.	orbiter	11 Dec, 1998	23 Sept, 1999	crashes on arrival, no data returned
Mars Polar Lander	U.S.A.	lander	3 Jan, 1999	3 Dec, 1999	fails upon arrival, no data returned
Deep Space 2	U.S.A.	impactor	3 Jan, 1999	3 Dec, 1999	travels with Polar Lander, searches for subsurface ice
Asteroids					
Galileo	U.S.A.	fly-by	18 Oct, 1989	29 Oct, 1991	first close-up images of an asteroid, 951 Gaspra, show craters
Galileo	U.S.A.	fly-by	18 Oct, 1989	28 Aug, 1993	asteroid 243 Ida: survey of cratered surface, finds moon, Dactyl
NEAR	U.S.A.	fly-by	17 Feb, 1996	27 June, 1997	asteroid 253 Mathilde: reveals big craters, low density
NEAR	U.S.A.	fly-by	17 Feb, 1996	23 Dec, 1998	asteroid 433 Eros: survey of craters and features
Deep Space 1	U.S.A.	fly-by	24 Oct, 1998	29 July, 1999	asteroid 9969 Braille: study of magnetic field, surface composition
NEAR	U.S.A.	orbiter	17 Feb, 1996	14 Feb, 2000	asteroid 433 Eros: first spacecraft to orbit an asteroid
Jupiter					
Pioneer 10	U.S.A.	fly-by	3 Mar, 1972	3 Dec, 1973	first detailed study of a gas-giant planet
Pioneer 11	U.S.A.	fly-by	6 Apr, 1973	3 Dec, 1974	studies polar regions of Jupiter, magnetic environment
Voyager 1	U.S.A.	fly-by	5 Sept, 1977	5 Mar, 1979	first detailed images of planet and moons, discovers ring system
Voyager 2	U.S.A.	fly-by	20 Aug, 1977	9 July, 1979	follow-up on Voyager 1's discoveries
Galileo	U.S.A.	orbiter & entry	18 Oct, 1989	7 Dec, 1995	first atmosphere probe, orbital tour of planet and moons
Saturn					
Pioneer 11	U.S.A.	fly-by	6 Apr, 1973	1 Sept, 1979	first spacecraft visit, discovers new rings
Voyager 1	U.S.A.	fly-by	5 Sept, 1977	12 Nov, 1980	detailed portraits of clouds, rings and moons
Voyager 2	U.S.A.	fly-by	20 Aug, 1977	25 Aug, 1981	follow-up on Voyager 1's discoveries
Cassini	U.S.A.	fly-by	15 Oct, 1997	July, 2004	orbital tour of planet and moons, lander for Titan
Uranus					
Voyager 2	U.S.A.	fly-by	20 Aug, 1977	24 Jan, 1986	first spacecraft visit, studies rings and moons, finds new moons
Neptune					
Voyager 2	U.S.A.	fly-by	20 Aug, 1977	25 Aug, 1989	first spacecraft visit, studies storms, finds geysers on Triton
Pluto					
no mission yet flown					
Comets					
Giotto	European	fly-by	2 July, 1985	14 Mar, 1986	photographs nucleus of Halley's Comet
Stardust	U.S.A.	fly-by	7 Feb, 1999	2 Jan, 2004	sample collection & return from comet Wild 2
Deep Space 1	U.S.A.	fly-by	Oct, 1998	Jan/Sept, 2001	fly-by of comets Wilson-Harrington and Borrelly

CONSTELLATION FACTS

CONSTELLATION	MEANING	HEMISPHERE	HIGHLIGHTS
Andromeda	the Princess	Northern	spiral galaxy M31 (Andromeda), double star Gamma Andromedae, open cluster NGC 752
Antlia	the Air Pump	Southern	planetary nebula NGC 3132, spiral galaxy NGC 2997
Apus	the Bird of Paradise	Southern	double star Delta Apodis, variable star S Apodis, variable star Theta Apodis
Aquarius	the Water Carrier	equatorial	globular cluster M2, planetary nebulas NGC 7009 (Saturn) and NGC 7293 (Helix)
Aquila	the Eagle	equatorial	bright star Altair, variable stars Eta Aquilae and R Aquilae, open cluster NGC 6709
Ara	the Altar	Southern	open cluster NGC 6193, globular cluster NGC 6397
Aries	the Ram	Northern	double stars Gamma Arietis, Lambda Arietis, and Pi Arietis
Auriga	the Charioteer	Northern	bright star Capella, open clusters M36, M37 and M38, double star Omega Aurigae
Boötes	the Herdsman	Northern	bright star Arcturus, double star Mu Boötis
Caelum	the Chisel	Southern	double star Gamma Caeli, variable star R Caeli
Camelopardalis	the Giraffe	Southern	double star Beta Camelopardalis, variable star VZ Camelopardalis, star cluster NGC 1502
Cancer	the Crab	Northern	open clusters M44 (Beehive) and M67, double stars Zeta Cancri and Iota Cancri
Canes Venatici	the Hunting Dogs	Northern	spiral galaxies M51 (Whirlpool) and M94, globular cluster M3
Canis Major	the Big Dog	Southern	bright star Sirius, open clusters M41 and NGC 2362
Canis Minor	the Little Dog	equatorial	bright star Procyon
Capricornus	the Sea Goat	Southern	double stars Alpha Capricorni and Beta Capricorni, globular cluster M30
Carina	the Keel	Southern	bright star Canopus, emission nebula Eta Carinae, open clusters NGC 3532 and IC 2602
Cassiopeia	the Queen	Northern	variable star Gamma Cassiopeiae, open cluster M52
Centaurus	the Centaur	Southern	bright star Alpha Centauri, globular cluster Omega Centauri, elliptical galaxy NGC 5128
Cepheus	the King	Northern	variable stars Delta Cephei and Mu Cephei
Cetus	the Sea Monster	equatorial	variable star Mira Ceti, Seyfert galaxy M77
Chamaeleon	the Chameleon	Southern	double star Delta Chamaeleontis, planetary nebula NGC 3195
Circinus	the Drawing Compass	Southern	double star Alpha Circini
Columba	the Dove	Southern	variable star T Columbae, globular cluster NGC 1851
Coma Berenices	Berenice's Hair	Northern	globular cluster M53, spiral galaxies M64 (Black-eye) and NGC 4565
Corona Australis	the Southern Crown	Southern	double star Kappa Coronae Australis, globular cluster NGC 6541
Corona Borealis	the Northern Crown	Northern	double star Nu Coronae Borealis, variable star R Coronae Borealis
Corvus	the Crow	Southern	variable star R Corvi, galaxies NGC 4038 and NGC 4039 (Antennae galaxies)
Crater	the Cup	Southern	—
Crux	the Southern Cross	Southern	bright star Acrux, open cluster NGC 4755 (Jewel Box), dark nebula the Coalsack
Cygnus	the Swan	Northern	bright star Deneb, double star Beta Cygni, emission nebula NGC 7000 (North America)
Delphinus	the Dolphin	Northern	double star Gamma Delphini
Dorado	the Goldfish	Southern	irregular galaxy the Large Magellanic Cloud, emission nebula NGC 2070 (Tarantula)
Draco	the Dragon	Northern	double stars Psi Draconis and 39 Draconis, planetary nebula NGC 6543
Equuleus	the Little Horse	Northern	double star Gamma Equulei
Eridanus	the River	Southern	bright star Achernar, triple star Omicron 2 Eridani
Fornax	the Furnace	Southern	barred spiral galaxy NGC 1365 (Great Barred Spiral)
Gemini	the Twins	Northern	bright stars Castor and Pollux, open cluster M35, planetary nebula NGC 2392 (Clownface)
Grus	the Crane	Southern	double stars Delta Gruis and Mu Gruis
Hercules	the Strongman	Northern	variable star Alpha Herculis, globular clusters M13 (Hercules) and M92
Horologium	the Clock	Southern	variable stars R Horologii and TW Horologii
Hydra	the Sea Serpent	equatorial	double star 27 Hydrae, open cluster M48, planetary nebula NGC 3242, spiral galaxy M83
Hydrus	the Water Snake	Southern	double star Pi Hydri
Indus	the Indian	Southern	double star Theta Indi
Lacerta	the Lizard	Northern	—
Leo	the Lion	equatorial	bright star Regulus, double star Gamma Leonis, spiral galaxies M65 and M66
Leo Minor	the Little Lion	Northern	—
Lepus	the Hare	Southern	double star Gamma Leporis, globular cluster M79
Libra	the Scales	Southern	double star Alpha Librae, variable star Delta Librae
Lupus	the Wolf	Southern	open cluster NGC 5822, globular cluster NGC 5986
Lynx	the Lynx	Northern	—
Lyra	the Lyre	Northern	bright star Vega, variable star Beta Lyrae, planetary nebula M57 (Ring)
Mensa	the Table	Southern	—
Microscopium	the Microscope	Southern	double star Alpha Microscopii
Monoceros	the Unicorn	equatorial	open cluster M50, nebulas NGC 2237 (Rosette) and NGC 2264 (Cone)
Musca	the Fly	Southern	double star Theta Muscae, globular clusters NGC 4372 and NGC 4833
Norma	the Level	Southern	open clusters NGC 6067 and NGC 6087
Octans	the Octant	Southern	pole star Sigma Octantis, double star Lambda Octantis
Ophiuchus	the Serpent Carrier	equatorial	open clusters IC 4665 and NGC 6633, globular clusters M10 and M12
Orion	the Hunter	equatorial	bright stars Betelgeuse and Rigel, emission nebula M42 (Orion), dark nebula IC 434 (Horsehead)
Pavo	the Peacock	Southern	variable star Kappa Pavonis, globular cluster NGC 6752
Pegasus	the Flying Horse	Northern	double star Epsilon Pegasi, globular cluster M15
Perseus	the Hero	Northern	variable star Algol (Beta Persei), open clusters NGC 869 and NGC 884 (Double Cluster)
Phoenix	the Firebird	Southern	double and variable star Zeta Phoenicis
Pictor	the Painter's Easel	Southern	—
Pisces	the Fishes	equatorial	double star Rho and 94 Piscium, spiral galaxy M74
Piscis Austrinus	the Southern Fish	Southern	bright star Fomalhaut
Puppis	the Stern	Southern	variable star L2 Puppis, open clusters M46 and M47
Pyxis	the Compass	Southern	—

CONSTELLATION	MEANING	HEMISPHERE	HIGHLIGHTS
Reticulum	the Reticle	Southern	double star Zeta Reticuli
Sagitta	the Arrow	Northern	globular cluster M71
Sagittarius	the Archer	Southern	globular clusters M22 and M23, emission nebulas M8 (Lagoon), M17 (Omega), M20 (Trifid)
Scorpius	the Scorpion	Southern	bright star Antares, double star Beta Scorpii, open cluster M7, globular clusters M4 and M80
Sculptor	the Sculptor	Southern	spiral galaxies NGC 253 and NGC 55
Scutum	the Shield	Northern	open cluster M11 (Wild Duck)
Serpens	the Serpent	equatorial	double star Nu Serpentis, emission nebula M16 (Eagle), globular cluster M5
Sextans	the Sextant	equatorial	double star 17 and 18 Sextantis, elliptical galaxy NGC 3115 (Spindle)
Taurus	the Bull	equatorial	bright star Aldebaran, open clusters M45 (Pleiades) and Hyades, supernova remnant M1 (Crab)
Telescopium	the Telescope	Southern	double star Delta Telescopii
Triangulum	the Triangle	Northern	spiral galaxy M33 (Pinwheel)
Triangulum Australe	the Southern Triangle	Southern	variable star R Trianguli Australe, open cluster NGC 6025
Tucana	the Toucan	Southern	double star Beta Tucanae, globular cluster 47 Tucanae, irregular galaxy the Small Magellanic Cloud
Ursa Major	the Big Bear	Northern	double star Mizar and Alcor, spiral galaxies M81 and M101, peculiar galaxy M82
Ursa Minor	the Little Bear	Northern	Polaris the Pole Star, double star Gamma and 11 Ursae Minoris
Vela	the Sails	Southern	double star Gamma Velorum, open clusters IC 2391 and NGC 2547
Virgo	the Maiden	equatorial	bright star Spica, elliptical galaxies M47, M87 and M104 (Sombrero), quasar 3C 273
Volans	the Flying Fish	Southern	double star Gamma Volantis, barred spiral galaxy NGC 2442
Vulpecula	the Little Fox	Northern	planetary nebula M27 (Dumb-bell)

BRIGHTEST STAR FACTS

STAR	CONSTELLATION	COLOUR AND TYPE	COMPANION STARS	APPARENT MAGNITUDE	ACTUAL MAGNITUDE	DIAMETER (SUN = 1)	DISTANCE FROM EARTH	WHAT YOU NEED TO SEE IT
Sirius	Canis Major	white main sequence	1 companion	−1.44	+1.4	2.4	8.6 ly	naked eye
Canopus	Carina	white giant	0 companions	−0.72	−3.5	80	117 ly	naked eye
Alpha Centauri	Centaurus	yellow main sequence	2 companions	−0.28	+4.4	1.0	4.3 ly	naked eye
Arcturus	Boötes	red giant	0 companions	−0.05	−0.27	20	36.7 ly	naked eye
Vega	Lyra	white main sequence	0 companions	+0.03	+0.48	2.4	25.3 ly	naked eye
Capella	Auriga	yellow giant	1 companion	+0.08	−0.60	10	42 ly	naked eye
Rigel	Orion	blue-white supergiant	1 companion	+0.14	−6.8	55	773 ly	naked eye
Procyon	Canis Minor	white subgiant	1 companion	+0.40	+2.68	1.3	11.4 ly	naked eye
Betelgeuse	Orion	red supergiant	0 companions	+0.41	−5.5	800	427 ly	naked eye
Achernar	Eridanus	blue-white main sequence	0 companions	+0.45	−2.5	3.9	144 ly	naked eye

VARIABLE STAR FACTS

STAR	CONSTELLATION	TYPE	MAGNITUDE RANGE	PERIOD (DAYS)
R Canis Majoris	Canis Major	eclipsing	5.7–6.3	1.1
Algol (Beta Persei)	Perseus	eclipsing	2.1–3.4	2.9
Delta Cephei	Cepheus	Cepheid	3.5–4.4	5.4
Eta Aquilae	Aquila	Cepheid	3.5–4.3	7.2
Beta Lyrae	Lyra	eclipsing	3.4–4.3	12.9
Alpha Herculis	Hercules	semi-regular	3.0–4.0	50–130
L2 Puppis	Puppis	pulsating	2.6–6.2	141
Mira (Omicron Ceti)	Cetus	pulsating	3.4–9.3	332
R Hydrae	Hydra	pulsating	3.4–10.7	389
RX Leporis	Lepus	irregular	5.4–7.4	irreg.

NOTES ON CONSTELLATION FACTS.

HEMISPHERE: This tells you where the constellation is most easily seen – in the Northern Hemisphere, the Southern Hemisphere, or around the Equator. Depending on where you live, you might be able to see a constellation that is not listed for your part of the world. Refer to the star maps, pages 94–109.

NOTES ON STAR & STAR CLUSTER FACTS

COMPANIONS: This tells you whether the star is part of a double or multiple system.

APPARENT MAGNITUDE: This is how bright the planet appears in the sky. Brighter objects have smaller numbers than dimmer objects.

DISTANCE FROM EARTH: The figures for distance (and for the diameter of star clusters) are in light-years (ly).

STAR CLUSTER FACTS

CLUSTER	CONSTELLATION	TYPE	NUMBER OF STARS	APPARENT MAGNITUDE	DIAMETER	DISTANCE FROM EARTH	WHAT YOU NEED TO SEE IT
Hyades	Taurus	open	100	0.8	17 ly	150 ly	naked eye
Pleiades	Taurus	open	several hundred	1.6	13 ly	375 ly	naked eye
Beehive	Cancer	open	50	3.9	15 ly	590 ly	binoculars
Double Cluster	Perseus	open	350	4.3	61 ly	7,000 ly	telescope
47 Tucanae	Tucana	globular	460,000	4.4	125 ly	16,000 ly	telescope
Omega Centauri	Centaurus	globular	1,100,000	4.5	180 ly	17,000 ly	telescope
Jewel Box	Crux	open	50	5.2	24 ly	6,800 ly	telescope
Hercules cluster (M13)	Hercules	globular	220,000	6.4	110 ly	21,000 ly	telescope
M15	Pegasus	globular	410,000	7.0	120 ly	34,000 ly	telescope
M4	Scorpius	globular	44,000	7.1	50 ly	14,000 ly	telescope

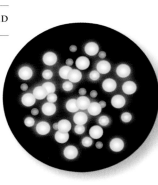

NEBULA FACTS

NEBULA	CONSTELLATION	TYPE	APPARENT MAGNITUDE	DIAMETER	DISTANCE FROM EARTH	WHAT YOU NEED TO SEE IT
NGC 7293 (Helix nebula)	Aquarius	planetary	6.5	2 ly	600 ly	telescope
M27 (Dumb-bell nebula)	Vulpecula	planetary	8.1	2 ly	815 ly	telescope
M57 (Ring nebula)	Lyra	planetary	9.0	0.4 ly	1,140 ly	telescope
IC 434 (Horsehead nebula)	Orion	dark	—	20 ly?	1,200 ly?	telescope
M42 (Orion nebula)	Orion	emission	4.0	40 ly	1,500 ly	telescope
NGC 2264 (Cone nebula)	Monoceros	dark	—	50 ly	3,000 ly	telescope
M20 (Trifid nebula)	Sagittarius	emission/reflection	8.5	40 ly	5,000 ly	telescope
M8 (Lagoon nebula)	Sagittarius	emission	5.8	130 ly	5,200 ly	telescope
M1 (Crab nebula)	Taurus	supernova remnant	8.4	13.7 ly	6,520 ly	telescope
M16 (Eagle nebula)	Serpens	emission	6.0	315 ly	7,000 ly	telescope

GALAXY FACTS

GALAXY	CONSTELLATION	TYPE	GALAXY CLUSTER	APPARENT MAGNITUDE	DIAMETER	DISTANCE FROM EARTH	WHAT YOU NEED TO SEE IT
M81	Ursa Major	spiral	Coma-Sculptor cloud	7.9	30,000 ly	4,500,000 ly	telescope
M83	Hydra	spiral	Coma-Sculptor cloud	8.2	52,000 ly	15,000,000 ly	telescope
M51 (Whirlpool)	Canes Venatici	spiral	Coma-Sculptor cloud	9.0	50,000 ly	15,000,000 ly	telescope
M101	Ursa Major	spiral	Coma-Sculptor cloud	7.9	120,000 ly	17,500,000 ly	telescope
NGC 6946	Cepheus	spiral	Coma-Sculptor cloud	8.9	78,000 ly	18,000,000 ly	telescope
NGC 5128 (Centaurus A)	Centaurus	giant elliptical	Coma-Sculptor cloud	7.0	138,000 ly	26,000,000 ly	telescope
M87	Virgo	giant elliptical	Virgo cluster	8.6	147,000 ly	55,000,000 ly	telescope
NGC 1365 (Great Barred Spiral)	Fornax	barred spiral	Fornax cluster	9.5	157,800 ly	55,000,000 ly	telescope
M104 (Sombrero)	Virgo	spiral	Virgo cluster	8.3	160,000 ly	65,000,000 ly	telescope
NGC 4038/4039 (Antennae)	Corvus	spiral	Crater cloud	10.7	220,000 ly	82,800,000 ly	telescope
NGC 1275	Perseus	Seyfert	Perseus cluster	11.6	175,000 ly	230,000,000 ly	telescope
3C 273	Virgo	quasar	unknown	12.0	unknown	1,900,000,000 ly	telescope

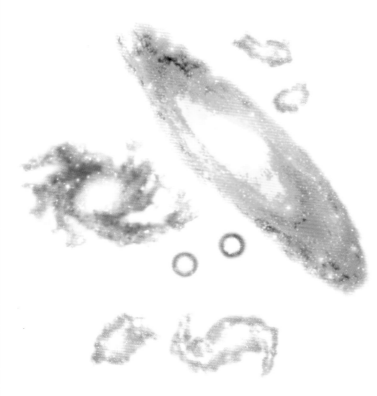

LOCAL GROUP FACTS

GALAXY	TYPE	APPARENT MAGNITUDE	DIAMETER	DISTANCE FROM EARTH
Milky Way	spiral	—	100,000 ly	—
SagDEG	elliptical	3.6	unknown	80,000 ly
Large Magellanic Cloud	irregular	0.6	34,000 ly	179,000 ly
Small Magellanic Cloud	irregular	2.8	17,000 ly	210,000 ly
Sculptor dwarf	irregular	9.1	1,400 ly	284,000 ly
Sextans I	elliptical	10.3	3,000 ly	300,000 ly
Ursa Minor dwarf	elliptical	10.0	1,000 ly	300,000 ly
Carina	elliptical	10.6	500 ly	300,000 ly
Draco dwarf	elliptical	10.9	500 ly	300,000 ly
Fornax dwarf	elliptical	8.5	3,000 ly	500,000 ly
Leo I	elliptical	11.8	1,000 ly	600,000 ly
Leo II	elliptical	12.3	500 ly	600,000 ly
NGC 6822	irregular	9.3	8,000 ly	1,700,000 ly
Wolf-Lundmark-Melotte	irregular	11.3	7,000 ly	2,000,000 ly
IC 5152	irregular	11.7	5,000 ly	2,000,000 ly
NGC 205	elliptical	8.6	10,000 ly	2,200,000 ly
NGC 147	elliptical	10.4	10,000 ly	2,200,000 ly
NGC 185	elliptical	10.1	6,000 ly	2,200,000 ly
M32	elliptical	9.0	5,000 ly	2,200,000 ly
Andromeda III	elliptical	13.5	3,000 ly	2,200,000 ly
Andromeda I	elliptical	14.4	2,000 ly	2,200,000 ly
Andromeda II	elliptical	13.0	2,000 ly	2,200,000 ly
M31 (Andromeda)	spiral	4.4	128,000 ly	2,500,000 ly
IC 1613	irregular	10.0	12,000 ly	2,500,000 ly
M33 (Pinwheel)	spiral	6.3	50,000 ly	2,600,000 ly
DDO 210	irregular	15.3	4,000 ly	3,000,000 ly
Pisces	irregular	15.5	500 ly	3,000,000 ly
IC 10	irregular	11.7	6,000 ly	4,000,000 ly
Sextans A	irregular	—	unknown	4,000,000 ly?
SagDIG	irregular	15.6	5,000 ly	4,000,000 ly
GR 8	irregular	14.6	200 ly	4,000,000 ly
Antlia	elliptical	14.8	unknown	4,100,000 ly?
Pegasus	irregular	12.4	8,000 ly	5,000,000 ly
Leo A	irregular	12.7	7,000 ly	5,000,000 ly
Tucana	elliptical	15.1	unknown	unknown

NOTES ON NEBULA, GALAXY AND LOCAL GROUP FACTS

APPARENT MAGNITUDE: This is how bright the planet appears in the sky. Brighter objects have smaller numbers than dimmer objects.

DIAMETER/DISTANCE FROM EARTH: The figures given are in light-years (ly).

• A question mark indicates that the value is an unconfirmed estimate.

UNIVERSAL RECORDS

HOTTEST PLANET SURFACE IN OUR SOLAR SYSTEM
The surface of Venus, 470°C (880°F). At its hottest, Mercury comes pretty close: 427°C (800°F). Venus' thick atmosphere traps the Sun's heat, so midnight temperatures are as hot as those at noon. (And the rocks are hot enough to glow dull red.)

COLDEST PLANET SURFACE IN OUR SOLAR SYSTEM
Pluto when furthest from the Sun. The actual temperature at that point has not yet been measured because Pluto has not made a full orbit since it was discovered in 1930. Pluto will reach the furthest point in its orbit in February 2114. At present, Pluto's surface temperature is –233°C (–387°F) – and it is slowly falling.

BIGGEST CRATER IN OUR SOLAR SYSTEM
South Pole-Aitken Basin on the Moon, roughly 2,500 kilometres (1,600 mi) in diameter. This ancient impact scar is so heavily marked with smaller craters that it was not discovered until the Clementine probe visited the Moon in 1994. Scientists used data from Clementine to carefully map the Moon's surface. This mapping revealed the basin, a broad depression in the lunar far side that is more than 12 kilometres (7 mi) deep.

TALLEST MOUNTAIN IN OUR SOLAR SYSTEM
Olympus Mons on Mars, rising 24 kilometres (15 mi) above its base. The second tallest is Maxwell Montes on Venus, which rises 11 kilometres (7 mi) above the planet's average surface. Earth's officially tallest peak is Mount Everest, 8.8 kilometres (5.5 mi) above sea level. However, Hawaii's Mauna Kea can also claim to be the tallest, since it rises about 9 kilometres (5.6 mi) above the ocean floor it stands on.

BIGGEST CANYON IN OUR SOLAR SYSTEM
Valles Marineris on Mars, roughly 4,000 kilometres (2,500 mi) long, with a maximum width of about 600 kilometres (370 mi) and a maximum depth of 8 kilometres (5 mi). In Europe, it would stretch from Paris, France, to Russia's Ural Mountains. If it were in the United States, this canyon could extend from San Francisco on the west coast to the Appalachian Mountains in Virginia near the east coast.

BIGGEST MOON IN OUR SOLAR SYSTEM
Jupiter's Ganymede, 5,268 kilometres (3,273 mi) in diameter. If Ganymede orbited the Sun instead of Jupiter, it would easily qualify as a planet. It is larger than either Mercury or Pluto.

BIGGEST PLANET IN OUR SOLAR SYSTEM
Jupiter, with 317.8 times the mass of Earth, and about 11 times its diameter. Jupiter contains more mass than all the rest of the planets, moons, comets and asteroids put together.

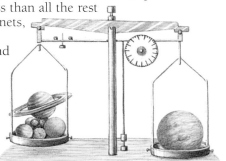

BIGGEST KNOWN PLANET
An unnamed planet orbiting the star HD 114762. This planet appears to have 11 times the mass of Jupiter, but some astronomers think it may actually be a brown dwarf, an object that is like a small, dim, cool star. If it is a brown dwarf, then the most massive planet would be one with 6.6 times Jupiter's mass that orbits the star 70 Virginis. (This Universal Record is very likely to change as research continues.)

GREATEST METEOR SHOWER
The Leonids on 13 November, 1833, with up to 200,000 meteors per hour. Onlookers said that the meteors 'fell like snowflakes', and many uneducated people thought the world was about to come to an end. The remarkable display helped astronomers realize that meteors were entering Earth's atmosphere from outer space, and were not just an Earth-based event like rain.

BIGGEST METEORITE
Hoba meteorite in Namibia, weighing 60 tonnes (65 tons) – about as heavy as nine elephants! Discovered in 1920, this iron meteorite almost 3 metres (10 ft) long still lies in the ground where it landed. It was originally even larger – the discoloured soil surrounding it shows that part of the meteorite has weathered away.

BIGGEST ASTEROID
1 Ceres, 913 kilometres (567 mi) in diameter. This largest of all asteroids was also the first one to be found – on the first day of the 19th century: 1 January, 1801. The discoverer of Ceres was Giuseppe Piazzi (1746–1826) and the place was the Palermo Observatory in Sicily.

CLOSEST COMET TO EARTH
Comet Lexell in 1770, at a distance of 2.2 million kilometres (1.4 million mi) from Earth – less than six times the distance to the Moon. Despite coming so close, this comet never developed much of a tail and its head looked no bigger than five times the size of the Moon in our night sky.

LONGEST COMET TAIL
Great Comet of March 1843, 300 million kilometres (190 million mi) long. This tail was long enough to reach from the Sun to well past the orbit of Mars. When it passed closest to the Sun, the comet was only about 130,000 kilometres (80,000 mi) above the Sun's surface. Planetary scientists call such comets 'sungrazers'.

BRIGHTEST STAR IN OUR NIGHT SKY
Sirius, –1.46 magnitude. Sirius is actually a double star, and its dim companion was the first white dwarf star to be discovered.

BROADEST STAR
Betelgeuse in Orion, about 800 times the Sun's diameter. If it replaced the Sun in our Solar System, this bloated red super giant star would reach past the orbit of Jupiter.

LARGEST STAR
Eta Carinae, about 150 times as large as the Sun. Astronomers are not certain if Eta Carinae is really one star or two.

SMALLEST STAR
Gliese 105C, about 10 per cent as large as the Sun. This is about as small as a star can be and still be a true star (an object that fuses hydrogen into helium).

NEAREST STAR
Proxima Centauri, third member of the Alpha Centauri system. This cool red dwarf star lies about 4.2 light-years away, about 0.1 light-year closer to us than the other two stars in the system.

GLOBULAR STAR CLUSTER WITH THE MOST STARS
Omega Centauri, with 1.1 million stars. This globular cluster measures about 180 light-years in diameter.

LARGEST GALAXY
Giant elliptical M87 in the constellation of Virgo, with at least 800 billion Suns worth of mass. M87 is a member of the Virgo cluster of galaxies.

SMALLEST GALAXY
The Pegasus II dwarf elliptical, about 10 million solar masses. Smaller galaxies may exist, but because they are not very luminous, astronomers cannot detect them unless they also lie close to us.

NEAREST GALAXY
Sagittarius dwarf elliptical, 80,000 light-years away. This galaxy is the current record holder, but surveys find new dwarf elliptical galaxies every year or so, and an even closer galaxy may yet be found.

MOST DISTANT OBJECT VISIBLE TO THE NAKED EYE
Andromeda galaxy (M31), 2.5 million light-years away. When you look at this galaxy, you are seeing light that left the galaxy when the most recent great Ice Ages were beginning on Earth.

MOST DISTANT OBJECT DETECTED
An unnamed galaxy in Ursa Major, 12.6 billion light-years away. This galaxy may not hold the record for very long. Astronomers working with giant telescopes on Earth and the Hubble Space Telescope find a new and more distant record-holder once or twice a year.

Timeline of Astronomy

30,000 BC Lunar phases scratched on bone – the oldest astronomical record?

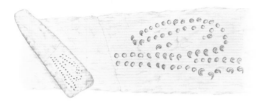

4,000 BC Sumerians of Mesopotamia make the first records of Leo, Taurus and Scorpius, the oldest constellations still used today.

600 BC Greek philosopher Thales probably knows the cause of solar and lunar eclipses.

525 BC Greek philosopher Pythagoras recognizes that Earth is round.

350 BC Greek philosopher Aristotle provides a scientific explanation of why Earth is round.

325 BC Greek mathematician Eudoxus explains celestial motions in terms of several crystal spheres with Earth at their centre.

300 BC Greek astronomer Aristarchus proposes a Sun-centred model for the universe. But his ideas are ignored until Copernicus' time, almost 2,000 years later.

200 BC Greek astronomer Eratosthenes measures the circumference of Earth, getting a result close to the modern one.

150 BC Greek astronomer Hipparchus creates system of magnitudes to measure star brightness, discovers a slow wobble in Earth's axis (precession) and creates the first star catalogue.

AD 150 Greek astronomer Claudius Ptolemy publishes the *Almagest*, a detailed summing-up of all the ancient world's astronomical knowledge. It dominates the subject for more than 1,000 years.

AD 165 Chinese astronomers make the first accurately dated observations, recording sunspots on the face of the Sun.

AD 635 A Chinese scholar records the rule that a comet's tail always points away from the Sun.

1543 Nicolaus Copernicus publishes his book *On the Revolutions of the Celestial Spheres*, proposing a Sun-centred Solar System.

1572 Tycho Brahe sees a supernova in Cassiopeia and determines that it lies beyond the Moon. This discovery conflicts with ancient ideas of the heavens being unchangeable, and it encourages Tycho to make a whole new set of accurate observations.

1576 Tycho builds his Uraniborg observatory on an island in the Baltic Sea and begins compiling the world's most accurate observations of the motions of stars and planets.

1600 Tycho Brahe hires Johannes Kepler as his mathematical assistant to work on the observations.

1608 Hans Lippershey in the Netherlands invents the telescope.

1609 Using Tycho Brahe's observations, Kepler determines that Mars' orbit is elliptical, a key advance over ancient astronomy, which had insisted on circular orbits. Galileo Galilei hears of the telescope and, following the reported description, builds his own. He is the first person to use the telescope for astronomy.

1610 Galileo publishes his telescope discoveries of moons orbiting Jupiter, craters on the Moon and stars in the Milky Way. He starts promoting a Copernican model of the Solar System.

1616 The Roman Catholic Church bans Copernican ideas as 'false and absurd'.

1619 Kepler discovers a simple mathematical relationship between the length of a planet's year and its distance from the Sun.

1633 Galileo is put under house arrest by the Church for promoting Copernican ideas.

1665 Isaac Newton starts developing mathematical physics.

1687 Newton publishes his book *The Mathematical Principles of Natural Philosophy*, which links astronomy with physics and puts both on firm mathematical ground.

1727 James Bradley discovers the aberration of starlight, an apparent shift in the positon of a star caused by the motion of Earth. It is the first physical proof that Earth moves around the Sun.

1758 Halley's Comet returns as forecast by Edmond Halley, the first predicted return of a comet.

1781 William Herschel discovers seventh planet, Uranus. This is the first planet to be discovered since pre-historic times.

1833 A spectacular Leonid meteor shower shows astronomers that meteors come from space and do not originate in the atmosphere.

1835 The Roman Catholic Church removes books by Copernicus and Galileo from its list of banned works.

1838 Friedrich Bessel measures the parallax of 61 Cygni, the first direct measurement of a star's distance.

1846 Johann Galle and Heinrich d'Arrest find the eighth planet, Neptune, following predictions made by Urbain Leverrier (and, independently, by John C. Adams).

1860s The spectroscope begins to show astronomers what stars and nebulas are made of.

1880s Photography becomes an important tool for astronomy because it can detect things in the sky that people cannot see and it provides a permanent record.

1905 Albert Einstein's special theory of relativity is published.

1908 Ejnar Hertzsprung divides the population of stars into two groups, giants and dwarfs. It is the first step in learning how stars change as they age.

1910 The return of Halley's Comet creates the world's first media event.

1912 Henrietta Leavitt discovers that Cepheid variable stars with long periods of variation are systematically brighter than those with shorter periods.
Vesto Slipher discovers that most 'spiral nebulas' are flying away from Earth, the first detection of an expanding universe.

1916 Einstein publishes his general theory of relativity, which predicts that the universe is expanding.

1917 2.5 metre (100 in) Hooker reflector telescope completed at Mount Wilson, California, U.S.A.

1919 Einstein's general theory of relativity is confirmed by observations of a total solar eclipse seen from Brazil and West Africa.

1923 Edwin Hubble uses Cepheid variables to show that 'spiral nebulas' are galaxies lying outside the Milky Way.

1929 Hubble presents observational evidence for an expanding universe and provides the first estimates of its age and rate of expansion.

1930 Clyde Tombaugh discovers the ninth planet, Pluto.

1931 Karl Jansky builds a rotating aerial and discovers radio waves coming from space. These radio waves had been predicted in the 1880s but were not found because astronomers had no way to detect them.

1937 Grote Reber discovers radio waves coming from the centre of the Milky Way, using a radio telescope built in his own garden.

1938 Hans Bethe publishes a theory explaining how the Sun and other stars shine because of nuclear reactions.

1942 John Hey and colleagues discover radio noise coming from the Sun.

1946 Hey and colleagues identify the most powerful radio source in the sky, the radio galaxy Cygnus A.

1948 George Gamow, Ralph Alpher and Robert Herman describe how chemical elements were formed in the Big Bang. 5 metre (200 in) Hale Telescope is completed at Palomar Mountain, California, U.S.A. Jan Oort proposes that comets come from a vast cloud orbiting far beyond Pluto.

1952 Walter Baade announces that galaxies are twice as far away as astronomers had previously assumed.

1957 Launch of Sputnik 1 satellite by the Soviet Union (now Russia) starts the Space Age.

1959 First photographs of the Moon's farside returned by Soviet probe, Luna 3.

1961 Yuri Gagarin from the Soviet Union is the first person to fly in space.

1962 Mariner 2 spacecraft flies past Venus, first probe to visit another planet, discovers dense atmosphere and verifies hot surface. Orbiting Solar Observatory, the first astronomical satellite, is launched.

1963 Maarten Schmidt discovers that quasars are objects with big redshifts and must lie very far away.

1965 Arno Penzias and Robert Wilson discover the cosmic background radiation – the faded glow of the Big Bang explosion in which the universe began. Mariner 4 spacecraft is the first to fly past Mars. It discovers lots of craters.

1967 Jocelyn Bell-Burnell discovers pulsars, which are soon identified as neutron stars, one of the objects that massive stars can become.

1969 Apollo 11 astronauts Neil Armstrong and Edwin Aldrin make the first manned landing on the Moon.

1971 Mariner 9 is the first spacecraft to orbit another planet, Mars. Finds evidence of past water.

1973 Pioneer 10 makes first fly-by of Jupiter and detects powerful radiation belts.

1974 Mariner 10 makes first two of three fly-bys of Mercury (third in 1975). Finds evidence of massive iron core and giant impacts.

1975 Venera 9 takes the first photos from the surface of Venus.

1976 Viking 1 and 2 land on Mars. They find no signs of life.

1977 Charles Kowal finds Chiron, the first comet discovered in the outer solar system. Uranus' rings are discovered by astronomers aboard the Kuiper Airborne Observatory.

1978 James Christy discovers Charon, Pluto's moon.

1979 Voyager 1 and 2 spacecraft fly past Jupiter. Make detailed survey of planet and moons and find its rings. Pioneer 11 makes first fly-by of Saturn.

1980 Alan Guth proposes a period of extremely fast expansion in the early history of the universe, which he calls cosmic inflation. Voyager 1 spacecraft makes first detailed study of Saturn system. Very Large Array radio telescope starts working in New Mexico, U.S.A.

1983 Infrared Astronomical Satellite (IRAS) completes the first full survey of the infrared sky.

1985/6 Halley's Comet's return is met by a fleet of space probes.

1986 Voyager 2 makes first fly-by of Uranus.

1987 Supernova 1987A appears in the Large Magellanic Cloud.

1989 Voyager 2 spacecraft makes first fly-by of Neptune. Captures details of the planet and its moons – and its rings, suspected to exist since 1981. Margaret Geller and John Huchra announce evidence for walls and voids in the distribution of galaxies in the universe.

1990 Hubble Space Telescope is launched.

1991 Galileo spacecraft on the way to Jupiter makes first asteroid fly-by, passing 951 Gaspra. Compton Gamma-Ray Observatory begins survey of universe at high-energy wavelengths, seeking cause of mysterious bursts of high energy.

1992 COBE satellite observatory confirms predictions of Big Bang theory.

1993 First 10 metre (394 in) Keck telescope begins operation on Mauna Kea, Hawaii. Hubble Space Telescope repaired in orbit.

1994 Comet Shoemaker-Levy 9 crashes into Jupiter.

1995 Discovery of first planet to orbit ordinary star other than the Sun, orbiting 51 Pegasi. Galileo spacecraft sends probe into Jupiter's atmosphere, begins tour of Jupiter's moons.

1996 Black hole confirmed at centre of Milky Way galaxy.

1997 Burst of gamma rays tracked to source far from Milky Way, perhaps caused by colliding neutron stars. Mars Pathfinder lands on Mars with Sojourner Rover.

1999 Chandra X-Ray Observatory is launched to look for X-rays from distant objects.

Glossary

A

active galaxy ~ A galaxy that emits a lot of radiation, perhaps from gas falling into a central black hole.

antenna ~ A device used to collect radio waves from the universe. Many antennas are made of an open mesh of aluminium or steel.

asteroid ~ A small rocky or metallic object orbiting the Sun, sometimes called a minor planet. Most asteroids orbit in the main asteroid belt between Mars and Jupiter.

astronomical unit (AU) ~ The average distance between Earth and the Sun, about 150 million km (93 million mi).

astronomy ~ The scientific study of the universe, including the Solar System, stars and galaxies.

atmosphere ~ A layer of gas surrounding a planet, moon or star.

aurora ~ A colourful glow in Earth's upper atmosphere caused by the impact of high-energy particles from the Sun. Sometimes called the aurora borealis (or Northern Lights) and the aurora australis (or Southern Lights).

axis (as in rotation axis) ~ The imaginary line through the centre of a planet, moon, star or galaxy around which it rotates.

B

belt ~ A band of dark clouds on a gas-giant planet. Also, a region of the Solar System, such as the asteroid belt between Mars and Jupiter.

Big Bang ~The extremely hot explosion that produced all the matter in the universe about 12 to 15 billion years ago, according to the best current theory of the universe's origin.

Big Crunch ~ One possible future fate for the universe. According to this theory, at some far distant time, gravity would stop the current expansion of the universe and then pull all matter back together into a single, highly compressed black hole.

billion ~ A million million. In numerals, it is written as 1,000,000,000,000.

binoculars ~ Two low-power telescopes yoked together. Binoculars make a good 'first telescope' for beginners.

black hole ~ A massive, infinitely dense object whose gravity is so strong that no light or other radiation can escape from it. Black holes can be large or small, depending on how much mass they contain.

brightness ~ The intensity of light (or other radiation) emitted by an object. On Earth we see the object's apparent brightness, which depends on how bright it really is and how far away it lies. Astronomers also calculate an actual (or absolute) brightness based on how bright an object would be at a standard distance of 32.6 light-years.

brown dwarf ~ A star-like object not quite large enough to start hydrogen fusion reactions and shine like a true star. It has less than 10% of the Sun's mass.

C

canyon ~ A long channel in the surface of a planet or moon caused by geological faulting or by erosion.

capture ~ The process in which the gravity of a planet or moon attracts and holds onto another body. Astronomers think Neptune captured its moon Triton early in the planet's history.

celestial object ~ Any natural object that appears in our sky. Planets, moons, asteroids, comets, stars and galaxies are all celestial objects.

celestial poles ~ The imaginary points among the northern and southern stars where Earth's rotation axis, if extended, would touch the sky.

cluster ~ A group of stars or galaxies that is held together by their gravity.

coma ~ The gaseous atmosphere that surrounds the icy nucleus of a comet. It forms as the comet's ice evaporate in the warmth of sunlight and can be thousands of kilometres wide.

comet ~ A small body made of ice and dust that orbits the Sun on an elongated path. When near the Sun, its ice grow warm, and the comet develops a large coma and streams off long tails of dust and gas.

command module ~ The main part of the Apollo spacecraft that carried the crew. It did not descend to the Moon's surface.

constellation ~ One of the 88 officially recognized patterns of stars that divide up the entire night sky. Most constellations that we use today came from the star myths and legends of ancient civilizations.

continent ~ The largest kind of land mass on Earth, and perhaps on other planets as well.

convection ~ A heat-driven process in which hot material moves up in an atmosphere, in a star or even in a planet whose rocks are softened by heat. Water boiling in a pot moves by convection.

convective zone ~ A region in an atmosphere, a star or a planet where convection occurs.

Copernican model ~ The model of the Solar System that places the Sun at the centre with the planets in orbit around it. It is named after Nicolaus Copernicus (1472–1543), the Polish astronomer and churchman who described it in his book *On the Revolutions of the Celestial Spheres*.

core ~ The central part of an object. Earth's core contains nickel and iron. The Sun gets its energy from nuclear fusion reactions in its core. The Milky Way galaxy may have a black hole in its core.

corona ~ The high-temperature outer atmosphere of the Sun. It is visible from Earth only during a total solar eclipse.

cosmic background radiation ~ A very low-temperature radiation coming from all parts of the sky. It is the fading glow of the Big Bang explosion.

cosmos ~ The universe – which is to say everything, including you!

crater ~ A dish- or bowl-shaped depression in the surface of a planet, moon or asteroid. Most are geological scars caused by the high-speed impact of a meteorite.

crescent Moon ~ The narrow curved phase of the Moon that appears between new Moon and First Quarter, or between Last Quarter and new Moon.

crust ~ The outer layer of a rocky planet, moon or asteroid. We live on Earth's crust.

D

dark nebula ~ A cloud of interstellar dust that blocks the light of more distant stars. The Horsehead nebula in Orion is a dark nebula.

day (rotation time and solar day) ~ A planet or moon's sidereal day is its rotation time, the time it takes to make one full spin on its axis. Its solar day lasts from one noon to the next.

debris ~ The remains of something that has been destroyed or broken. The material thrown out by the impact of a meteorite is called debris. Debris can also refer to any material drifting through space.

deep space ~ A term generally used to include everything beyond the Solar System.

disk (of a galaxy) ~ The broad region of a spiral galaxy that surrounds the nucleus. The Sun lies in the disk of the Milky Way.

Doppler shift ~ A change in the colour of light produced by a planet, star or galaxy as it moves toward or away from us.

double star ~ Two stars linked by gravity and orbiting each other.

E

earthshine ~ Sunlight reflecting from Earth that gently lights the part of the Moon that is not in direct sunlight. Earthshine produces what some people call 'the old Moon in the new Moon's arms'. For someone standing on the Moon, earthshine is exactly like moonlight is for us on Earth.

eclipse ~ When one celestial body passes in front of another, dimming its light. Solar eclipses occur when the Moon lies between Earth and the Sun, and lunar eclipses occur when Earth lies between the Sun and Moon.

eclipsing binary ~ A double star that appears to dim and brighten regularly. When one star moves behind the other and is eclipsed, its light is cut off and the combined light we see dims. When the star comes out again, the combined light brightens.

electromagnetic spectrum ~ The full range of radiation in waves produced by celestial bodies. It runs from very long-wavelength radio waves through visible wavelengths to high-energy gamma rays.

ellipse ~ The oval path followed by celestial objects in orbit. Planets and comets travel through space in ellipses.

elliptical galaxy ~ A ball- or oval-shaped galaxy that lacks a disk with spiral arms and is made up of older reddish stars. Elliptical galaxies include the largest galaxies as well as the least massive. For example, M87 is a giant elliptical galaxy, while the Sculptor dwarf is a tiny dwarf elliptical galaxy.

emission nebula ~ An interstellar cloud of gas (mainly hydrogen) that glows from the radiation of nearby hot stars. The North America nebula in Cygnus is a famous emission nebula.

entry probe ~ A robot spacecraft designed to enter the atmosphere of a planet or moon and collect information as it falls. Some entry probes survive to land on the surface, but most are destroyed by increasing heat and pressure, as the Galileo mission's entry probe was at Jupiter in 1995.

Equator ~ The imaginary line on the globe of a planet, moon or star that lies half-way between its two poles.

equinox ~ The moment when the Sun appears to stand directly above a planet's equator. This is the date when day and night are equally long at any point on the planet.

extraterrestrial ~ Anything that comes from outside planet Earth.

F

fireball ~ A meteor that is bright enough to cast a shadow.

First Quarter ~ The lunar phase when the Moon looks half-lit in the evening sky and has travelled the first quarter of its orbit around Earth.

fly-by ~ A spacecraft visit to a planet or moon in which the probe does not land or orbit. This is usually the first stage of investigation, followed by an orbiter and then a lander craft.

full Moon ~ The lunar phase when the Moon's disk is fully lit by the Sun.

G

galaxy ~ A collection of millions or billions of stars plus lots of gas and dust, held together by gravity. There are spiral, elliptical, and irregular types of galaxies.

Galilean moon ~ Any of the four largest moons of Jupiter: Io, Europa, Ganymede or Callisto.

The name honours Galileo Galilei (1564–1642), an Italian astronomer who discovered the moons in 1610.

gamma rays ~ The electromagnetic radiation with the shortest waves and highest energy. Gamma rays come from the most violent astronomical processes, such as active galaxies, supernovas and black holes.

gas giant ~ A large planet composed mainly of hydrogen. In the Solar System, Jupiter, Saturn, Uranus and Neptune are gas-giant planets.

geyser ~ A jet of gas or hot liquid that erupts from the ground. Geysers on Earth send up streams of boiling water, but geysers on Neptune's moon Triton erupt warm nitrogen gas.

gibbous Moon ~ The partly rounded lunar phase that appears between First Quarter and full Moon, and between full Moon and Last Quarter.

globular star cluster ~ A spherical cluster bound by gravity that may contain up to a million stars. The Milky Way contains more than a hundred known globular clusters.

granule ~ A bubble of hot gas at the Sun's surface. The smallest granules are about 500 kilometres (300 mi) in diameter.

gravitational lens ~ A galaxy (or other massive object) between Earth and a more distant object. The massive object's gravity bends the light from the distant object and creates distorted or multiple images of it.

gravity ~ The force that attracts one object to another. Gravity holds galaxies together and it holds planets, moons and spacecraft in orbit. It also holds you on the ground.

greenhouse effect ~ The warming of a planet's surface by trapped solar heat. Sunlight passes through the atmosphere and heats the surface. But since the warmth can't easily escape through the atmosphere, the surface grows hotter.

H

hemisphere (northern and southern) ~ One half of a planetary globe. Earth is divided into the Northern and Southern hemispheres by the Equator.

Hertzsprung-Russell diagram ~ A graph that shows the brightness and temperature for all stars.

horizon ~ The distant line where the ground and sky meet.

I

infrared radiation ~ Invisible radiation that travels in slightly longer waves than visible light does. We feel infrared radiation as heat when we are near a fire or radiator.

interferometry ~ A technique for linking two or more telescopes together so they work to give a much sharper picture of astronomical objects.

interstellar matter ~ Any material drifting through space between the stars. Some interstellar matter is dust, some is gas. Eventually much of this gas and dust will end up making new stars.

irregular galaxy ~ A small galaxy that has no obvious shape or structure, such as the Small Magellanic Cloud. Most irregular galaxies have lots of gas and dust.

K

Kuiper Belt ~ A region beyond the orbit of Neptune where multitudes of icy comets orbit the Sun.

L

lander ~ Any spacecraft that sets down on another planet. Lander missions, which may carry rovers to explore areas away from the lander, usually follow fly-by and orbiter missions.

Last Quarter ~ The lunar phase when the Moon looks half-lit in the morning sky and is about to begin the last quarter of its orbit around Earth.

lava ~ Molten rock that has erupted from the interior of a planet or moon through a volcano or a crack in the surface.

light-year ~ The distance that light travels in one year. One light-year equals about 10 billion kilometres (6 billion mi)

Local Group ~ A cluster of about 35 galaxies to which the Milky Way galaxy belongs. Other Local Group members include the Large and Small Magellanic Clouds and the Andromeda (M31) and Pinwheel (M33) galaxies.

long-period comet ~ Any comet with an orbit lasting longer than 200 years.

lunar module ~ The part of the Apollo spacecraft that carried two astronauts to the Moon's surface.

M

magma ~ Molten rock that remains underground. If it erupts, it is called lava.

magnetic field ~ A region of space where an object exerts a detectable magnetic force.

magnetic poles ~ The two opposite points on a spinning planet, moon or star where magnetic fields pass from the surface into space.

magnitude ~ The unit for measuring the brightness of celestial objects. Brighter objects are given smaller magnitude numbers than dimmer objects – a star of magnitude 1 is brighter than a star of magnitude 6, for example. Very bright objects are given negative magnitude numbers – the Sun shines at magnitude –26.8. Apparent magnitude describes how bright a star looks in Earth's night sky. Actual (or absolute) magnitude is the brightness the star would have if it was placed at a distance of 32.6 light-years from Earth.

main sequence ~ The strip on the Hertzsprung-Russell diagram that includes the Sun and most other stars. On the diagram, it runs from upper left (high temperature, high brightness) to lower right (low temperature, low brightness).

mantle ~ The layer inside a planet or moon that is below the crust, but above the core. It may be entirely rocky or a mixture of ice and rock.

mare (plural maria) ~ (Pronounced MAH-ray and MAH-ree-ah.) One of the smooth dark patches on the Moon. The maria are old lava flows. Early astronomers thought the patches were the beds of dried-up oceans, so they named them *mare*, the Latin word for 'sea'.

meteor ~ The bright streak of light produced by a bit of space debris burning up as it enters the atmosphere at high speed. Meteors are also called shooting stars.

meteorite ~ A piece of solid debris that lands on the surface of a planet or moon. It may be stony or metallic or a mixture of the two. Most are pieces broken off from asteroids.

meteoroid ~ Any small debris travelling through space. Larger meteoroids are usually pieces of shattered asteroids. Smaller meteoroids are mostly dust particles shed by comets.

meteor shower ~ A large number of meteors that appear to come from one small area of sky. A meteor shower happens when Earth runs into the debris thrown off by a comet. Meteor showers are named for the constellation from which they appear to come. The Perseids, for example, which are most active around 12 August, appear to come from the constellation of Perseus and are debris from comet Swift-Tuttle.

Milky Way ~ The galaxy that contains our Solar System and all the stars you can see in the night sky with the naked eye. Also, the softly glowing band of light, made from faint stars, that arcs across the night sky.

moon ~ A natural object orbiting a planet. Also called a satellite.

multiple star ~ Three or more stars that are linked by gravity and orbit one another. The star nearest the Sun is the multiple system of Alpha Centauri, which has three stars: Alpha Centauri A and B, plus Proxima Centauri.

N

naked eye ~ What you can see with just your ordinary vision, without using a telescope or binoculars.

near-Earth asteroid ~ Any asteroid that comes close to Earth. Astronomers think that thousands of asteroids may have near-Earth orbits.

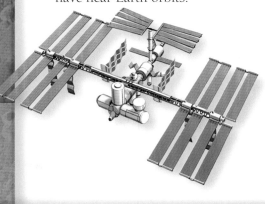

nebula ~ A cloud of interstellar gas and dust that may be bright or dark. Nebulas are the birthplaces of stars.

neutron star ~ The highly dense remnant of a star that has blown up in a supernova. Neutron stars are about the size of a city and spin rapidly. When we detect a neutron star, it is called a pulsar.

new Moon ~ The lunar phase when the Moon passes between Earth and the Sun and is not lit up in the sky. Many people also call a crescent Moon low in the evening sky a 'new Moon', although by that time several days have passed since the true moment of new Moon.

night vision ~ Changes that occur in your eyes to help you see more in the dark. The changes take about 15 minutes, and will be cancelled if you glance at a bright light for even an instant.

nova ~ A white dwarf star in a double-star system that brightens suddenly by several magnitudes. The outburst happens when gas pulled from the companion star falls onto the white dwarf and explodes in a nuclear reaction.

nuclear reaction ~ A process in which a star fuses simple elements into more complex ones, releasing huge amounts of energy.

nucleus ~ The core of a comet or galaxy. In a comet, the nucleus is the lump of ice and dust that forms its central part. In a galaxy, the nucleus is the collection of stars and gas that lie at its centre.

O

Oort Cloud ~ A swarm of billions of comets believed to extend from the Kuiper Belt out roughly half-way to the nearest star, or about 2 light-years.

open star cluster ~ A group of several hundred to a thousand stars bound by gravity and moving through space together.

optical telescope ~ Any telescope that collects visible light.

orbit ~ The path of an object, such as Earth, as it moves around another object, such as the Sun. Also, to move around another object under the control of its gravity, as in 'Mars orbits the Sun'.

orbiter ~ A spacecraft that orbits a planet or moon. Generally, an orbiter is the second stage of exploration – fly-by probes go first, then orbiters provide more detailed views, then landers explore the surface.

P

phase ~ The changes in the appearance of an object, such as the Moon, as we see more or less of it lit by the Sun.

photosphere ~ The visible surface of the Sun or any other star.

planet ~ A large object, such as Mars or Jupiter, that orbits a star, such as the Sun. Planets shine by reflecting sunlight – they do not produce their own light as a star does.

planetary nebula ~ A cloud of gas released by a dying star. It has no relation to planets, but is called a planetary nebula because it appears pale and round in a telescope, roughly like the planet Uranus or Neptune.

planetesimal ~ A small body that formed in the early stages of the Solar System's evolution. Planetesimals were the building blocks of planets. They were mostly rock or mostly ice.

plate tectonics ~ A theory that explains changes in Earth's crust by the movement of about two dozen stiff crustal plates. These collide and separate slowly, driven by the motion of molten rock in Earth's mantle.

poles ~ Two opposite points on the surface of a spinning planet, moon, or star. The axis of the planet, moon or star passes through the poles.

probe ~ An unmanned spacecraft sent from Earth to explore an object in the Solar System. Its data are sent back to Earth as radio signals.

prominence ~ On the Sun, a cloud of cooler gas lying above its surface. Prominences are held up by the Sun's powerful magnetic field.

proto-Sun ~ The body that formed at the centre of the solar nebula and later became the Sun.

Ptolemaic model ~ The ancient world's vision of the universe, as described in a work by Greek astronomer Claudius Ptolemy around AD 150. In the Ptolemaic model, Earth lies in the centre, while the Sun, planets and stars all move around it. This model was accepted for nearly 1,500 years, but was replaced by the Copernican model.

pulsar ~ A neutron star that sends out beams of radio waves as it spins. These produce regularly timed pulses of radio signals in radio telescopes on Earth.

pulsating variable ~ A star that changes in brightness as it expands and shrinks every few days, weeks or months.

Q

quasar ~ Short for quasi-stellar radio source, quasars are believed to be the active cores of very distant and very luminous galaxies. Probably powered by matter falling into black holes, quasars emit incredible amounts of energy.

R

radar astronomy ~ The study of solar system objects by bouncing radio waves off their surfaces with a radio telescope.

radiation ~ Energy that is carried through space as waves or particles. Also, the process that carries energy through space.

radiative zone ~ The middle zone of the Sun (and other stars) where energy travels by radiation. Below it is the core, above it is the convective zone.

radio energy ~ Invisible radiation that travels in longer waves than infrared and visible light.

radio galaxy ~ A type of active galaxy that is a strong source of radio energy.

radio telescope ~ A telescope designed to collect radio waves.

ray ~ A bright streak of shattered rock that surrounds a fresh impact crater. The Moon's longest rays extend from the crater Tycho.

red giant ~ A large, cool star that is in a late stage of its life. Red giants are often pulsating variable stars.

red super-giant ~ The red giant stage in the life of a very large and massive star.

reflection nebula ~ A cloud of interstellar dust that shines by reflecting the light of nearby stars.

reflector ~ A telescope that collects light and forms an image using a mirror.

refractor ~ A telescope that collects light and forms an image using a lens.

relativity theory ~ A theory by Albert Einstein (1879–1955) that explains properties of the universe, such as mass, space, time and motion, as they are seen by different observers moving relative to each other.

rings ~ Small particles that fill an orbit around a planet. Rings are believed to be the remains of broken-up moons.

rocky planet ~ One of the four small planets (Mercury, Venus, Earth and Mars) that is made mostly of rock. Sometimes called a terrestrial planet.

rotation ~ The spin of a planet, moon or star on its axis.

rover ~ An unmanned spacecraft that can move around on the surface of a planet or moon. Also, a four-wheeled 'car' driven by Apollo astronauts on the Moon.

S

satellite ~ Any object that orbits a larger object. A moon is the natural satellite of a planet, while a spacecraft orbiting a planet is an artificial satellite.

satellite galaxy ~ A small galaxy that orbits a larger one. The Large Magellanic Cloud is a satellite of the Milky Way galaxy.

satellite observatory ~ A telescope placed in orbit around Earth or the Sun to make observations without the interference of Earth's atmosphere.

season ~ Regular changes in the weather on a planet, caused by the tilt of its rotation axis. As the planet moves around the Sun, this tilt means that the amount of solar energy falling on any particular region varies.

service module ~ The part of the Apollo spacecraft that provided the fuel, rocket engine and living supplies for the command module and the astronauts.

Seyfert galaxy ~ A kind of active galaxy with unusual, often violent core activity. Discovered by American astronomer Carl Seyfert in 1942.

short-period comet ~ Any comet with an orbit lasting less than 200 years.

sidereal day ~ A planet's rotation time, that is, the time it takes to spin once on its axis. Earth's sidereal day lasts 23 hours 56 minutes.

skylore ~ Myths and legends about stars and constellations.

solar day ~ The time from one noon to the next. Earth's solar day lasts 24 hours.

solar flare ~ A powerful explosion from a small region on the Sun. Often an aurora will appear in Earth's night sky a day or two later when the particles ejected by the solar flare reach Earth.

solar nebula ~ The swirling cloud of gas and dust that condensed to form the Sun and planets.

Solar System ~ Originally, this referred only to our Sun and the planets, moons, comets and asteroids that orbit it. The term is now also used more generally for other stars and their families of planets.

solar wind ~ A high-speed stream of charged particles flowing from the Sun in all directions.

solstice ~ The time in the year when a planet's pole tilts most directly towards (or away from) the Sun, and the Sun reaches its highest (or lowest) position in the sky at noon. The solstice marks the beginning of summer and winter.

space ~ Everything above Earth's atmosphere.

space shuttle ~ A reusable NASA spacecraft that carries people and cargo into orbit around Earth. NASA's space shuttle fleet consists of four craft: Columbia, Discovery, Atlantis and Endeavour.

space station ~ A large satellite that orbits Earth and can be occupied by people for long periods of time.

space telescope ~ In general, any telescope placed in space. The Hubble Space Telescope, named after American astronomer Edwin Hubble (1889–1953), was launched by NASA in 1990 and has made many discoveries, studying everything from lunar craters to the furthest galaxies.

spectrograph ~ An instrument that breaks the light from a celestial object into its component colours for analysis.

spectrum ~ The rainbow of colour from an object such as the Sun or a star. It is produced by breaking the light into its component colours using a spectrograph.

spiral arm ~ The curving arm of a spiral galaxy. Spiral arms are rich in stars and gas. The Sun lies in a spiral arm of the Milky Way galaxy.

spiral galaxy ~ A large galaxy with several starry arms reaching out from a dense core, like a pinwheel. Some spiral galaxies have a roughly oblong-shaped centre that resembles a broad bar. These are called barred spiral galaxies.

star ~ A large ball of hydrogen gas that produces light and heat by means of nuclear reactions in its core. The Sun is a star.

star cloud ~ A patch of Milky Way where the stars lie so close together that they look like a glowing cloud.

stellar association ~ A group of up to a hundred young stars that formed together and are now scattered across hundreds of light-years. The bright stars of the constellation Perseus belong to several associations.

supercluster ~ A loose collection of several clusters of galaxies, all bound by gravity. The Local Supercluster contains the Local Group, the Virgo cluster and other galaxy clusters.

supernova ~ The explosion of a massive star in which it blows off its outer atmosphere, temporarily equalling an entire galaxy in brightness. Supernovas occur when a giant star runs out of fuel, or when a star collects too much gas from its companion star.

supernova remnant ~ An expanding cloud of gas that has been thrown into space by a supernova explosion.

T

telescope ~ Any instrument that collects light or other forms of radiation so astronomers can study celestial objects better.

tide ~ The distortion of one body by the gravity of another that is nearby. The Moon raises tides in Earth's oceans, and the Sun does also. When the solar and lunar tides combine, the effect is stronger and is called a spring tide.

tonne ~ A metric ton, equal to 1,000 kg or about 2,200 lb.

trillion ~ A million million million. In numerals, it is written as 1,000,000,000,000,000,000.

Trojan asteroids ~ Two groups of asteroids that orbit the Sun in the same orbit as Jupiter. One group travels ahead of Jupiter, the other behind.

U–Z

ultraviolet radiation ~ Invisible radiation that travels in slightly shorter waves than visible light does. The Sun's ultraviolet radiation causes sunburn.

universe ~ Everything that exists – all the galaxies, black holes, stars, nebulas, moons, planets, comets, asteroids, meteoroids and dust scattered through space. This includes you!

variable star ~ Any star whose brightness appears to change over periods ranging from minutes to years. A variable can be an eclipsing binary or a pulsating variable.

visible light ~ Radiation that the human eye can see.

wavelength ~ The distance between two successive waves of energy passing through space.

white dwarf ~ A small, very hot star near the end of its life. It is essentially the leftover core of a red giant star.

X-rays ~ Invisible radiation that travels in shorter waves than ultraviolet and visible light. X-rays are emitted by very hot objects and energetic events, such as exploding stars and colliding galaxies.

year ~ The time it takes a planet to orbit the Sun. Earth's year lasts 365.25 days.

zodiac ~ A band of 12 constellations that the Sun appears to move through during the year. The zodiac constellations are: Pisces the Fishes, Aries the Ram, Taurus the Bull, Gemini the Twins, Cancer the Crab, Leo the Lion, Virgo the Maiden, Libra the Scales, Scorpius the Scorpion, Sagittarius the Archer, Capricornus the Sea Goat and Aquarius the Water Carrier.

zone ~ A band of bright clouds in the atmosphere of a gas-giant planet.

Index

Acknowledgments

Weldon Owen would like to thank the following people for their assistance in the production of this book: Helen Bateman, Mike Croll, Michael Hann, Veronica Hilton, John Mapps, Stuart McVicar, Cliff Watt.

Photographic credits: AAO = Anglo-Australian Observatory, AF = Akira Fujii, ESO = European Southern Observatory, NOAO = National Optical Astronomy Observatories, ROE = Royal Observatory, Edinburgh, SPL = Science Photo Library, STScI = Space Telescope Science Institute, TPL = The Photo Library, Sydney, TS =Tom Stack & Associates
t=top, b=bottom, c=centre, l=left, r=right
3, Oliver Strewe/Weldon Owen; 8t Superstock; c TPL/Rev.Ronald Royer/SPL; b TPL/NASA/DVR/SPL; 9 TPL; 10bl AAO/ROE; br TPL/STScI/SPL; 11tr TPL/Kim Gordon/SPL; 12bl TPL/NASA/SPL; br The Observatories of the Carnegie Institute of Washington; 13tl NOAO; cr ESO; 14 The Bridgeman Art Library/British Museum, London; 15tl William Austral/MacQuitty/Camera Press; tr The Granger Collection; c TPL/Paul Thompson; 18c ASP/Mt Wilson and Las Campanas Observatories; 19tl Malin/IAC/RGO; tr TPL/Hale Observatories/SPL; 20tl Richard J. Wainscoat; tr Corbis/Roger Ressemeyer; 21bl TPL/David Nunuk/SPL; br TPL/NASA/SPL; 22l TPL/Max Planck Institute/SPL; r STScI/NASA 25 t TPL/NASA/SPL; cl Novosti, London; cr TPL/NASA/SPL; b TPL/NASA/SPL; 27 TPL/NASA/SPL; 32tr Tony & Daphne Hallas/Astrophoto; cl TPL/NASA/SPL; cr TPL/SPL 33 bl TPL/Geoff Tomkinson/SPL; 34 TS/JPL/TSADO; 36cl NASA; cr TPL/SPL/David P. Anderson/NASA; 38tl Auscape/Maurice & Katia Krafft; tr TPL/Ted Mead; 39c NASA; b TPL/SPL/NASA; 40c A; b NASA; 42cl TPL/SPL/BMDO/NRL/LLNL; tr NASA; 44tr TPL/Fred Espenak/SPL; cr TPL/John Sanford/SPL; br AF; 46tr TPL/John Sanford/SP; cr TPL/David Nunuk/SPL; 48cl TPL/USGS/SPL; cr TPL/NASA/SPL; 50t NASA; cr NASA; cl John Hopkins University Applied Physics Laboratory; b TPL/NASA/SPL; 52t TPL/NASA/SPL; cl NASA; cr NASA; b TPL/NASA/SPL; 56 NASA/JPL;

58 NASA; 60 TPL/STScI; 62 TPL/John Chumack; 63bl TPL/SPL; br TPL/European Space Agency/SPL; 64bl NASA/STScI; br NASA/STScI; 64-65 NASA/STScI; 65tc NASA/STScI; bl AAO/David Malin; br TPL/Fred Espenak/SPL; 66t TPL/ROE; c AAO/David Malin; b TPL/STScI/NASA; 67tr TPL/I.M House; c TPL/STScI/NASA; bl AAO/David Malin; br AAO/David Malin; 68br TPL/Lick Observatory; 70bl NASA/STScI; 71br AF; 72cl AAO/ROE; cr NASA/STScI; 76t AF; 78t NASA/STScI; tc NASA/STScI; c TPL/Tony Hallas/SPL; bc AF, b AAO/David Malin; 79bl TPL/NASA/SPL; br TPL/Fred Espenak/SPL; 80t AAO/David Malin; c NASA/STScI; 82 AAO/ROE; 83tl TPL/NASA/SPL; tc AAO/ROE; tr TPL/SPL; 84t NASA/Chandra X-Ray Observatory/MFSC; ct NASA/STScI; cb TPL/SPL/AAO/David Malin; b TPL/Max Planck Institute/SPL; 86c NASA/STScI; 87c TPL/NASA/SPL; 88t David Miller; c Jerry Schad; bl Oliver Strewe/Weldon Owen; br AF; 90-91 The Granger Collection, New York; 91t Alan Dyer; c British Library, London; 92bl TPL/Pekka Parviainen/SPL; 94t AF; c AF; 95t A; c TPL/SPL; 96t TPL/Kim Gordon; c NOAO; 97 AF; 98cl TPL/Celestial Image Pict/SPL; cr Bill and Sally Fletcher; 99t TPL/SPL; cr TPL/Kim Gordon/SPL; 100tc TPL/Kim Gordon/SPL; bc TPL/Tony Hallas/SPL; 101t TS/Bill and Sally Fletcher; c TPL/John Sanford; 102cl TPL/SPL; cr TPL/SPL; 103c AAO/David Malin, cr TPL/Fred Espenak/SPL; 104 AF; 105t AAO/David Malin; c AF; 106t TPL/Tony Hallas/SPL; c TPL/J. Hester & P. Scowen/SPL; 107cl TPL/SPL; cr AAO/ROE; 108t AAO/David Malin; c TPL/NOAO/SPL; 109c TPL/SPL; t AAO/David Malin; 121 TPL/NASA/SPL.

Illustration credits: Wildlife Art Ltd.
18-25, 120cr, 121br, 121cr, 124bl, Tom Connell; 1(constellations), 14-17, 94-109, 116cr, 117tr, 120cl, 120bl, 120c, 123tr, 125bl Luigi Gallante; 68-73, 78-83, 117bl, 118cl, 121tr, Lee Gibbons; 1c, 3, 8-13, 26-65, 66-67 (digital manipulation), 74-78, 84-87, 90-93, 112cr, 113-115, 117br, 118tr, 119tr, 120r, 121tl, 121cl, 121c, 121bc, 122, 123b, 124br, 124tr, 125tr, David A. Hardy; all Projects & Amazing Facts, 119bl, 120tl, 12tr, Sandra Pond; 38bc, 38br, 39bl, 39br, 88-89, Jonathon Potter.